PRAISE FOR SURV

"A bold and full account of a remarkable (
—Yvon Chouinard

"A deeply human portrait of an alpine climbing legend that extends well beyond Jim Donini's visionary ascents, and ventures into more complex terrain: the layers of beauty, tragedy, and purpose in a remarkable life."
—Kelly Cordes, author of *The Tower*

"The climbing dictionary definition of 'hardman' only needs to be two words: Jim Donini."
—Rick Ridgeway, author of *Life Lived Wild*

"Portraying such a complex and iconic personality as Jim Donini is a daunting task, but Geoff Powter pulls it off with grace, powerfully combining his skills as a writer, climber, and clinical psychologist. He takes us along on a wild journey, both physical and emotional, to understand his subject. Reading this book feels like listening to intimate conversations as Powter encourages his interviewees to dig deep, revealing the many facets of Donini's character and the triumphs and tragedies of his life."
—Maria Coffey, author of *Instead*

"Jim Donini is a wild mountain lover and a legitimate legend for all he has achieved, and his remarkable story is written right into his skin. . . . Spend just a little while with Jim and you can see why he connects so well with the new generations of climbers: because under that wise old skin, there is still a wild boy who imagines towering walls; long, cold leads; and big storms, and still knows what those mountain moments bring.

For anyone who wants to understand what it takes, and what it can cost, to have the fullest mountain life, this book is a wonderfully compelling, insightful, and honest guide."
—Thomas Huber

"Powter's account of an extraordinary person's extraordinary climbing life is vivid and acute. More moving still is his morally complex exposé of how the intoxication and solace offered by climbing can change the course not just of a single person's life, but the lives of all of the people around them. This book is a great, totally unique achievement."
—David Smart, author of *Royal Robbins*

"This is one of the best reads of climbing and exploration literature, and of the complex psychology that drives adventure. Powter has accomplished the remarkable feat of compassionately revealing an exemplary and charismatic mountain life that is also filled with terrible tragedies and very human complexities. Powter's skill, and willingness, to explore both sides of the story is a humane victory for both the writer and his subject."
—Sharon Roberts, psychoanalyst, lifelong adventure traveler

Powter has accomplished a feat nearly as impossible as one of the epic climbs contained in this book—unpacking the multi-faceted and complicated life of Jim Donini with clean, well-crafted prose. Powter's insight, painstaking research, and superb writing cracks open Donini's heart, revealing the manifold triumphs and cataclysmic tragedies that have defined the life of one of America's true alpine heroes.
—Gregory Crouch, author of *Enduring Patagonia*

SURVIVAL IS NOT ASSURED

THE LIFE OF CLIMBER JIM DONINI

GEOFF POWTER

Foreword by Michael Kennedy

MOUNTAINEERS
BOOKS

 **MOUNTAINEERS BOOKS** is dedicated to the exploration, preservation, and enjoyment of outdoor and wilderness areas.

1001 SW Klickitat Way, Suite 201, Seattle, WA 98134
800-553-4453, www.mountaineersbooks.org

Printed in the United States of America

27 26 25 24   1 2 3 4 5

Design and layout: Jen Grable
Cover photograph: *Jim on the first ascent of Torre Egger, Patagonia, 1976* (Photo by Jay Wilson)
Frontispiece: *Jim on the first ascent of Cerro Chueco, Aysén, Chile, 2018* (Photo by Tad McCrea)

Library of Congress Control Number: 2023951100

Mountaineers Books titles may be purchased for corporate, educational, or other promotional sales, and our authors are available for a wide range of events. For information on special discounts or booking an author, contact our customer service at 800-553-4453 or mbooks@mountaineersbooks.org.

ISBN (paperback): 978-1-68051-537-4
ISBN (ebook): 978-1-68051-538-1

An independent nonprofit publisher since 1960

There are three sorts of people:
Those who are alive, those who are dead,
and those who are at sea.
—Anacharsis

CONTENTS

Foreword by Michael Kennedy 9

Author's Note: Finding Jim 13

1	A Man on One of His Mountains	19
2	Non Il Sogno Americano	31
3	American Idyll	36
4	The Bridge	40
5	Special Forces	43
6	Finding a Way Up	50
7	The Summer of Love and Mountains	53
8	A Young Man Gone West	61
9	Apprenticeship	65
10	Days in Eden: The Yosemite Years, Part One	68
11	Work, Whisky, and an Unexpected Offer	78
12	Days in Eden: The Yosemite Years, Part Two	86
13	An Obscene Journey to an Unseen Mountain	90
14	Towers of Patience	98
15	Life of a Salesman	111
16	Latok I: The Magnificent Failure	116
17	The Sadness of Valleys, Part One	128
18	Siguniang: The Ugly Americans	132

19   City Ways... 148

20   Tackle, Part One 151

21   Tackle, Part Two... 157

22   Del Mar a las Tormentas 164

23   Tackle, Part Three.. 172

24   The Sadness of Valleys, Part Two 180

25   Reinvention: Crouch 186

26   The Sadness of Valleys, Part Three 212

27   The Mentor... 218

28   The Reluctant Elder... 238

Acknowledgments 247
Selected Climbs 251
Notes 253
Selected Bibliography 266

FOREWORD

JIM DONINI IS a force of nature, a constant in the climbing world akin to the whisper of wind through a distant mountain pass, the early sun etching the features of a high mountain wall, the inexorable march of a glacier toward the valley below.

In other words, he's ancient.

His climbs span three distinct generations, and in his ninth decade Jim still exhibits an enthusiasm for the vertical that exceeds that of partners fifty years his junior. He has always exhibited a commitment to technical difficulty, small teams, and excellent style, as well as a fine-tuned sense of the great risks—and immense rewards—fundamental to operating in the alpine environment.

A skilled storyteller, Jim also recognizes and celebrates the absurdity of our pursuit. After a 2023 misadventure in Patagonia during which he suffered "an unintended swim down a major icy cold glacial river . . . followed by a sleepless night in a dense rain forest fighting off hypothermia," he concluded: "It seems the older I get, the easier it is for me to epic."

With his razor-sharp wit, strongly held opinions—often loudly shared—and willingness to call a spade a spade, Jim can be an intimidating figure. Yet behind a sometimes-crusty exterior (it is not without reason that some of his friends refer to him, affectionately, as "Jim Dameanie") lies a person who values friendship above all else, someone who exemplifies the ideals of "the brotherhood of the rope."

Forty-five years ago, we were well into our third week on the north ridge of Latok I in Pakistan when Jeff Lowe fell grievously ill in the cramped snow cave of our highest bivouac. We'd become a tightly knit team, having suffered together through the doubts and fears of stepping into the unknown, challenging route-finding and multiday storms, and many uncomfortable nights out. But George Lowe and I could only watch in awe as Jim nursed Jeff through three painful, stormbound days in that snow cave, then shepherded him closely during the four days we spent getting back down from our attempt. Like a loving mother or a benevolent guardian angel, Jim never left Jeff's side.

In *Survival Is Not Assured*, Geoff Powter weaves a masterful tale of an American original. His nuanced and sympathetic narrative reveals much I was never aware of despite having known Jim for decades. It almost makes me feel as if I've led a boring life, one thankfully devoid of many of his missteps, challenges, and tragedies. As Jim says early in the book, when asked why it bothers him when people say they envy his life:

> *Sure, many things about it have been great: I've had some incredible adventures. I've traveled everywhere. . . . I'm nearly eighty and I'm still climbing. But I promise you, no one would want to go through what I've gone through just to have this life.*

One of the tragedies Jim and I have in common is the loss of a son. Montana Donini died from a drug overdose on August 17, 2000, a few months shy of his twenty-first birthday. At the time, I couldn't conceive of the pain Jim felt, nor could I offer him anything more than cursory comfort and understanding. We spoke little of Montana in the years to come although in retrospect Jim's later friendship with our son, Hayden, seemed a profound echo of an earlier, happier time.

After Hayden took his own life in October 2017, Jim offered what would be the best counsel in dealing with sudden, unimaginable grief:

> *Yes, it is very, very difficult to have your child precede you in death. Some acceptance will come but, I'll be honest, it is a long process.*
>
> *Please do not make the mistake I did. It was so painful I found myself trying to shut out all memories of Montana. Perhaps in some weird way I thought that would make it feel like it didn't happen. It took me two years before I could easily look at pictures of him and recall some of the great times we had together. It was much better for me to celebrate the joy that he brought to my life while he was here.*

Our lives are short, and we need to live in the present and be all that we can be to the ones we care about. We also need to celebrate the love and beauty that those no longer here were able to give us.

In Jim's case, the loss of his beloved son was followed by that of his troubled older daughter, Sage. The two had reconnected shortly before she died of metatastic melanoma in 2021. Geoff's telling of Jim's relationships with Montana and Sage are among the most poignant and vital passages in the book, revealing a deeply conflicted yet genuinely loving father who wished only for his children to find peace and happiness.

That Geoff has been able to get well beyond a sometimes deliberately crafted persona is a tribute to his skill as a writer, his experience as a clinical psychologist, and his willingness to invest so much of himself in the process. "Writing this book has been by far the most difficult and most rewarding work I've ever done," he told me when we spoke about an early draft.

For Jim, too, this biography became an opportunity "to join the two ragged halves" of his life. His candid appraisal of his strengths and weakness, the idiosyncrasies that played such a critical role in both his successes and failures, is a moving testament to Jim's complicated, messy, wonderful humanity. *Survival Is Not Assured* is a gift to all who know its subject and to anyone interested in how one might navigate the ups and downs of an unconventional and adventurous life.

—Michael Kennedy
Carbondale, Colorado

FINDING JIM

JUST BEFORE DAWN on a snappy autumn morning, my partner and I saddled up for another day climbing in the tower lands of Utah. Puffs of chilled breath misted up through the beams of our headlamps, reminding us it was too late in the year and too early in the morning to be climbing, but we had a plan: Three times before Guy and I had waited too long for the sun and other parties had beaten us to the punch. *This* time we'd be the first team on the spire looming in the shadows above. So, with knees creaking in the cold, we left the road and once again began our way up the long chain of sandy switchbacks, certain no one would be in front of us.

Gauzy light seeped over the rim of Castle Valley, and the ground began to take on the familiar colors of the desert: ochre dust on desiccated greens of saltbush, white slabs of rock with the brown-baked bubbles of soda crackers.

It was light enough now to see the outline of the pinnacle lurking overhead, and I paused to catch a breath. A thin fog floated below; a lonely truck wove along the valley floor. High above, Castleton Tower, our objective, turned a muted tan as the top of the spire snagged the first rays of the day. An orange halo circled the summit.

Guy was now well ahead, and I shifted gears to catch up. He crested the long ridge between Castleton and its squatter neighbor to the north, the Rectory, then stopped, looking up at our planned line on the north face of Castleton.

He cursed. We had company. We heard laughter and the tinkle of gear, saw a climber well up the opening pitch. We could make out a second on the ground, huddled in a big red jacket in the maroon shadows. The party had either spent the night at the base of the climb or they were very fast.

We growled and shifted our plans yet again. As we started to walk away, we heard the leader call down to his belayer, asking for slack. The command was a deep, gruff bark, with a theatrical projection.

"That's Donini," Guy said.

I'd never met the man, but I'd been hearing stories for years. He was well into his sixties by this time, but if anyone of any age was going to be up this early, climbing this hard, while it was still this cold, it was going to be Donini.

Guy headed off along the long red ridge toward the Rectory; I sat and watched. In the fifty-plus years I've been in the climbing world, I've had the chance to see some of the world's best dancing their vertical ballet, and I recognized that magic at play that cold morning. The pitch Donini was sorting out was the crux of the *North Face* of Castleton, a demanding riddle of steep, sharp sandstone cracks and thin edge moves, but he moved with a fluency that belied the 5.11 grade. Most climbers' hands and feet would have performed like blocks of wood in the cold, but Donini drifted up, buoyant as a fish in water. It looked like he had placed only one piece of gear, and I felt for the belayer who had to be gulping in the shadows below, watching the potential fall grow from thirty feet to fifty to a ground fall. But in a few minutes, Donini was at the belay, bellowing, "Secure!"

I moved to catch up to Guy, and as we walked away from Castleton, I reeled off what I knew of Donini. In the 1970s, he was one of the pioneers of hard crack climbing, and he was still climbing hard things fifty years later. He'd been a top-shelf ice climber for decades. He'd mixed the two skills together in the elusive alchemy of alpine climbing, completing important first ascents, many of which remain unrepeated decades later, on some of the hardest peaks on the planet in Patagonia, Alaska, Asia, and the Karakoram Range. He'd been involved in some legendary epics of mountain survival and endurance.

Guy, always to the point, quipped, "He's a nice man, too."

In the end, the route we climbed was far more than a consolation; it was an outstanding route, blessed with all-day sun. From the top of our tower, I turned to look back at Castleton, still haunted by shade, and saw that a party was starting another route where I'd spotted Donini. When I heard voices, I realized it was Donini again, back for another route on the face.

Hours later, as a posse of us told tales around a campfire, the sweeping traces of headlamps bounced down the switchbacks above. It was Donini again, finally finishing his day. He joined our circle, smiled, laughed, and

A familiar space, a familiar look: Jim on Goretta Pillar, Cerro Fitz Roy, in 2006 (**Photo by Thom Engelbach**)

shook a few nearby hands. I recalled he'd once been described as "an alpine Ichabod Crane," and in the flicker of the fire, it didn't seem an unfair description. He's tall, gaunt as a gecko, with an air of the undertaker about him, and the firelight scooped out the hollows of his cheeks a little deeper.

But I'd also heard the man called "brooding" and "unapproachable," and that night he was anything but. Stories—alternately hilarious and gripping— poured out of him. We all knew we were standing there with one of the greats, but none of us felt the distance we might have expected. He insisted that we'd all love the climbs he was talking about, even though none of us would ever think about trying them. He made it sound like we were all just part of the same vertical family. Then, as quickly as he'd appeared, he looked at his watch, said, "Oh, shit," and walked off into the night.

I never did find out who his partner was that day, nor where he'd gone.

WE MET AGAIN a few years later on a bright winter's day at the Banff Mountain Festival, the great gathering of mountain lovers that happens every November in the Canadian Rockies. I have the privilege of interviewing guests each year at the festival, and in 2011 Jim joined me for a taping in a TV studio. As soon as the room lit up, so did he. Jim is a consummate performer, and as our conversation progressed his tales got better, the lessons learned richer. A few of the stories I knew, but there were surprises: That he had been a Green Beret but also enjoyed a raucous journey through the counterculture excesses of the 1960s and 1970s. That he lived the complex realities of the American Dream in a family of immigrants. That he had children. As is the case for many climbers, those more human, everyday parts of his story weren't as quick to surface as the climbing accounts.

After the interview ended, I told him that it surprised me how little had been written by him or about him, and I asked why he'd never penned an autobiography. He smiled, turned toward his wife Angela, and said, "She'll tell you it's because I'm too lazy."

Angela shook her head and laughed. "No," she said. "It's because you always choose to go climbing instead."

"True," said Jim.

They walked off, hand in hand, and I was left thinking—as I would several times over the next ten years—that if Donini didn't want to tell his story, I would.

THERE ARE TWO questions that simmer—and sometimes boil over—in a project like this: Why does a biographer choose this person's story to tell? And why would the subject ever let a writer burrow into their life and then share it with the world?

The first question was easy to answer: Donini has been a part of many landmark moments in climbing history with some of the best climbers of our time. Those climbers universally laud him, calling him *the toughest, strongest, fastest, smartest, most natural* climber they'd roped up with. And more than a few talk about how his climbs inspired them and how welcoming he's always been.

There was also a historical attraction to the project: In many ways, Donini is an icon of a special time, not just in climbing history, but America's, too. He comes from a generation of climbers that shifted the way mountain adventure is perceived and practiced, a shift that also reflected uniquely American ways of seeing and walking through the world.

But it was when I started to explore the second question—*Why would he let someone dig into his story?*—that I was truly hooked. I began to understand how much more there is to the man's life than mountains: how much more utterly human than heroic it has been, how much more tragic and moving, and, ultimately, how much more compelling.

I also started to see that if these more complex sides to Jim's story aren't known, that's largely been both a guarded choice—for a long time he wasn't willing to share the harder things—and a theatrical one: while he does tell stories of legitimately grand deeds, he's just as happy to spin self-deprecating yarns about acting out in the ways at which men—particularly men of his time—excel. It's consequently easy to feel that you've been entertained, but it's just as easy to feel that you actually know little about the man who just entertained you, other than he's climbed some mountains and had a thunderous time of it.

For much of his life, that's been the way that Jim wanted it. Even as a child, his sister told me, he preferred to have things simple and to ignore the inconvenient complexities of life. That made things easier. "That ability," she insightfully suggested, "is probably something that got him up all those damn climbs of his."

But Jim's fuller story has included twists that make it hard to pretend that life isn't complicated. Terrible, tragic things happened that he couldn't just ignore, and he had to make sense of it all. Participating in this book, he said, was part of that sense-making.

It's always bothered Jim when people tell him that they *envy* his life. "Sure," he acknowledges, "many things about it have been great: I've had some incredible adventures. I've traveled everywhere. I have a house in Ouray, Colorado, a fantastic place to climb, and another one in Patagonia. I have a super supportive and understanding wife, and I get to go all over the world, and see friends in this great community of ours. I'm nearly eighty and I'm still climbing.

"But I promise you, *no one* would want to go through what I've gone through just to have this life."

It didn't take many conversations to appreciate what he meant. The image that kept coming to my mind was two halves of an unfinished jigsaw puzzle, one of the halves built of the bright pieces of the mountain side of Jim's story, painted with sunny summits, great friendships, and grand adventures, the other half shades darker, with pieces colored by bone-deep sadness, tragedies of loss, addiction, mental illness, death, and incarceration.

For years, Jim has been trying to understand how to join the two ragged halves, but that's not an easy task: even to him, the two seem like pictures of separate lives, with the joining pieces hard to fit, as though they belong to different puzzles. Putting those pieces on the table and sorting through them included many difficult conversations spread over a couple of years, as well as some hard looks by Jim on his own at the turns of his life.

Even sorting out the climbing stories had its own puzzles, with so many partners remembering the pieces differently. Most of the events recounted here happened a long time ago, and Jim comes from a generation of climbers who were reluctant to crow about, or even document, their accomplishments. Many of them didn't keep journals and wrote only spare accounts of their trips—largely because, they insisted, they'd rather *climb* than talk about it. Combined with Jim's natural yarn-spinning, the unfortunate, albeit sometimes hilarious, result is that many of the stories that follow had many different, and even contradictory, versions, even out of Donini's own mouth. (As his longtime friend and climbing partner Greg Crouch plainly put it, "No story of a climb with Donini was ever told the same way twice.")

Still, Jim was willing to remember as best he could, heed the meanings of the alternate takes on his story, and dive into this adventure of self-understanding with all the enthusiasm, courage, and tenacity he brought to his exploration. He was impressively candid and seemed more than willing to critically assess the role he's played in both his successes and his failings, calling this journey inside as difficult and fulfilling as any trip he'd ever taken.

In the end, I hope this is a fair telling of the forces and choices that shaped one American climber's life.

CHAPTER 1

A MAN ON ONE OF HIS MOUNTAINS

MAY 21, 1999. 5 p.m. South Face, Thunder Mountain, Alaska Range.

One step at a time. He had to keep moving, just as he had all afternoon. He kept his eyes on the sun-scorched glacier below, hoping it would be warmer down there. He kept his weight on his good leg, avoiding all but the softest touches on the bad one.

Donini had been at this for six hours now and had dropped nearly 3,000 feet down the wall. There had been a lot of difficult travel down steep bands of friable rock and brittle ice, and he'd been living a hard truth every step of the way: Climbing down is always more challenging than climbing up. It's awkward, the feet are blind, ice tools are not designed for descent, and it's all the worse when you have a leg that isn't working properly and a badly broken partner high above you.

Keep moving.

After descending another short pillar of ice, he reached the final snow-slope. The angle eased, only fifty-five degrees now instead of ninety, but that wasn't entirely a good thing: Yes, it meant he was finally getting closer to the bottom of the wall and the safety of the tent they'd left early that morning, but it also meant that he had to put more weight on his bad leg. He shifted his balance back to the good one.

One step at a time.

As welcoming as the sun below was, and as tantalizing as it was to see the tent so close, his injured leg was stiffening more with each step kicked. The protective cocoon of shock was wearing off, and he still had 800 feet to descend down dangerous, rotten snow.

Just get it done.

Donini had always been good at compartmentalizing. It had served him well, again and again, on walls like this, but also, he'd come to understand, in other parts of his life. He'd always been able to push discomforts aside, and this afternoon he'd been able keep away dark thoughts of how badly his partner Malcolm Daly must be suffering. *But don't think about that. Just focus on what needs to be done now. Every moment in all your years in the mountains has been preparation for this. Just get down. Deal with the glacier when you get there. Then deal with whatever the hell comes next.*

He knew he'd been impossibly lucky. It seemed ridiculous that Malcolm could have fallen more than 200 feet and slammed into Jim, crampons first, down at the belay, and left him with nothing more than a single spear hole. But that seemed the verdict: they both could have died when Malcolm fell, but instead Jim only had one tear in the right leg of his Gore-Tex suit, a stain of crimson on the ragged edges, a bruise swelling on his thigh.

Malcolm's condition was an entirely different matter.

Everything had gone so wrong, so quickly. They'd been climbing well that morning and seemed to have the first ascent of this huge Alaskan wall in the bag. They'd cruised the poor snow at the bottom and the rockband. They'd made quick work of the big triangular snowfield midway up the wall and then sailed up the first pitches of the beautiful ribbon of blue water ice that led to the summit ridge. The climb was *done*. Nearing the top, Jim offered his friend a gift: the final leads that would take Malcolm to his first Alaskan summit. Malcolm happily grabbed the honor and the rack and set off. He was fast and solid, and he raced up the block of technical pitches.

An hour later, far out of sight on the last pitch, Malcolm scratched his tools at the top of the face, just a step away from easy ground.

Then Jim felt the rope go slack. There was a scream, a sickeningly long loop of rope arcing through the air, followed by Malcolm, splayed out against the sky. Malcolm slammed into him, then fell past, until the rope finally caught him seventy feet below the belay.

Then, silence.

ON A BEAUTIFUL desert evening twenty years later, Jim poured a glass of decent Italian red as we sat outside his teardrop trailer and looked up at the dome of Arizona granite we'd spent the day climbing. The last of the fires that plagued the American Southwest that summer were still smoldering, and the sky and the rocks glowed with the colors of flame.

We sat in rapt silence, until I asked a question that I realized I'd never asked in any of our conversations: *Of all the climbs he'd done, which truly captured the spirit of the mountains he'd known?* I expected him to bring up one of the big, hard lines he's best known for, but he surprised me. Without a pause, he said, "Thunder Mountain."

I asked why he'd choose Thunder—a smaller Alaskan peak that isn't a well-known mountain, and an ascent that could arguably be described as a glaring failure—and the answer came quick. "Thunder was all about partnership, and that's what matters more than anything else. Thunder was trust, commitment, and having faith. I learned as much from that one day as I did from any other day I've had in the mountains—or any other day in my life, for that matter."

As he started the Thunder story, I understood his point.

WHEN JIM FINALLY touched the bottom of the wall, he took stock of the sickening predicament. He was down but Malcolm was alone, thousands of feet above, tied into the wall with a shattered right foot, compound fractures of his left leg, and blood pooling in his boots.

Committing to descending alone had been a terribly difficult decision, breaking two of the bedrock rules of climbing: you don't leave your partner, and you don't leave your ropes. But, really, what choice did they have? No one was going to look for them. The pilot who'd brought them into the Tokositna Glacier a week before, Jim's friend Paul Roderick, had already flown by that morning, doing his daily check. But even if Roderick came back, the gully where Malcolm fell was tight and dark. It would be hard to see the climbers unless he knew exactly where to look.

At first they thought about staying together, lowering Malcolm down pitch by pitch. But after just one rope length it was clear that this plan wasn't going to work. Getting Malcolm down from the bottom of his fall to the ledge where he was now tied in had been an epic of engineering and pain. A splint

Jim belaying on Thunder Mountain in the Alaska Range in 1999 (Photo by Malcolm Daly)

of ice axes and duct tape had fallen apart the first time Malcolm weighted it, and whenever his foot touched the wall, his screams echoed round the valley.

So, up on the four-foot-wide ledge of ice stained with far too much blood, the pair agreed that Jim needed to get down alone, somehow, despite the complicated technical terrain and his ripped-up leg, while Malcolm waited above.

But waited for what? They were the only party for miles, and they didn't have a radio. In the noble moments of planning for the trip, they'd agreed that a radio would be cheating. That was one of the *Donini-isms* that Jim's always happy to share, maxims that chart the proper path in the mountains— or at least proper according to him: No oxygen in the Himalaya. No fixed ropes in Patagonia. No radios in Alaska. Both men agreed to the righteous principle that they'd fight the mountain cleanly. And now they were paying the price.

They made a plan. Jim would leave Malcolm with all the food, all the extra clothes, and painkillers. They'd join their two ropes together and Malcolm would lower Jim down to the bottom of the large, steep, triangular snowfield below. Then Malcolm would untie and let the ropes drop, and Jim would start down alone, leaving the ropes behind on the most technical sections of rock below in case he, or rescuers, needed to climb back up to Malcolm.

With miles of crevasses to navigate alone should he reach the glacier, it was unclear how Jim would actually contact those rescuers, but that was a problem for later, and as Jim set up the ledge, Malcolm's characteristic sunniness helped. When Jim first reached him after the fall, Malcolm had ignored the bloody, broken mess of his legs, held up a pinky torqued at a sickening angle, and joked. "Uh-oh," he said, "I think I broke a finger!" Then, when he saw the gouge in Jim's leg that his crampon had made, Malcolm laughed again, thinking it was hilarious that when he designed crampons for his gear company, Trango, he'd branded them *Harpoons*. "Look," he said, "I *Harpoon*ed you!"

The first part of Jim's mission went as well as anyone could have hoped. He reached the bottom of the snowfield, the ropes fell cleanly, and he disappeared into the rockbands. For a time, Malcolm could hear the tap of tools on rock and ice, and agonized grunts when Jim caught his leg wrong, but soon both men were as alone as anyone ever was.

Jim settled into the painstaking work of the descent. He'd never faced a predicament close to this. While a bad fall, high on a wall, is so much a part of what *can* happen in the big mountains, in Jim's forty years of serious climbing, this was the first time he or anyone with him had been injured.

Just before 6 p.m., he stepped onto the glacier. The sun was just a few steps away now, but the line of shadow painted by the ridge of Thunder was racing toward their tent, a hundred yards out on the wash of ice.

Up on the wall, Malcolm could see Jim again. He watched his friend hop and drag his leg, fall and crawl as he chased the sun, finally reaching the tent. He was glad Jim was safe.

Down in the tent, Jim peeled off his bright orange windsuit and assessed the rough-lipped triangle of the cut in his leg and the black lump of the hematoma that was swelling beneath it. He put his head down onto the sleeping bag, realizing how profoundly exhausted he was, but then felt something even more profound: guilt. He had two big sleeping bags to keep warm. He had weeks of food. He had left his friend, and there was a very good chance that friend might die before the night was done. Long ago and far from any mountains, another friend had died beside him, and he never wanted to live through that again.

Jim had been lying in the tent for barely ten minutes when off to the west, where he shouldn't have heard a thing on such a windless day, he caught a mechanical whine, growing distinctly louder. He crawled out, hobbled to his feet, and started frantically waving his windsuit in great arcs at the unmistakable outline of a plane drifting down into the valley.

MALCOLM HAD PROPOSED the adventure. A couple of months before, they'd both been at an outdoor trade show where Malcolm was showing people new products from Trango and Jim was working the room as a sales rep for Trango and other manufacturers. Malcolm bought Jim a beer and complained: work was stressful and the rest of his life was paying the price. He needed a big-mountain fix, going climbing himself instead of selling climbing gear to strangers. Jim knew the feeling.

They'd climbed together on day trips for years, and Jim had always thought that Malcolm would be a great partner for a bigger adventure, but Malcolm never had the time. So when his friend suggested they run off to Alaska, Jim happily said yes.

His partners love that: Donini always says yes. But these same people also say that he's able to be that spontaneous because he doesn't always prepare for mountains like other climbers do. He's not much of a researcher. He doesn't obsess about details, hunt for photos, or look at maps, and he doesn't usually read other people's accounts. He says he likes to learn a peak by *climbing* it, not by hearing what others think. Indeed, he's rarely interested in considering routes that have been done before. He can't see the point: "Why follow someone's else footsteps when there are so many things that no one else has ever seen, let alone touched?"

This time, not long after Jim said yes to Malcolm's proposal, he came up with at least half a plan: Why not have a look at the south ridge of Mount Hunter, one of the magnificent unclimbed lines of the Alaska Range? At 14,573 feet, Hunter is the third highest mountain in the range, a monster of a peak with a massive footprint. The south ridge would be a mammoth undertaking of both difficulty and distance, perfectly suiting Jim's penchant for hard, remote, and serious climbs.

Just how serious the route on Hunter was became clear when Jim and Malcolm landed on the Tokositna Glacier at the base of the peak. Their planned line looked chaotic, threatened by rock- and icefall, and complicated to reach. It appeared, according to Malcolm, "stupid and dangerous." Jim's ambitious plan wasn't going to happen.

But their decision to forsake a radio meant the pair was going to be stuck in the big amphitheater until the scheduled pickup a couple of weeks later, so they looked for another objective. Across the valley, they spotted a far more modest but still intriguing line of barely connected snow and ice features up a steep wall of black rock. Jim started imagining how to connect the uncertain dots of the wall: up a big cone of snow at the base, then puzzle through the rock to a large triangle of snow, then a final stretch of ice leading to the summit ridge.

Jim guessed the climb might have some difficult moments, but he had faith in Malcolm. Much of the unwritten but oft-told "Donini Alpine Manifesto" circles around the chemistry of partnership. Jim will always say nothing matters more than *who* you choose to climb with. Drive and technical competence are never the full picture: many physically brilliant climbers can't handle the hazards and the isolation of big-mountain routes or the grinding boredom of expedition life, stuck in stormbound tents with the very likely possibility that they may never get to touch, or even see, the mountain. You want someone who climbs with unbounded enthusiasm, but it's just as important to have a partner who can walk away without regrets, because regret can incite fatal choices. Malcom ticked all the boxes.

THE NEXT MORNING, the pair walked across the glacier from their base camp, ready to start up the gloomy face. They soloed together up several hundred feet of moderate ground and then Jim passed Malcolm the rack of ice screws at the base of a steeper section. Malcolm barely left the belay before realizing that this stretch, which looked inconsequential from below, was actually frothy slush you could punch your arm through. "It was the worst, most dangerous climbing I'd ever done," he remembered.

He called down, "Jim, I don't think I can do this . . ."

"Alright, I'll do it," Donini grumbled back.

Malcolm descended, sheepishly passing over the rack. It was, he thought, an awfully feeble beginning to his first Alaskan climb, so he felt great relief when Jim got twenty feet up and swore, "I can't believe you just tried to climb this!"

The two started looking for another route up, but this proved complicated—they were forced up, down, left, and right for nine pitches to avoid the bad snow, but at least the rock proved better than it had looked from below. They were soon at the base of the big snowfield, which they now saw led up to a beautiful, unexpected solution to the steep upper headwall: a fine thread of ice that hadn't been visible from below.

But up on the snowfield they ran into a frustrating hitch. Jim pointed down at one of his feet and cursed. The front points of his crampons were completely bent back. It was puzzling that the crampons had failed so easily—particularly to Malcolm, whose company had made them—but the men had little choice but to descend.

Back down in base camp, they unraveled the mystery of Jim's gear. Lack of planning again. Packing for the trip, he'd grabbed demo crampons from the Trango warehouse that hadn't been heat-treated. He obviously hadn't bothered to check the crampons, which sported a "Do not use—samples only" stamp on the heel. Malcolm rolled his eyes and passed Jim his spare pair of real crampons.

The following morning, the pair headed back up the face. With knowledge of the line, they climbed faster, quickly reaching the ice runnel that arced to the top of the wall. But the fates were against them yet again. This time, a chunk of ice caromed down the gulley, smashing into Malcolm's arm. He couldn't move or feel the limb for nearly thirty minutes and worried about continuing. They headed down again.

All of this was taken in stride, simply accepted as tolls to pay for the ascent. Early the next morning, with the last stars fading out of the short northern night, the pair headed back up for a third go. They were quickly at speed, reaching the high ice by 9:30 a.m. Jim offered Malcolm the rack for the beautiful series of final pitches, and Malcolm danced up the delicate mix of ice and rock. When we spoke about the climb twenty-one years later, Malcolm told me these were some of the best pitches he'd ever climbed, anywhere. The gully ended and he moved onto an easier snow slope that led to a fifteen-foot pillar of ice and the top of the face.

"But that last little bit of ice," Malcolm remembered, "turned out to be the same crap that stopped me cold days before at the bottom of the climb." He placed an ice screw that he guessed wouldn't hold and hacked his way to the top of the pillar, only to find that the sun creeping over the top of the wall was further rotting the ice. He placed a crampon unsteadily on one wall, slammed his other foot into a hole in the snow, and hooked the pick of an axe over the lip of Thunder Mountain.

And then it all happened: the pillar collapsed, Malcolm fell backward, the screw pulled out without a tug. He slid down the snow, ricocheted through the long gully, and continued on and on until he speared Jim's thigh—and then flew past him. One of screws far above finally held and Malcolm slammed to a stop.

He had fallen nearly 200 feet. The rope caught him, but barely: seven of its eleven core strands had been cut. He passed out from the pain.

The wall went silent.

DONINI'S DESCENT FROM Thunder has become a legend of climbing, called a heroic, even impossible, feat.

Jim brushes that appraisal off with a touch of irritation, saying, "It wasn't that hard. I'd already been down the wall twice. I wasn't that badly injured. I really didn't do anything. Malcolm's the hero, not me."

That's both true and not. Yes, Malcolm had to suffer through incredible pain alone and came all too close to a terrible end on the ledge. But if Donini hadn't made it down the wall, or if he'd simply said, "I'll stay with you," there's a good chance that neither man would have lived.

Jim's insistent modesty about his climb down Thunder has the tenor of most of his stories: He consistently says that what *he* does isn't much of anything, while the people around him are remarkable. He swears that luck has played just as big a part as his talent has in his successes. He insists that the real thing that matters in this and any other story about his climbing is the way that his community—the family of climbers—has always come together to do what needs to be done, without a thought for themselves.

And that's what happened next on Thunder Mountain.

AFTER DROPPING CLIMBERS off below Denali around 6 p.m., Paul Roderick felt the hairs on the back of his neck standing up. After years of flying in the Alaska Range, he'd learned to trust his instincts, and somehow he knew it was the Thunder team that was in trouble. He thought he'd better fly by.

The man down on the glacier was waving what seemed to be an orange flag. He was something of a stick figure, so Roderick assumed it was Donini rather than his heftier partner. If Donini was asking for help, something was very wrong. Roderick landed, and the man hobbled over. Roderick had never seen look Jim so ragged, and the pair were airborne again in an instant, bound for Talkeetna.

Looking down from the darkening wall, Malcolm breathed a sigh of relief when he heard the plane whine back down the valley, but he already knew things were going to get a lot worse before they got better. He would be spending the night on the wall. The temperature was falling and the wind was rising. Waves of cramps in both his legs brought searing pain. He started to shiver as clouds mustered on the horizon.

IT WAS 1 a.m., Saturday, May 22, before Jim was free of his responsibilities with the Denali National Park rescue team and could call Malcolm's wife in Boulder. He wanted to be as clear as he could, so he began the call by simply telling Karen Daly, "There has been a fall. A very serious fall." Karen pressed for details, but they only confused her. Thunder Mountain? Malcolm was climbing *Hunter*. Why was Donini talking about Thunder?

Jim explained as best he could, then promised he'd keep her posted. An hour later, she got a call from J.D. Swed, the chief climbing ranger for the park. Swed helped Karen understand that she should probably come to Alaska. By four that afternoon, she was on a plane to Anchorage.

Jim then started trying to reach his own wife. That took some time. Angela, a medical researcher, was attending a conference in San Diego and was reveling in the rare privilege of being able to turn off her phone. Jim's purist insistence on disconnecting from the outside world during his expeditions meant there was no reason to look for messages from him.

So she was stunned when she turned her phone back on at the end of the conference that weekend and discovered she had nine voicemails from Jim. She called him right away and heard the struggle in his voice the moment he picked up. He didn't say much about the accident but just wanted to share the latest news: A plane had flown by Thunder that morning, Malcolm's second morning on the ledge, and Malcolm had waved his arms. A rescue was underway, but it was complicated. Jim's voice caught when he told her how bad he was feeling that *he* was safe, but unable to help, while Malcolm was up there in worsening weather. He didn't tell her that a paramedic was treating a hole in his leg. He said she didn't need to worry and didn't need to come to Alaska; he'd be home soon.

After Jim was finished with the paramedic, he went down the street to the Fairview Inn and had a beer and a meal. He sat in the bar, as alone and helpless as he'd ever felt. "It was incredibly frustrating," Jim remembered, "to feel that useless and to know there was nothing to do but wait."

Mountain rescues involve a complex mix of people and emotions—a combination of fate, endurance, creativity, and talent—and more ingredients than usual were thrown into Malcolm's extraction. The rescue team had just completed a multiday search on Denali and were exhausted. The amount of blood that Malcolm had lost meant time was ticking. The weather was turning poor, and growing winds would make it hard to land a rescue team on the summit ridge. The rangers consequently felt that climbing up to Malcolm was the best option, until Jim explained how difficult the route was.

The rescue was finally mounted at the end of Malcolm's third day on the ledge, and it was an impressive feat of engineering, risk, and luck. A ranger on the end of a 200-foot longline cable swung wildly in the wind and had to climb up, tied to the line, to reach Malcolm's perch. By the time the chopper got Malcolm to the hospital, storms that would rage for a week had engulfed the mountain.

There was one last moment that reinforced Jim's choice of Thunder as his iconic mountain moment. When the rescuer finally climbed onto the ledge, Malcolm took one look at his ice axes and laughed: "Hey, cool, you're using Trango tools!"

"Can you imagine," Jim said twenty-two years later, "going through all that and still having the inner strength to joke? Having a partner like that— *that's* what makes a climb great."

THUNDER HAS BECOME part of the lore of alpinism, both as a cautionary tale and an inspirational one. It's pulled out to demonstrate that the worst can happen, to the best climbers, at the least expected times, but also to show that wells of endurance and resilience can carry us through those times.

Thunder is also a reminder of the potentially lasting consequences of the choice to go into the mountains. As much as he managed a remarkable feat of survival, Malcolm's injuries continue to plague him. He endured six surgeries and the eventual amputation of his right leg below the knee, as well as a series of heart attacks and strokes due to complications in the years that followed.

"But Malcolm is this amazing man who never stops impressing me," Jim told me. They've stayed very close over the years and, with Malcolm using a prosthetic, have even been able to climb together. He's not at 100 percent, but it's remarkable how far Malcolm has come. When I spoke to him in the fall of 2020, Malcolm had just returned from a road trip with Jim to the granite spires of City of Rocks, Idaho. The first thing he said was, "I wouldn't be here if Jim hadn't saved my life that day. There's no one else [who's] better in that kind of situation. No one could make you feel safer or offer a better hope for the outcome. That climb down was pretty incredible. I sure as hell couldn't have done it if Jim was the one who fell."

Then, he said, "I'm really glad that Donini's life is getting told. More people should know the whole story . . ."

CHAPTER 2

NON IL SOGNO AMERICANO

We all carry, inside us, people who came before us.
—*Liam Callanan,* The Cloud Atlas

WHEN JIM PULLS on the threads of his family story, looking for hints of his life of mountain adventure, the line that holds the most weight runs back to his paternal grandfather. He never met the man—Giacomo Donini died in 1921, twenty-one years before Jim was born—but Jim heard enough stories around the Donini dinner table to see something of himself in his grandfather's own twisting tale.

"He was an interesting man," Jim said. "Tough. Smart enough to survive some pretty hard times. Took a lot of chances. Didn't like to live by rules; didn't like to be told what to do or think. Freedom was important. He was an *anarchist*."

And then, with a laugh, the greatest compliment from the mountain clan: "He sounds like a *climber*."

When Giacomo Donini arrived in New York in 1891, he was at the early edge of the largest single-country migration the United States had ever seen. In the three decades after Giacomo sailed from Marseille, France, on the SS *La Bretagne*, more than four million other Italians followed.

The pattern of the Italian immigration was unique in American history: While most other immigrants who arrived in the centuries before came with hopes of building a new life, virtually all the Italians who flooded the country from 1890 to 1921 (when federal legislation staunched the flow) referred to themselves as *i ritornati*: the returning. Almost all of them were men who came for work not available in Italy after the failures of Italian unification—and most of them planned to, and did eventually, return to Italy when they'd earned enough money.

Until that money came, the fabled promises of a welcoming, free America eluded most Italian migrants. Many came indentured to *padroni* (bosses) who worked them mercilessly and kept them isolated in urban ghettos in New York and Philadelphia or in rural work camps with terrible conditions. Few bothered to learn to speak English, and most experienced shocking prejudice in their interactions with Americans. The press often took vile stances toward them, and the public listened, sometimes rabidly. The year that Giacomo arrived, the *New York Times* ran an editorial lamenting the "filthy, wretched, lazy, criminal dregs" coming, and later that year eleven Italians who had been found innocent of the shooting of a cop were hung from trees by a raging mob outside a New Orleans courthouse. It was the largest mass lynching in American history.

Jim's grandfather had to navigate all that, and his journey to America had an added twist: as much as Giacomo wanted to go home, he could not be a *ritornato*, because he would never be welcome in Italy again.

Giacomo was born in Castel d'Aiano, a picturesque hill town of red slate roofs, limestone walls, and tight, cobbled alleys west of Bologna, in the northern province of Emilia-Romagna. Though he was born into relative comfort and privilege, he grew up in a time of great disruption sparked by the troubled attempts in the 1800s to unify the Italian peninsula's fragmented city-states.

Like many educated young men of the time, Giacomo was swept up in a movement that fought to create a very different Italy than the unifiers had in mind. By midcentury, anarchist groups had formed across Italy and were seeking, sometimes violently, to build a country without a centralized government, without a corrupt papacy, and with individual liberty as the only true guiding principle.

It's unclear what role Giacomo played in the anarchist uprising, but he was active enough that he was forced to escape the country in 1889, with court records showing that he was facing a life sentence of hard labor or death if he remained. He fled to France, spent a year as part of the Italian diaspora in Algeria, returned to France, then ran again just a few days later, catching passage on the *La Bretagne*. On May 20, 1891, after a nine-day trip in the third-class bowels of the ship, Giacomo Donini landed in New York, uncertain how long he'd stay.

As a talented cabinetmaker, Jim's grandfather made the most he could of America—he moved to Philadelphia and built a thriving business in Germantown, an Italian enclave in the heart of the city—but his revolutionary roots stayed strong, and they easily found water. There was an active cadre of anarchists in Philadelphia, still committed to changing Italy but also to spreading the anarchist manifesto in an America that they felt was not free enough, especially for people who sounded and looked like them. It's unclear whether Giacomo ever played a role in the movement's most violent actions (which included bombings across the country and, most dramatically, the assassination of King Umberto I by the United States–based anarchist Gaetano Bresci in Monza, Italy, in 1900), but Jim grew up hearing stories of dramatic characters, clandestine meetings, and guns stashed in the family home.

Most of these tales were told by the woman that Giacomo eventually married—Jim's grandmother Ermentina, whose own American story was just as compelling and twisted.

By 1900, Giacomo decided it would be worth risking a brief return to the home country to find a proper bride to bring back to America. Ermentina Banorri, then twenty-two, grew up in a village across the valley from Castel d'Aiano, and when the thirty-four-year-old Giacomo appeared, her parents saw him as a solution to a vexing problem: their daughter had fallen in love with a Jew, and that was simply not acceptable. Marriage to a wealthy American, fugitive anarchist or not, was a far better option, so Ermentina's parents packed her up and shipped her off with Giacomo.

Ermentina's resentments about losing her love and being sent across the sea were amplified by her experience arriving at Ellis Island, New York, which she'd come to fear. On the boat, she'd heard whispers about *l'Isola delle Lacrime*, the Island of Tears, a terrible place where families could be permanently separated by capricious authorities if paperwork was confused, motives for immigration were questioned, or illness was suspected. Giacomo was let through as a citizen, but Ermentina's papers took days to sort out.

When she was finally released from Ellis Island and taken to Philadelphia, there was more reason for tears. Bustling Germantown couldn't have been more different from the quiet village she'd left barely a month before, and she soon saw that there was much to dislike about Giacomo and the anarchist company he kept. "Let's just say," said Jim's sister, Sandy Yanosov, who heard many stories at Ermentina's knee, "that our grandfather wasn't a nice man."

Tensions only grew when the couple had children. Jim's father, Ugolino, came first in 1901, followed by Bruno a year later and then Ida three years after. But Giacomo was doing well enough in his business that the couple could afford a détente that lasted for years: each summer, Ermentina would take the children back to Italy, and Giacomo would stay in Philadelphia.

The child most influenced by the connection to Italy was Jim's father. Ugo Donini was a quiet, studious boy, and Ermentina feared that both Giacomo and America might uniquely corrupt him. So in 1912, when Ugo was eleven, his mother sent him off for an extended stay with her family in the hills of Emilia-Romagna, believing he'd be there three or four years. Ugo studied, mastered Italian, and, to the joy of his mother, became more fully immersed in the Catholic church than Giacomo would have ever allowed. Jim laughed when he recounted how church connections set his father up to serve for several months as an altar boy for the Archbishop of Bologna, Giacomo Paolo Giovanni Battista della Chiesa, and then how, a few months later, della Chiesa was elected Pope Benedict XV. Though Ugo had only attended him for a short time (and later strayed far enough from the faith to call himself an agnostic), he always took pride in telling people that he had once been an altar boy to a pope.

THE FIRST WORLD War, and the prejudices that followed it, complicated Ugo's return to America. Though Italians had fought alongside the United States and the Allied powers, in the aftermath of the war Americans were suspicious of anyone deemed "other," and it was more than two years after Armistice Day before Ugo was able to come home.

When Ugo finally arrived back in Philadelphia in 1920, Giacomo wanted him to join the family business, but Ermentina was having none of that. In Italy, Ugo had become an intellectual, with a special talent for mathematics, and she wanted her boy to continue his education.

She started an impressive campaign to fight the prejudices Ugo experienced every day and get him into the US Naval Academy in Annapolis, Maryland. She got the required letter of support for the application from their congressman—despite the great challenge that Congress was in the middle of passing the Emergency Quota Act, summarized in the popular press as "no more Jews and Italians"—and, in 1922, Ugo Donini became the first Italian American admitted to Annapolis.

He despised his time there. He said he was "treated like garbage" by teachers and students alike because of his heritage, and after only a few months, he left Annapolis in a fury.

A transfer to the University of Pennsylvania didn't go much better. Ugo was treated especially poorly there by a senior professor in mathematics who publicly shamed him for being Italian, and he always insisted this led him to abandon math and shift his major to the history of the Renaissance. Jim revels in the irony of the story: "That math professor belittled my father for being Italian, and he responded by becoming an expert in the greatest flourishing of civilization in history, which was Italian. That was a great big 'Fuck you,' and I was proud of him for it."

Ugo's expertise was impressive enough that when he graduated from the University of Pennsylvania, he was admitted into graduate school at La Salle University, a private Catholic school on the edge of Germantown, and was later asked to join the faculty. He taught in the history department at La Salle to great acclaim for the rest of his life.

Though Ugo spent his days in the bucolic commons of the La Salle campus, at night he returned to the bustle of the Italian community, sharing a small apartment above a butcher shop with his parents and his brother and sister and their partners, until the mid-1930s, when he finally met the woman who would redraw the map of his life.

Elizabeth "Betty" Deatore was a striking catch. Beautiful, charismatic, and effervescent, Betty was sixteen years younger than Ugo and came from what Jim describes as "a very blue-collar family" in central Philadelphia. Though they both shared Northern Italian roots, Betty was petite, blonde, and blue-eyed, while Ugo was taller and darker. The pair were married not long after they met at a dance, and their daughter, Alessandra (Sandy), arrived in 1941.

On July 23, 1943, James Ugo Donini was born, and twenty-seven minutes later, Jim's fraternal twin, William Bruno, followed.

CHAPTER 3

AMERICAN IDYLL

THE SHIFT INTO a new America was dramatic. With three children and a tenure-track position at La Salle, the Doninis had the incentive, and the means, to reach for the grand aspiration of the time: a suburb where you could build a dream home with a big yard on a broad street lined with trees, where your children would be free and safe and could live out the sparkling promise of America, no matter where you came from.

In the early 1950s, the freshly budded town of Blue Bell, just fifteen miles northwest of Philadelphia but immeasurably far culturally from Germantown, was just that kind of place. When the Doninis started building their two-story stone colonial on Valley Road in 1947, the wavy crescent on the north side of town seemed indeed to be a new frontier, with grand homes butting up against hundreds of acres of forest and farmland. The Doninis had an acre-and-a-half lot, and the twins were outside all day long, up in their tree fort, playing endless ball games. The creek that ran through their yard teemed with crayfish, Jim won 4-H medals for the chickens that he raised behind the house, and he kept a three-legged muskrat that he'd trapped as a pet.

It was a sublime place to be a boy. "Bill and I were allowed to just run free," Jim remembered. "I could walk through those woods for hours, convinced that I was exploring places that no one had ever been. Valley Road was where I learned how important wild places are to me."

Valley Road was also the place where the Doninis were finally stirred into the melting pot that had seemed out of reach for his mother's and father's families. There were still small slights—Jim recalls how the local priest, Father Kelly, always openly favored the Irish kids over the Italians, and he knew there were other places around Philadelphia where someone with a name like Donini would be less welcomed—but on Valley Road, Jim was an unhyphenated American.

Still, the family's roots became more obvious when Ermentina moved in when Jim was six. His grandmother's presence changed how things looked, sounded, and worked in the home. Italian was suddenly being spoken between Ugo and Ermentina, and village values followed, including elevating the boys in status above their older sister. Sandy remembered, "They could never do any wrong, and I was there to serve them. Jim couldn't even tie his own shoelaces when he started grade one . . ."

Jim's mother had her own struggles with her powerful and opinionated mother-in-law, but she turned that tension into an opportunity to chart an unusual, and newly American, path. If Ermentina wanted to rule the roost, do all the cooking, and take over raising the children, that was fine; Betty would build a life outside the home. She took a job at a local country club and quickly rose to a senior position that was a perfect fit for a woman who was so outgoing.

All of this explains Jim's social and competitive sides, but it's harder—especially for him—to uncover the roots of his passion for the outdoors and high places. He didn't have any of the formative family adventures that many of his mountain peers did. "The opposite," he insists. "We went a couple of times to the Poconos, and we'd visit relatives out on the Jersey Shore, but we never did any camping anywhere, and we really had little to do with nature as a family." The only mountain moment Jim could conjure from childhood was a faint recollection of seeing a newspaper when he was nine years old that announced that Everest had finally been climbed. "All I thought," Jim laughed, appreciating the foresight into his later approach to mountaineering, "was how disappointing that was, because I thought that meant there was no reason for anyone to ever climb it again."

One of the more puzzling aspects of Jim's childhood—and indeed, much of his adult life as well—was what it meant to be a twin. He doesn't tell typical twin stories that suggest he and Bill were joined at the hip, living strange coincidences of similarity and fate. Instead, most of the family stories about the brothers circle around how different they were: in temperament and action, in build, in drive, and in interests. There was little that suggested that Bill and Jim were siblings, let alone twins, especially when they were teenagers, and a strong thread of disappointment runs through Jim's early

Ugo, Jim, Sandy, and Betty Donini at their home on Valley Road in 1960 (Donini family collection)

stories about his brother. Both he and his sister were discomfortingly blunt in the critical judgments they held about Bill's failures.

Much of Bill's struggle, Sandy and Jim both suggested, seems to have been a response to the easy and continuous successes that Jim always enjoyed. He excelled, effortlessly, in school and sports, while Bill barely waded his way through. Jim was an accomplished middle-distance runner; by the end of high school, Bill weighed over 200 pounds and wasn't much accomplished in anything. "If I'm being honest," Jim said, "when it was just the two of us, I liked him fine, but out in the world, I was embarrassed to be his brother."

The boys' father wasn't any easier as a role model. In Ugo's forties, at a time when few senior adults were active, the bookish professor took up running. He was "one of the original health nuts," Jim said, and was impressively fanatic about running. "He ran seven miles nearly every day," Jim said, "picked dandelion leaves from our lawn for the salads that other families weren't eating then, [and forbade] us from having soft drinks. It was all great for me, but pretty hard on my brother, who just wasn't driven the way our father, or I, was."

Bill eventually escaped all these pressures in the way that many young men of his time did: as soon as he graduated high school, he joined the army. Bill headed off to Korea, while Jim took the very different, very expected, path of starting college at La Salle.

CHAPTER 4

THE BRIDGE

Yes, terrible things happen, but, sometimes,
those terrible things, they save you.
—*Chuck Palahniuk,* **Haunted**

IN ONE OF our strolls around his home in Ouray, Jim walked me along the south rim of the Uncompahgre River Gorge, a steep-walled canyon that's home to the Ouray Ice Park and Ice Festival and to a recently constructed *via ferrata* that he uses to stay fit on summer days when he's not out climbing. Jim was keen to talk about the climbs in the canyon and up on the snowy peaks that glimmered off in the high distance, but I pushed him to talk again about earlier days.

"There was never any question whether I'd go to university," he finally said as we stopped for a minute atop one of the bluffs. "My brother went away to the army, my sister got married, and I started at La Salle. It was all mapped out.

"But at university, for the first time in my life, I was lost. I was immature, I didn't know how to handle myself. Things were hard for me, and I'd never experienced that."

At college, aiming for a psychology degree, he just couldn't find his pace. He was getting poor grades and he understood for the first time what it was like to run in the back of the pack—in class and on the trails. But he didn't respond by working harder; he slacked off and had fun. He got soft in ways that surprised everyone who knew him.

That first year of college, Jim also started to see shadows darken his extended family. By the time he was leaving his teens, some of Jim's relatives were leading exemplary lives, while others were showing troubling patterns. Substance abuse problems surfaced. One of Jim's maternal uncles had a violent streak and served prison time.

When Jim was lost that freshman year at La Salle, the hardest thing was knowing how deeply he was disappointing his family—especially his father. But one stable comfort was Jim's best friend, Tom Dardis. The Dardis family— Greek, the other immigrants on the block—had moved onto Valley Road a few years before, and Tom had always been a voice of reason when Jim wavered.

At the end of his freshman year, Jim returned to Valley Road, struggling to make sense of what was happening, and Tom was there for him again. They played baseball, they joked around, they chased girls, and one night that spring, the two of them and a couple of other boys drove off to find a place they could have a beer. In Montgomery County, where Blue Bell sat, they were too young to drink, but in Schuylkill County, a few hours to the north, the rules were less strict. The four of them got into Jim's father's car and drove up for the evening.

When they started for home several hours later, Jim drove while the others slept off the beers. He left the turnpike, then started down the back roads to Blue Bell. He was tired. His eyes started to close. He rolled down the window for some air.

Everything went black.

JIM WOKE ON the side of the road, on his back. He was surrounded by flashing lights and the chaotic noise of shouts and whining machinery. He was vaguely aware of his car, off in the distance, the front end of its passenger side crumpled like tinfoil around the parapet of a small bridge.

Tom had been in the front seat on that side.

Sixty years later, when we sat on the edge of the Uncompahgre River Gorge, tears still came. "I killed my friend," Jim said with a catch in his throat. Tom Dardis died of catastrophic injuries at the scene, and one of the other young men who been in the back seat died a few days later. The third boy was battered but survived. With little more than a badly bruised chest, Jim was the least injured of all, at least on the outside.

Driving away from the gorge later that morning, heading into the high country above Ouray, where Jim wanted to show me some roadside rock climbs, I felt I had to push about the accident again. I asked the most difficult question to understand how the accident had been woven into the fabric of his life: Was he drunk at the wheel that night? The answer came without much of an edge. He's asked himself the same question a thousand times: Yes, he'd had a few beers, but he felt okay to drive and believed he'd simply dozed off. The policemen at the scene never even asked if he'd been drinking. In 1961, people drank and drove. The officers took Jim home.

More stinging tears came to Jim's eyes as he expressed his remorse about what he *didn't* do next. "I'm not a person that has regrets," he explained, "but the one thing that I've lamented every day of my adult life is that I never spoke to Tom's parents after the accident. Never told them what happened that night; never owned it. I just didn't know how to face them. I felt so much guilt in taking their son from them. Not going over to see them was the most cowardly thing I ever did."

Tension about the accident simmered along close-woven Valley Road, and it burned in the Donini house. Everyone tried to talk to Jim, but as his sister, Sandy, explained, "No one could get through to him. It was like he completely disappeared into himself, and it was terrible for our parents." The family thought it might help if Jim could get away for a time, so he was sent to live with Sandy, her husband, and their new baby for a few weeks. "But it was the strangest time," Sandy told me. "He never said a word about the accident, just acted as though nothing had happened at all."

That wasn't at all how that summer felt for Jim. He said he simply had no idea how to begin any conversations about what had happened, how he felt, or what to do. "I was a complete mess," he said with a slow shake of his head. "Nothing was the same anymore. I couldn't face anyone. I couldn't be around that neighborhood and those people—not even my family—anymore. And there was no way I could go back to school.

"I knew I had to do something *entirely* different with my life. So I did."

CHAPTER 5

SPECIAL FORCES

STRUCTURE. DISCIPLINE. PURPOSE.

Those were the simple ingredients that Jim decided would get him past the accident, and there was an obvious place he could find all three: the army. Nothing in his life to that point had hinted that he'd end up in the military, but in the limbo that he was suffering, it made perfect sense. Someone else would be in control. He'd get constant feedback about his worth. There was an element of self-punishment, too: as a good Catholic boy, he could atone for his wrongs through suffering and abasement, and the army offered both those expiations almost as well as the church.

But there was still enough of the honors student in him, still enough of the competitive runner, that he wasn't going to settle for simply being a grunt like his brother was. Jim went to a recruitment office and told them that he wanted to join the Special Forces, the newly formed elite units known for their green berets.

The recruiters laughed. You don't *sign up* for the Green Berets, they told him. You go through Basic Training, and *if* you survive that, *we* decide where you end up. He stayed adamant: No, I *will* be going into the Special Forces.

He thrived in Basic. He loved the order, the predictability, the hard physical days. There wasn't time to think about the bad year at college or the bridge. He didn't talk about the accident any more than he had at home, but in Basic, that didn't matter. There, no one's past mattered; you were all part of a noble cause much greater than yourself. All that counted was that you believed in that cause, and in the men that you spent every breathing moment with.

Jim completed Basic, then got accepted, as he said he would, into Special Forces. But when he was told that he could move through Special Forces training faster if he was willing to serve as a radio repair technician, attitude burned to the surface again. "No way," he told his officers. "That's bullshit. I'm not a support person. I want to be on an operational detachment team. An A-Team."

He won all those sparring matches, and when he was finally admitted as a full Special Forces candidate, he knew he'd found his people. This was a really smart group; one of them had just come out of Cornell Law School. "They were strong, really good men, ready to learn as much as they possibly could," Jim said. He'd never been around a team of people who worked so hard and so well together and who could trust each other so unconditionally. He was sold on the honor of serving with them. "I'd had lots of friends growing up," Jim said, "but as someone who's always preferred to do individual sports like running, and often preferred to just be out in the woods on my own, I'd never really been part of a *team*." The men spent twenty-four hours a day together. They were pushed physically, but they also spent long stretches in the classroom. Jim saw it all as a privilege: "This was like a university program, except that you completed it in months rather than years. It's really where I learned the critical ingredients of climbing: how to wholly commit to an objective and completely trust my partners."

Jim joined a team of trainees at Fort Bragg, North Carolina, home of the 7th Special Forces Group (Airborne). The operational detachments within the battalions helped to cement small, tight squads: twelve men, two of them officers, and a master sergeant, who, as Jim underscored, "is the fucking dude." Each team had two members who specialized in one of five disciplines—weapons, demolitions, communications, intelligence, and medical—to ensure redundancy in the field.

Jim chose the medical specialty, which had the longest training course. He spent forty-six weeks at the Brooke Army Medical Center at Fort Sam Houston, Texas, followed by eight weeks of practical instruction, which included sitting in on human autopsies and performing amputations and bullet extractions on dogs and goats. Forty-four students began the course with him; fourteen graduated, and Jim was at the top of the class. When he returned to Bragg, he joined the 1st Operational Detachment of the 7th— the A-Team he'd been looking for.

When Jim signed up in 1962, joining the army wasn't as freighted with moral complexity as it soon would be. The draft and the first anti-war protests were still a couple of years away, and, as Jim explained, "People still believed it was a privilege to serve and enlisting was an honorable thing to do." Still, Jim did ponder his choices: "I was a lifelong liberal raised by two liberal parents, and no one expected I'd ever wear a uniform. People could see Bill in the army, but not me."

By the time Jim joined the Green Berets, Vietnam was smoldering, but Vietnam wasn't the only place, nor even the most likely place, that Jim's unit might head to. Through the early 1960s, the world was becoming more tangled, with more guerilla insurgencies—exactly the thing the Green Berets were being trained to suppress—springing up. There was a chance that Special Forces teams could be sent to any number of hot spots, but stepping onto foreign soil was a very delicate political process, and everyone on the team understood it could be a long wait before they'd see action.

While they waited, the team went through every kind of preparation imaginable. They paddled whitewater, bivouacked through cold winter nights, and endured survival weeks in the ersatz jungle of the Blue Ridge Mountains. They became experts at difficult parachute insertions, pioneering new techniques. They tried jumping from as low as 600 feet and as high as 4,000. "Every time," Jim said, "we could get eleven of us where we were supposed to be, but there was always that twelfth guy who was way off somewhere else, hung up in a tree." People got injured on jumps; one sergeant broke his back.

The off days were just as important for team building as the long days of training were. Several of the men on the team shared an apartment in Greensboro, North Carolina, intentionally far from the base and close to the coeds at the University of North Carolina, Greensboro. Jim has endless stories of the trouble they got up to.

But even on those infamous days off, the men had to be ready to spring into action. One memorable Sunday night at the apartment in Greensboro, Jim recalled, "We'd been partying for two days when the master sergeant called and said, 'You guys have to get back here right away. We've got a training mission.'

"No one was in any condition to drive, but when the sergeant says go, you go. We grabbed our stuff, chugged coffee, drove ninety miles to Pope Airfield, hurried into our uniforms, and jumped on a C-130 at two in the morning."

They were told that they were going to be practicing a coastal jungle insertion, flying below radar altitude (1,000 feet) the entire way. "It was bumpy, and we'd all been drinking for two days," Jim said with a guffaw. "Everyone was puking the whole time."

Their target was Isla de Vieques, a barren, mangrove-rimmed island southeast of Puerto Rico that had been used as a naval training range since the 1940s. The plan was to drop the team into the mangroves behind the beaches on the south coast, but in the dawn light, the pilot misjudged both his altitude and the width of the narrow island, and the jump went spectacularly wrong.

"I ended up on the beach," Jim said, "but most ended up in trees, or, worse, in the ocean, and they had to swim, which was pretty dangerous with all the crap we were carrying.

"But that's the army. When the green light comes on and tells you to jump, you jump. There were lots of lessons like that, about just stepping up and doing what's needed in the moment. That's served me well for a long time."

OF ALL THE life-changing experiences that Jim had in the Special Forces, there was one that took time to percolate but truly altered the path of his life. One summer day, Jim's Special Forces unit got sent to the Linville Gorge, a pretty quartzite canyon northwest of Charlotte, North Carolina. They were told they were there to learn to rock climb, something Jim had never heard of.

The instructors—members of a British Special Air Service mountain team imported to train US soldiers—set up topropes, and Jim tied in without expecting anything other than another physical challenge. Instead, something clicked. "It really felt from the first moves that this is where I *belonged*," Jim said. "I can't explain why, but I remember thinking, in a way that I'd never felt, *I have done this before* . . ."

He loved the movement and the way that he seemed to be built for the flow of climbing. Being off the ground, with air under his feet, didn't spook him, and all through the afternoon he leapt at the chance to try harder things. "That day," he believes, "changed everything. I never climbed in the army after that one afternoon, and I didn't get the chance to tie into a rope again for two years, but it was in my head now. I never stopped thinking about how I felt on that rock."

After nearly three years of perpetual training, Jim's unit finally received a live order in September 1964. With little advance notice, they were going to be front and center in a politically charged mission to rescue US citizens, most of them consular personnel, held hostage by Simba rebels in the US Embassy in Stanleyville (now Kisangani), capital of the newly independent Republic of the Congo.

The Pentagon brass responded to the siege of the embassy with two options for a rescue, one of which was christened Operation Golden Hawk. The bold scheme would see Jim's unit parachuted in at night near Stanleyville, dropping with rafts that they'd use to float into the city. They'd sneak in, rescue the hostages at dawn, and then raft out to a rendezvous with a helicopter.

An explosion of last-minute preparation kicked in, but just before the team was set to leave, the mission was questioned. Hawks in Lyndon Johnson's cabinet were keen to win political points with the rescue, but Johnson himself was reluctant to intervene, given concerns starting to surface about US involvement in Vietnam.

The final nail in the coffin of the plan was pounded during a serendipitous conversation at a Washington dinner party. A general involved in the mission and a woman who was raised in Stanleyville were talking about Golden Hawk, and the woman said that the maps for the mission had the direction of the flow of the Lualaba River wrong and didn't account for Boyoma Falls, a sixty-mile-long chain of fifteen-foot-high cataracts east of the city. If Jim's team had followed the plan, the rescue attempt would have failed catastrophically. The mission was quietly scrapped.

After Golden Hawk dissolved, it was time for Jim to consider reenlistment. Not long before, he'd been promoted to buck sergeant, and he was now told that he'd be made staff sergeant if he signed up again. "That was really flattering," he said. "The idea that I was worthy of being made sergeant was a huge thing for me, unheard of after only three years in the Forces."

But in those three years, the world had changed. Jim knew that he would be seeing a very different kind of action if he reenlisted. He wouldn't be completing one-off missions like Golden Hawk; he'd be going to Southeast Asia and stepping into a conflict already cloaked in some very dark shadows. This could be especially true for a Special Forces unit likely to be sent into the heart of that darkness.

It was a difficult choice: Jim was exceptionally close to the men on his team and felt a strong sense of obligation to them, but he also knew how hard his time in the service had been on his parents, who struggled with him joining a war that they opposed and still wanted him to return to college.

His parents' voices won out. Jim didn't reenlist, and he returned to Philadelphia just before his unit deployed to Asia. "They got into some really weird shit," he said. "I can't begin to imagine how my life would have turned out—or maybe even ended—if I'd decided to go." Not long after they arrived in Vietnam, Jim's unit disappeared into the underbelly of the war, joining ten other Special Forces teams in the covert fight against Pathet Lao paramilitaries on the Bolaven Plateau in Laos.

Because the Laotian campaign was classified and largely unknown by the public, Jim heard little about what his teammates faced during their two years in the hills. Despite how close they'd been in training, he had no contact with any of them other than Ross Johnson after he left the unit; not reenlisting was a boundary that was hard to reach across. It was years before he learned that three of his friends had been killed in action. Jim did not know, or would not tell me, their names.

EVEN IF HE doesn't discuss it much, Jim's time in the Special Forces figures large in the fabric of his climbing life. One of the more interesting threads is the way his time in the Green Berets has become part of the Donini legend in the climbing community. Many people—especially those who knew Jim through his time climbing in the early 1970s—assumed that he fought in Vietnam. I heard these people say things as vivid, and wrong, as "You could tell by the look in Donini's eyes that this was a man who had killed people." They said stories about Donini in Vietnam circulated around Yosemite campfires for years.

Those same people were clear, however, that Jim himself was not the source of those stories and had never hinted that he was in Vietnam or saw combat. Instead, people had simply connected the dots incorrectly—as they do when the subjects of stories don't tell the stories themselves.

The stories that Jim *has* told about being a Green Beret tend to be the same kinds of tales that he weaves about his climbing adventures: crazy moments of drinking and brawling and women, the screwups like the missed jump over Isla de Vieques, his love for his comrades.

Jim is quick to credit the military not just for giving him back his life after the accident on the bridge but also for teaching him foundational lessons—especially ones he would apply in the mountains. He learned to trust his decisions. He learned how to be tough. He swears his relationship with fear changed. "I faced enough scary situations during training," he said, including live weapons exercises and difficult jumps, "that I honestly don't get scared anymore. I learned how to appreciate and move through fear. I've honestly never gone into a climb feeling nervous."

It also taught him patience: "I know how to turn off, settle in, and just wait. We learned how to wait in the cold, in the rain, in the dark, and we learned how to turn off our minds humping big loads for hours, day after day. Those are great lessons for mountains."

Most of all, he said, the military taught him about the paramount importance of strong partnerships in risky situations. "I learned what you can do when you're with the right people. People you can absolutely trust, people who can step up when you can't, people who are easy to be with in difficult places."

CHAPTER 6

FINDING A WAY UP

WHEN JIM STEPPED away from the army at the age of twenty-two in 1965 and returned to Blue Bell, it seemed like his plan to straighten out his life had worked. He was ready to take the lessons that he'd learned, put the past behind him, and complete his degree in psychology at La Salle.

"Because I'd really learned to discipline myself, going back into school was incredibly easy," he said. "The pace was so much slower than it had been during Forces training, and I was really enjoying myself."

But there was a difference now: he'd become obsessed with climbing. The feeling of movement he'd experienced years before in the Linville Gorge had blossomed into a conviction that he had to try climbing again.

That wasn't an easy ambition in suburban Philadelphia in 1965. Information on where to climb was hard to come by, and outside the main venues in the East, like the Shawangunks and Adirondacks of New York and the White Mountains of New Hampshire, and isolated pockets in the South, like Seneca Rocks, West Virginia, and Stone Mountain, North Carolina, very few climbing areas had been developed, and partners were hard to find.

So Jim did what most people did at the time: he hunted down every climbing book he could get his hands on and tried to figure out the game by reading. Though he'd never seen a rock face higher than the topropes he'd done in the Linville Gorge, books convinced him that the real point of climbing was to summit *mountains*, and that rock climbing in a place like Linville was merely practice.

Jim was particularly drawn to the stories about the great climbers from the Alps—especially, in a nod to his heritage, the Italians like Giusto Gervasutti, Walter Bonatti, and Riccardo Cassin. These masters helped set a path for Jim that has lasted through his climbing career. They taught him the importance of style over success; of self-reliance, a minimalist approach, and small teams; and full but reverent commitment to bold objectives. They preached climbing as an act of supplication rather than conquest. "Connecting with them," he said, "made me the proudest I'd ever felt of being Italian."

Though actual mountains were years away for Jim, he was committed to mastering the skills he'd eventually need to climb them. He discovered there was climbing potential on a sedimentary formation on the Delaware River barely twenty-five miles from Blue Bell. These cliffs—now known as High Rocks—were as much as 150 feet high, and between classes at La Salle, Jim would sneak off and solo around or practice rappelling on a nylon sailing line that he'd scavenged. He never saw other climbers.

Jim's climbing dreams were better served when he started a new summer pattern with his Special Forces friend, Ross Johnson. Ross's father ran the maintenance crew at the University of Minnesota in Minneapolis, and every summer Jim would travel west, live with Ross's family, and work around the campus with Ross as unionized laborers making good money.

Jim had heard rumors that climbers were sometimes seen on the gunmetal gray walls of Interstate State Park near Taylors Falls, Minnesota, on the St. Croix River, and he dragged Ross along to explore. The river borders Minnesota and Wisconsin, and basalt cliffs half a pitch high line the shores of both states. Typical of columnar-basalt crags, the area offers both corner cracks and thin, technical face climbs, and Jim discovered right away that cracks, especially wide cracks, were going to be his specialty. There was something about his build—his long arms and broad hands, his reach, his flexibility—that was perfectly suited to the contortions of crack climbing, but nothing prophesied his lifelong preference for wide cracks better than his feet. They are one of first things you notice about the man, especially in rock shoes: he has flippers—long, thin, size twelve paddles, exaggerated by bony ankles, that seem almost purpose-built to bridge wide cracks.

Taylors Falls was also where Jim discovered that he seemed to have an unusually good head for the sharp end. "I basically started climbing by leading," Jim said. "I just ran the rope up and figured things out as I went." That could have been a frightening and terribly consequential introduction, but Jim instead reveled in his capacity to put fear aside—if he was experiencing it at all. "Right from the beginning, I loved being off the ground. I just wasn't feeling the same head things that people I saw around me were going through, and I progressed quickly," he said.

But there were limitations to his progress typical of the time. The first was a failure of Jim's own imagination. "In my mind," he said, "climbing was mountaineering, exploring big climbs on big peaks, and getting to summits. I still didn't understand rock climbing as an end unto itself." He enjoyed the movement and the challenge of the small walls, but he didn't believe he was doing the real thing.

The second hitch was that Eastern climbers of the era didn't travel much, not even to other regional areas, let alone the mountains of the West, so there was little sharing of information about better places, and other ways, to climb. It was years before Jim encountered anyone who could climb any better than he could, and until then, his skills flatlined.

CHAPTER 7

THE SUMMER OF LOVE AND MOUNTAINS

BY 1967, THE anchors of Jim's world were loosening. He wanted to honor his parents' dreams, so he stayed at La Salle, but he started making deals with himself that would allow him to take time off to climb while still completing his degree.

At twenty-four, he was the only one of the children still living at home. Sandy was raising her family, and while Bill had settled down somewhat, he still wrestled with how to make his life work. He'd started a career as a long-distance truck driver, and Jim was open in his disappointment about that choice. "The trucking life kept him stuck for years," Jim said. "He was a smart guy, but he always set his sights low, just never tried. He got into *bowling*, of all things. He met a troubled woman at an alley, then ended up having kids with her. He put on a lot of weight, and those kids were out of control."

Both Sandy and Jim were irritated and puzzled by Bill's choices—and frustrated by their inability to help him change. Jim particularly felt that he had found a solution that would work for anyone who wanted to live their best life—get active, get outside, eat better—but he had little hope that his brother would be willing, or able, to make those obvious changes. "It was increasingly hard to believe that we'd come from the same family," Jim said.

Sandy was feeling much the same about the changes she'd seen in her other brother: "It was really hard to understand what [Jim's] climbing thing was about," she told me. "You never heard about mountains then, and none of us understood what he was getting out of doing something that could kill him. He never really could explain that to me. Both my brothers seemed a bit lost."

Jim didn't see himself as lost in the least—in fact, he felt he was inching ever closer to a path of truer purpose. He wasn't interested in the life of home and children that his sister was preaching, and he feared the lazy seductions his brother had chosen. "It's just too easy," he said, "to fall into all those traps."

Importantly, Jim felt like he had his father's approval, even if Ugolino never came out and said it. "I think my father was happy to see me doing what I was doing, being free and having the kinds of adventures I was. I think that was the kind of life he himself wanted, but only got in the books that he read," recalled Jim.

Of course, in 1967, living alternative freedoms and questioning the status quo was happening far beyond the Donini family. By that summer, a rage had started to boil under the skin of American life, and the war in Southeast Asia was the clearest source of the heat. In 1967, the casualty count in Vietnam—11,153 American lives lost—was double what it had been in 1966, and more than six times what it was in 1965. There were nearly half a million US troops on the ground, and Americans, young and old, of all political stripes, were starting to openly question the justification for their country's involvement in a conflict that seemed to pose so little tangible threat to America.

Jim watched it all with curiosity. Given his military service, he had a more complex relationship with the Vietnam War than the average critic, but he opposed it without any sense of hypocrisy. After all, he chose to enlist for personal reasons that didn't include a belief in the righteousness of war, and he chose not to reenlist for the same reason that people were protesting across the country: he thought America had no legitimate role in a civil war on the other side of the planet.

Jim was also drawn to the kinds of people who were against the war, and to the social changes that they were bringing to America. A return to nature, revolution against authority, mind-expanding drugs, freer love—these were all things that he was seeing around him. Everyone at school seemed open in a way that he'd never seen before. It was a great time to be young, free, and ready to experiment.

At the end of that summer, Jim cajoled Ross Johnson into a spontaneous decision to skip the beginning of the fall semester and finally go find mountains. After their jobs were finished in Minnesota, Jim, Ross, and a couple of Ross's friends from high school, John Grahn and Brian Johnson, hopped into a big sedan and pointed west.

THE PEAKS OF Glacier National Park are perfect first mountains. When you've driven from the east and have spent days rolling through the endless grasses of the high prairies, the Rocky Mountains roar up and crack the western Montana sky, clearly proclaiming that a very different world lies ahead.

When Jim woke to the dawn of the second morning of the drive and looked out the car window, the Rockies were burning with alpenglow from one edge of the sky to the other. "I had never seen anything like that in my life, and I'd never *felt* anything like that," Jim remembered. "The thought that struck me, profoundly, was *I have been here before*. I knew right then that I would spend the rest of my life in the mountains. Nothing had ever seemed so clear."

What Jim was seeing was the wild country he'd been dreaming about since boyhood but had never been able to find in the East. All four of the men were ignited, and as they followed the last leg of Highway 2 through the rolling hills of Blackfeet country to the eastern edge of the park, they sang their astonishment. The scale of the vertical rise of the gray walls at the head of Saint Mary Lake was overwhelming. They jammed their packs with supplies in town, then drove up into the high heart of the range and started hiking.

Though they didn't know it when they started up the trail, it was an uneasy time for four young and inexperienced men to walk off into the Glacier backcountry. A couple of weeks before, two young women had been killed by different grizzlies on the same night, and those tragedies had shaken not just the park but the entire National Park Service (NPS). The maulings would change the way that wilderness access was managed across the country. The official report called the night of August 12, 1967, "the moment innocence was lost in our national parks."

Jim and his partners heard about the killings, but they weren't fazed. They thought what countless climbers before them had thought: *That won't happen to me*. They ignored the restrictions that should have stopped them from hiking, shouldered their packs, and set off toward a suitable-looking peak that was barely a mile from the location of one of the attacks.

It's unclear to Jim just what his first summit was, but his description suggests it was likely Mount Cannon, an 8,956-foot summit reachable via a moderate scramble. Cannon was visible from the road and didn't seem to have any snow or ice, which was critical, as none of the men had ever seen a glacier.

The foursome started up the trail, thinking that they'd bivouac and then tag the top the following day. Just after dawn, Jim, Ross, and Brian summited. It was an easy ascent, but Jim believes the day cemented his future. "Standing on top of that little mountain was everything that I'd been dreaming about for years," Jim said. "This was what climbing was supposed to be. All I wanted was to keep feeling like this."

The only thing missing was a view: smoke from the fires that had been plaguing the park all summer shrouded the peaks. That night, celebrating in the bar, they hatched a plan they were sure would include some real mountain vistas.

They'd find a place with clear skies and even more real wilderness.

They'd go to Canada.

"YOU MIGHT AS well aim high if you're going to aim at all," Jim recalled with a laugh. "We knew there were bigger, harder mountains up in the Canadian Rockies, so we figured we'd just go try one."

They passed hundreds of perfectly acceptable peaks on the 400-mile journey north, but they'd heard of a mountain town named Jasper, and they fixated on getting there. In Jasper, the first thing they did was go into the only climbing store in town and announce their plans. Jim laughed again: "We honestly said to the guy, 'What's the biggest, baddest mountain around here?'"

The clerk cocked his head. "That's Mount Robson, but . . ." He paused for a moment and took measure of the boys. "What kind of experience do you have?"

"We dodged that question," Jim said, "but then the salesman asked, 'What kind of gear do you have? You're going to need ice axes and crampons for Robson.'

"He eventually managed to convince us that we'd need real mountain gear to get up the highest peak in the Canadian Rockies—but he had to work to get us to listen. We had a high enough opinion of ourselves to believe that we could probably get up anything with what we had—which was basically jeans and hiking boots—and thought he might be taking advantage of us. Still, we bought a bit of snow gear and the next day set off up the trail."

I had to stop Jim there and ask whether he'd learned anything about the routes before starting the approach or had even looked at the regal peak from the trailhead. By any measure, Robson is a massive and serious undertaking. All sides of the peak are guarded by vertical walls of rock and ice, and the summit soars 9,300 feet above the road, with almost all of that gain on the mountain itself. No routes to the top are remotely suitable for novices, and there are often years when no one of any skill level reaches the top.

"None of that mattered," Jim said. "All I could think about was how incredible it would be to stand on that thing. Somehow, we honestly thought motivation was enough to get us up. Ignorance, as they say, is bliss . . ."

The men hiked the eight-mile fire road into Kinney Lake and only by chance pitched their two-pole pup tents below the great wall of slabs that begin Robson's easiest route, the *South Face*. They had no idea where the route went, but felt ready to start up, sure they could learn how to use axes and crampons as they went.

The big mountain laughed at their pretentions. As the men slept, a foot of snow fell. They were woken by the sound of climbers walking by early the next morning. Jim stuck his head out of his tent, saw that the world had gone white, and was greeted by an impressive figure with a strong accent. The man was Hans Schwarz, one of the renowned Canadian Swiss guides, who had enough experience on Robson that a feature on the route that Jim was about to try—the Schwarz Ledges—was named after him.

Schwarz announced that the Robson season was over and then, after hearing Jim's accent, asked, "You are Americans, *ja*?"

Jim nodded.

"Then you should go back to America."

Schwarz started to walk away, then turned and added a more gracious close: "Go to the Tetons. It's very good rock climbing, which is maybe better for Americans."

The boys walked out through calf-deep snow, pointed the car south, and started the 1,000-mile drive to Wyoming.

IT WAS HARD to say what the lesson of all of this back-and-forth running from range to range was. Be more reasonable? Don't come back until you're ready? Don't come back at all—this just isn't for you?

In Jim's mind, it was none of these. When the men finally arrived in Jackson Hole, Wyoming, after another marathon drive, he convinced the others that they should aim even higher. They were surrounded by many appealing, moderate peaks that would have been great accomplishments given their skill, but he somehow worked out that if the 12,972-foot Robson had chased them away, there was no reason not to target the 13,775-foot granite fang of the Grand Teton.

But they had dragged Robson's weather south and never even saw the Tetons. They stayed for a few days in town, dreamed and had some fun, then began the long drive home.

By the time they'd finished the journey, Jim had rewritten the experience in his mind and come to the conclusion that it wasn't a disappointment but rather the best possible first lesson: Mountains don't give a damn about your dreams, and that's fine. Plan accordingly.

The experience wrote Jim's future. The exploration, the uncertainties, the mysteries of what lay above the clouds, the views when those clouds blew away, the fact that people actually live in places like this—it was all magic to him. He knew when he turned back toward Minnesota that he wouldn't stay in the East. It might take a bit of time, and he'd finish his degree, but his life had changed.

THERE WAS ONE last chapter in that charmed year, a turning point in Jim's life that was also a turning point in American history. In mid-October, university friends suggested that Jim join them for a drive to Washington to take part in a massive anti-war demonstration. The organizers of the rally included the luminaries of the anti-war movement—Allen Ginsberg, Timothy Leary, Gary Snyder, Abbie Hoffman—and it was predicted that the turnout was going to be the largest yet seen for a protest.

The plan was to march on the Pentagon, and the organizing committee—perhaps tongue in cheek, perhaps not, given what was floating through the ether and the bongs of the times—told the media that they believed the energy of the crowd would vibrate itself into an "orange glow of peace" that would levitate the Pentagon and end the war.

Jim went along, partly out of solidarity with his friends and the movement, partly out of curiosity, and, less nobly, because he "knew there'd be all kinds of pretty girls there."

The march on the Pentagon, October 21, 1967 (Photo © Everett Collection Inc/Alamy Stock Photo)

He joined 100,000 other people at the Lincoln Memorial and listened to Peter, Paul, and Mary sing "This Land Is Your Land," and then he started following the throng south to the Pentagon.

Early on, Jim lost his friends and found himself pushed closer and closer to the front of the huge wave of people. "All good," he said. "There were these five beautiful women, and they invited me to walk with them." Caught up in the surf of the crowd closing on the Pentagon, Jim and his new friends passed barriers that had been pushed over by marchers ahead of them. As the swell of people started to wash in behind them, Jim and the women were pressed to the front of the crowd before jolting to a stop at the steps of the Pentagon, toe to toe with a cordon of paratroopers from the 82nd Airborne, who held bayonet-fitted rifles across their chests. A chain of military police stood close behind. "The soldiers were pretty controlled," Jim said, "but every once in a while, an MP would push through and start beating on someone, and I'd think, *What the fuck is wrong with you people? These are just kids . . ."*

Instead of pushing back, the women with Jim did what so many young women of the time did: they took flowers out of their hair and put them in the muzzles of the paratroopers' guns. "That could have been *me* holding one of those guns," Jim said, "but instead, I was staring the soldiers in the eye, and when other marchers pulled out their draft cards, I pulled out mine and burned it, too, because I was so angry.

"I never did tell those lovely women with the flowers in their hair that I'd once been on the other side of that line."

CHAPTER 8

A YOUNG MAN GONE WEST

IT WAS JUST a matter of time. While the first trip west had been a strange one, mountains had infected Jim and he was fully committed to going back as soon as he could. He was still doing fine at school, but university was increasingly secondary to his mountain dreams. He'd already decided that he'd never build a career out of his psychology degree. His only plans were to return to the Tetons and sort out how he could live in a place like that.

First, though, there was a very unexpected twist. Jim returned to Minnesota in the summer of 1968 to work for Ross's father, and he and Ross continued to explore the crags around Minneapolis, which Jim now viewed as "pretty pathetic." They also continued hitting the town. One night out, a couple of young women caught their attention. Jim was especially drawn to the petite blonde. Even from a distance, Sandy Squiers was striking, her hair and eyes and skin painted with the light Nordic colors so common in the Northwoods.

She was also sweet and kind, quiet and shy. It puzzled people when Sandy and Jim moved into a serious relationship—him such a gregarious extrovert and her so demure, off by herself reading while Jim told his loud, raucous tales. But however their chemistry might be explained, they were soon a true couple—the first real couple that Jim had ever been part of. But chemistry was hardly enough to stop him from heading back west, on his own this time, aiming again for the Tetons.

HE FELT SOLID, and the flow came easily. The sun had moved out of the long gully now, and that kept the snow crisp, letting him move fast. The line he soloed up the east face of the Tetons' Table Mountain was a straightforward snow route, but it was the first time he'd climbed with an ice axe in hand, and it was the longest thing that Jim had climbed yet, by far. He'd done more pitches that morning than he could do in a month at Taylors Falls or High Rocks.

An even bigger difference leapt out when Jim reached the summit and walked along the expansive ridgeline: he had magnificent views. Table's summit plateau is a balcony seat for the theater of the Teton Range, and in the early morning light the peaks were putting on an operatic performance. He started down, stunned by how beautiful this all was.

That night, Jim passed through another graduation of sorts: he entered the circle of the climbing family. After the descent from Table, he made his way to the Jenny Lake Campground and walked over to meet other climbers gathering at the end of the day. Stepping in wasn't always easy in those days. Some climbing areas were clannish and unwelcoming and had idiosyncrasies of style, ethics, and especially grading that could leave visitors cold.

But the scene in the Tetons was different. These were mountains that climbers all over the country traveled to. This was Mecca, and pilgrims were expected.

Until now, there hadn't really been a community for Jim to enter or a climbing culture to navigate, but this evening he stepped into a fully formed one, and he did fine. He was his mother's son, and he knew how to win people over. It took just a few minutes before he'd shared his experience on Table and then, when he asked for recommendations of what to do next, got an invitation for the following day.

George McKiehl was a more experienced climber who'd been making annual trips to the Tetons from Wisconsin for years. George asked Jim if he wanted to tag along on a solo of the *Durrance Ridge* on Symmetry Spire. Jim replied with an enthusiastic yes; George raised an eyebrow and said, "Are you sure?"

The next morning, Jim understood why George had checked. "It's an easy climb, maybe 5.6 on really good rock, but it's eight pitches long and starts above a couloir approach, so there's tremendous exposure," recalled Jim. The line climbs to a 10,565-foot summit, following blocks and flaring cracks along a sharp ridge. "I was over my head, but I had a great time," said Jim.

"It was really good to see how someone like George moved over that kind of terrain. I just followed and did what he did."

Soloing the *Durrance* was yet another milestone for Jim, showing him—and others—that he had a good head and the ability to keep pace with a leader in the clan.

A final crucial moment of the transformational trip came when he was about to head home. McKiehl listened one evening as Jim talked about wanting to become more of a mountaineer, and he offered a surprising piece of advice: "Instead of telling me that I needed to climb more *mountains*, like I'd concluded, George insisted that the very best thing I could do was to focus on rock climbing. He helped me understand that rock was the foundation of everything else."

A VERY DIFFERENT kind of transformation happened when Jim returned to Minnesota the following year, 1969. He had been seeing Sandy occasionally through the winter, but when he came back for the summer, he just couldn't decide what he wanted with her. But, always impulsive, instead of following his first instinct and ending the relationship, Jim proposed marriage. "I decided to just go for it," Jim said, "but we had to cross the state line to have a wedding that fast." In early July, he and Sandy headed off to South Dakota, with Ross in tow as best man.

Ross was not impressed. "Every time we stopped on the drive," Jim recalled, "he'd pull me aside and say, 'You can't do this. It doesn't make any sense. It's not right for you and not fair to Sandy.' But I'd made my mind up, and that was that. Sometimes you have to untie and just go for it."

And marriage to someone as passive as Sandy didn't require many changes. She was licensed as a court reporter, which let her find work just about anywhere. She followed Jim back to La Salle for his fall semester. They got an apartment together, and Jim convinced her—and himself—that he'd finish school.

But the pull of the mountains was too strong, and by November, Jim had another proposal: "Why not head west with Ross? We'll find work at a ski resort. I'll come back and finish school later." Sandy agreed, and so did Ross. They were gone by that afternoon.

"We got all the way to Colorado and pulled into the parking lot at Aspen, where we thought we'd be able to find work, and slept beside the car," Jim explained. "But when we woke up in the morning covered in snow, all we could think about was how California would be a much better place to spend the winter."

They threw their soggy sleeping bags in the car and drove on.

CHAPTER 9

APPRENTICESHIP

IF THERE IS an inevitable chapter in any American climber's story, it's that a climber like Jim Donini would eventually end up in Yosemite.

Then, as now, that magnificent valley—*the* Valley—was both measuring stick and testing ground. Yosemite was the place to go, learn, be humbled and fail, be challenged at an international scale, see really good climbers at play. But for a lot of players in the 1960s, and certainly as Jim understood the rules of the game, you didn't just *show up* in Yosemite. There was a ritual path that included an initial journey of humble internship.

"I did what we were all told to do," he explained. "[Yosemite master Yvon] Chouinard had written a piece for *Mountain* magazine in which he said that climbers should cut their teeth at Suicide and Tahquitz before even *thinking* of going to the Valley. So that's what I did."

The beautiful white granite walls of Suicide and Tahquitz rocks sit across from one another high above the town of Idylwild, California, in the ponderosa hills of the San Jacinto Mountains. With a mix of fine cracks and immaculate slabs, the big crags have, since the 1930s, been the premier multipitch playground for Southern California climbers, many of whom had their code of climbing shaped by the heady runouts so common there. As John Long, one of the gifted younger climbers who showed up in Idylwild in the same era as Jim, poetically framed the challenge, "Casting off on a Suicide testpiece had the feel and consequences of big game hunting with your bare hands."

Through the late 1960s, one of the most skillful climbers on these walls was Bud Couch, a teacher at a local community college. Couch had lived in Idylwild for years and was a master of the footwork that was so key on the twinned walls above the town. He rarely climbed elsewhere, and his familiarity with the polished ripples and dikes on the big white faces let him dance where others trembled.

To many, Couch wasn't an easy man to like. He had a high opinion of his own skills and an even higher opinion of the routes that he created. Both opinions were warranted—as Long pointed out, "Jesus, Couch could climb. He did stuff that people with the very best shoes still can't do today"—but it wasn't easy to hear those opinions from Couch himself. Long described Couch as "a high lama who lorded over Suicide with a flinty disdain."

Jim didn't find Couch difficult at all and happily embraced the opportunity to settle in under the local master's wing. Couch was the first person Jim climbed with who was truly more technically gifted, and he filled a much-needed space as Jim's mentor. Said Jim, "I'd grown up in sports and always had coaches, and then I was in the military and had great leaders, but I'd never had either of those in climbing."

Couch's brusque ways might have been hard for others, but they weren't foreign to someone who'd been a soldier. Jim ignored the bluster and learned as much as he could. Couch took Jim up his first 5.9 and 5.10 routes and schooled him in the intricacies of the Couch specialty: the steep, technical face climbs that Jim had always avoided. Jim's nearly free ascent that winter of *The Vampire*, a renowned four-pitch 5.11a testpiece up dime-thick edges on Tahquitz, was a clear sign that Couch's tutoring had paid off.

That first season in the Rocks was also the first time that Jim had spent an extended period immersed in a live-in climbing scene. He, Sandy, and Ross moved into a house together in Riverside, a high desert town in the Santa Ana Valley below Idylwild. Early on, Jim connected with Paul Gleason, who worked at the local climbing shop, and then with Gleason's brother, Phil.

The Gleasons introduced Jim to the granite boulders strewn over the slopes of nearby Mount Rubidoux, and they immediately saw how committed Donini was to moving up the learning curve. "Jim was still pretty raw when he first showed up," Phil told me, "but you could tell that there was a lot of talent there. He had an athleticism that set him apart, but he also worked harder than anyone else we'd ever seen. He could be out there for hours on those boulders, and you could actually *see* him getting better."

"That winter," says Jim, "was when I really started to see my future. I was with my people, doing just what I wanted, and I was really starting to understand how to climb better."

By spring, he felt had completed the apprenticeship that Chouinard had prescribed. It was time to reach for the prize.

CHAPTER 10

DAYS IN EDEN: THE YOSEMITE YEARS, PART ONE

This is our island. It's a good island.
Until the grownups come to fetch us, we'll have fun.
—William Golding, Lord of the Flies

IT RAINED THE spring of 1970—biblical rain that lasted for weeks. A climber could be forgiven for losing faith and going in search of sun, but Jim stayed put. He was finally in the Valley, and once he found *Generator Crack*, the rain didn't matter so much.

A few other climbers stuck around despite the deluge and played the game with him. Every morning they'd wake up to rain bleeding through the seams of their cheap pup tents, take their time with their coffee, maybe drift over to Yosemite Lodge and drape their sodden sleeping bags on the heaters along the wall. When they couldn't stand the itch of boredom any longer, they'd load ropes into cars and head down-valley to the big, sheltered boulders clustered around the old power station on Highway 140.

Jim knew it was absurd to be spending days on a fifty-foot-high boulder when he was surrounded by the best long climbs in the country, but he had a mission. The south side of the Generator Boulder overhung enough that it stayed dry even on the wettest days, and *Generator Crack*—a brawny, ragged fracture that splits the big boulder clean through—was a perfect place to master one of climbing's more arcane arts.

"Those rainy days taught me how to climb offwidths," Jim said. "First try, I couldn't even get off the ground. Then, I figured out how to climb it leaning to the left, the way everyone did, then I learned how to do it to the right, then I did it in tennis shoes, then I soloed it. When the monsoon finally ended, I could climb wide cracks for the rest of my life."

Jim had traveled up from Riverside a few weeks before, following the climbing pilgrims' trail north on Highway 41, through the Wawona Tunnel—a birth canal for so many climbers—to the magnificent first sight of El Capitan and Half Dome from Yosemite Valley View.

He felt like he was *home*.

Home, though, is never quite complete without *family*, and in Yosemite Jim found plenty of kin. It was a remarkable time to join the Valley clan. In the last few years of the 1960s, just before Jim arrived, Yosemite had gone through a lull, and there were fewer breakthrough climbs happening. Many of the stars of the 1960s—Royal Robbins, Warren Harding, Yvon Chouinard, Tom Frost, Chuck Pratt—had slowed or moved on. People said the Valley's "Golden Age" was over.

But seismic rumbles were starting. The committed leftovers who were the bridge between the 1960s and 1970s—especially Jim Bridwell, Barry Bates, Mark Klemens, and Peter Haan—as well as new climbers like Jim, who were showing up at the turn of the decade, were already setting new benchmarks. When Jim arrived, there was a new energy sparking Yosemite climbing, and a new culture fueling it. The earlier climbers had certainly had their bohemian ways, but the fresh crew were perfecting what would come to be called the "dirtbag life," and they were living it in a sinner's paradise.

The Valley had the giddy feel of a summer camp without counselors. There were no limits on stays—not enforced limits, anyways—and people lived in their vehicles or in dime-store tube tents for months. You could still drive right into the climbers' roost known as Camp 4, whose footprint was nearly twice as large as it is today, spreading climbers and their vehicles far out into the big trees. Some of the sites had long-term decorations and rustic furniture, giving the appearance of a half-built backwoods survivalist village. Some of the vans and cars hadn't been started for months.

The freedoms of the Yosemite climbing scene could be, literally and fig-uratively, intoxicating. There were great climbs, few climbers, and this was

Camp 4 in the halcyon days, 1971 (Photo by Steve Arsenault)

California, heart of the counterculture. As Jim summed it up, "Good drugs, bad wine, and pretty women were always available." It was easy for climbers playing on these walls to believe that they held a secret truth that elevated them above the tourists bound to the Valley floor, and they behaved accordingly.

The climbers' behavior could have drawn the ire of the NPS, but for the most part, relations were cordial—particularly because of the invaluable role that climbers played in the high-angle rescues that were regular occurrences in the park. The rangers needed the climbers far more than the climbers needed the rangers, and a détente of sorts evolved. Climbers were given much greater freedom, of many types, than other park users.

But, for Jim, those unbridled liberties were short-lived. As the weather finally improved in May 1970 and he prepared to leave for the Tetons, self-described hippies started to arrive in the Valley, and by Memorial Day, they had taken over Stoneman Meadow, a pristine lowland in the heart of the park, claiming they had the right, as Americans, to live in *their* park however they wanted.

Over the next six weeks, the NPS and the hippies waged a battle that came to an ugly head on Fourth of July weekend, when horse-mounted rangers carrying billy clubs and axe handles rode into the squatters' camp. Several people and several horses were injured, the whole thing was caught on national TV, and the scuffle spiraled into a multiday riot.

The Stoneman incident pushed a shift in NPS policy that had a lasting impact on Yosemite's climbers. Regulation and enforcement became priorities, and that included controlling climbers—even though the rangers knew that virtually none of them were involved in the riot and most were openly disdainful of the squatters. The climbers might *look* more like the hippies than they did the rangers, but they had far more in common with the rangers in their appreciation of the sanctity of the Valley.

Regardless, the NPS took steps to address the message of the visibly unruly Camp 4. They brought in fees, halved the size of the campground, restricted cars to the parking lot, banned permanent structures, and, to the irritation of climbers who had a historical connection to the Camp 4 name, blandly rechristened the campground "Sunnyside."

And then there were the changes in Yosemite climbing itself that were bubbling to the surface—changes Jim was very much a part of.

If it looked like Valley climbing had died when the Golden Age passed, that's perhaps because people were mistaking a chrysalis for a corpse. An evolution was taking place, particularly in the brilliant mind of Jim Bridwell, the new king of Camp 4. Bridwell had an enormous influence on every aspect of Valley life, from climbing standards to social mores. A talented and visionary man, he would go on to record more first ascents in the Valley than anyone else in history, and he was particularly known for necky big-wall routes. Bridwell was a nexus character who joined the past to the present and connected newcomers to the Valley and to one another. Better than anyone else, Bridwell understood three waves of the future—harder big-wall climbs, harder free climbs, and free ascents of long aid routes—and was uniquely responsible for promoting the use of skills honed in the Valley in the bigger ranges.

In the seven consecutive years that Donini spent in the Valley, from 1970 through 1976, these trends that Bridwell seeded reshaped climbing around the world, perhaps even more so than the advances set during the Golden Age.

All the changes certainly shaped Donini's future.

YOSEMITE IS WHERE Jim finally rose up in the climbing world, where he found his special talent, where he earned a name, where he set the pattern of his life. That first wet spring trip in 1970 begat a return that fall, and that became the rhythm: three months in Yosemite in spring, summer in the Tetons, then another three months in the Valley in fall. Like many others, Jim bent his life to that schedule.

Fifty years after Jim first arrived in the Valley, the climbs, the partners, and the long days on rock have started to blur together, but there are stories that he and others can pluck out of the weave. A lot of them have to do with the people who gathered there. Though some climbers experienced Camp 4 as a cold place to enter, chilled by cliques and elitism, that's not what Jim experienced. "King" Bridwell, who did not suffer fools, welcomed him warmly. "Bridwell was great," Donini said. "He came over right away when I showed up, introduced me around, told me what climbs I should be doing, where I should set up camp. I understood right away that if you were in with him, everything else fell into place. I have no idea why he bothered with me, because I sure wasn't climbing at a level that would have drawn his attention, but right from the start it felt like we connected."

Jim's first season helped link him to the core group of Valley climbers who were pushing at the edges of the possible. It was a tight, talented crew with much to teach someone as passionate as Jim. Two free-climbing geniuses influenced him greatly: Barry Bates, master of Yosemite's hard, thin cracks, and Mark Klemens, early sage of Valley offwidths. Jim had huge respect for Bates's talent, but he felt a stronger draw to Klemens, partly out of their shared affinity for wide cracks, partly because he was intrigued by Klemens's dark edges.

"Klemens," Jim said, "was a hardcore surfer in the off-season, and when he'd leave the Valley, he'd usually go to Hawaii and get into really heavy drugs. Then he'd come back in the spring, find some place to get clean, and then show up a few weeks later ready to climb. Really smart, really interesting guy, but pretty troubled. I think that stopped him from being as fully amazing as he should have been."

There were all sorts of lessons to be learned at the feet of people like Bridwell, Bates, and Klemens, and Jim jumped on every opportunity to get out with them. He was quick to impress with his willingness to try anything and push his limits. Phil Gleason, one of the Riverside Gleason brothers who climbed extensively with Jim in his second season in Yosemite, explained, "People were talking about him. You could see the phenomenal raw talent that Donini had. He was still on the learning curve at that point, still getting better, but there was so much strength and finesse in the way he climbed, especially on cracks. He was as good as anyone we'd ever seen."

The edgy façade that people sometimes experience with Jim became something of a legend around Camp 4. At first glance, he could appear stiff, dour, unapproachable—and a bit of a puzzle. He wasn't the typical California surfer kid like most of the new generation. He was older. He came from somewhere back east. There were those whispers that he'd fought in Vietnam.

But once you got past that veneer, Jim was also a proud and exuberant ambassador for Valley life. Bridwell's welcome had meant a great deal to him, and he decided to offer the same to others. He went out of his way to greet newcomers to Camp 4, tell them where the best climbs were, set them up with partners, and take them climbing himself.

In a few notable cases, Jim was the *only* advocate that some visiting climbers had, fighting against the harsh judgments of outsiders that occasionally came from Bridwell and the other Valley gods. The very talented Colorado climber Jimmie Dunn told me that Donini was the fiercest defender of his right to attempt a solo first ascent on El Cap. In 1972, when Dunn started working on what would become *Cosmos*, a difficult aid climb on the southwest face, Bridwell told him he had no business attempting the line, insisting only locals could do new climbs. Bridwell threatened to break Dunn's arms, or—if Dunn completed the route—throw him off the top. Donini intervened, telling Camp 4 that he'd meet Dunn at the summit and, if anyone else showed up, he'd throw *them* off. "Donini was the only reason that I went back up and completed that climb, and, yep, he was up there when I topped out," said Dunn. With Donini mediating, Bridwell shook Dunn's hand instead of breaking it when Dunn returned to the Valley floor, and he even made him dinner and came up with the name for the route.

The thing that caught most people's attention about Donini, though— and this is saying quite a bit, given the type A personalities of so many Valley climbers—was how constantly willing he was to climb. He'd climb anything he could, every single day, with anyone he could find.

Jim's hunt for partners included shepherding emerging climbers into the Valley fold, sometimes taking a dedicated mentoring role. Some of those connections shaped history. John Long remembered that when he was still a teenager, still developing what would become a stellar talent, he and two friends were bouldering at County Park in Idyllwild and saw this "older guy" working a problem. They ended up talking to Jim, who encouraged Long to come to Yosemite for the first time, saying he'd introduce him around.

When Long showed up in the Valley a few weeks later, he walked up to Donini and Bridwell at a Camp 4 picnic table. Donini, only half in jest, yapped at Bridwell, "This is John Long. He's a pretty good climber, but he's a loud-mouth punk and I don't want to deal with him!" Bridwell and Long's climb of a hard route on the Folly an hour later, matchmade by Donini, was an early step in a foundational role that Bridwell would play in sculpting the next generation of Yosemite climbers. For talented teenagers like Long, Bridwell acted as the guide who introduced them to the Yosemite Way, guiding the emergence of the new wave who styled themselves the "Stonemasters."

Donini played a lesser-known role in that emergence, too, often rustling up newly arrived young climbers to hold his rope. Ron Kauk, who'd go on to become one of the most talented of the Stonemasters, remembers that Jim took him up his first 5.11 when he was still in high school. Another of the Stonemasters, the Bay Area prodigy Mark Chapman, has very fond memories of Jim.

"[Donini] couldn't have been a better mentor at a better time," Chapman said. "He was keen, and he didn't mind dragging us along. For a kid like me, climbing with someone like that—one of the best climbers in the Valley at the time, probably one of the best in the world—was pretty amazing. There was no pretension in him, no sign that he felt he was too good for us. He'd just show up and say, 'Let's go climbing.'"

GIVEN ALL THE seasons that Jim spent in Yosemite, it's surprising that he spent almost no time on the Valley's famed big aid routes. As he explained that gap in his résumé, "I love the flow of free climbing, and there's not much of that when you aid climb. It's too slow, too mechanical, too much like work."

But there was the *Salathé Wall*. In 1971, fellow Northeasterner Steve Arsenault pulled Jim into an early ascent of the aid line up the massive southwest face of El Cap. Thirty-five pitches long, the *Salathé* was going to be not only the biggest climb by far that Jim had ever done but also the first time that he'd use any of the specialized techniques and tools of aid climbing, as well as the first time he'd sleep on a wall. When people asked Jim if the *Salathé* might not be too large a first bite, he had a typically perfunctory response: "I've done grade IVs. Isn't a grade VI just a bunch of grade IVs stacked on top of each other?"

That presumption might have been factually true, but it didn't exactly capture the reality the pair faced. The climb took five arduous days. They brought nothing but light sweaters and jeans and froze when cold rains hit. Poorly managed hauling slowed them to a crawl.

Worst of all was the food. Arsenault had also served in the military, and he suggested that he could get good value at a PX in Modesto. Their first night on the wall, when Jim asked what was for dinner, Arsenault proudly pulled out a can of military-grade SPAM and another of mandarin oranges. Jim begrudgingly accepted that first night's menu, but he was far less happy when he discovered the second night that Arsenault had brought nothing *but* SPAM and mandarin oranges. "I never let someone else choose my food for a climb again," Jim raged. "Ever!"

There was another lasting lesson from the wall. Before the climb, the only worry Jim had was the notorious bomb-bay chimney on the eighteenth pitch called The Ear, a three-sided bubble of granite that has no bottom and puts 2,000 feet of air below the climber's feet. Jim and Steve were attempting only the ninth ascent of the route, and previous ascensionists spoke with fear-filled reverence about the exposure. After the first ascent, Royal Robbins called the pitch "the most terrifying 5.7 in the world."

In the end, particularly because Jim was already a fine wide-crack climber, the supposedly horrifying feature turned out to be a nonevent. "I just launched up," Jim recalled, "and because I was expecting to need wide stuff higher up, I didn't place a single piece, and then it was over." In one of his told-a-thousand-times stories, Donini insists that single pitch was responsible for his lifelong preference for unclimbed routes: "Worrying about The Ear ruined that climb for me. After that, I never wanted someone else telling me how hard any pitch was going to be. I'd rather find out for myself."

When they finally pulled onto the summit, dehydrated and spent, Jim swore that he was done with big aid. He was, he told everyone who'd listen, a *free* man.

THAT COMMITMENT TO furthering his free-climbing skills fixed Jim's place in the Yosemite story. By the end of his sixth season, he had been part of the first ascents of several groundbreaking crack climbs. He was a full Valley local, welcomed back every season as part of the family.

One dramatic change during Jim's time in Yosemite was the increasingly visible role of women in Valley climbing—and in his own climbs. Though women had been involved in significant climbs since the early days of Yosemite, flat-out sexism kept their names out of accounts of first ascents, and where they were acknowledged, they were often unjustly cast as "wives or girlfriends" merely "along for a ride." But through the 1970s, a new cadre of women was far harder to dismiss. Very talented women like Bev Clarke, Liz Robbins, Sibylle Hechtel, Bev Johnson, Mari Gingery, Molly Higgins, Barb Eastman, and Lynn Hill were climbing with other women and were making the first all-female ascents and first ascents proper on free climbs and aid climbs around the Valley.

Jim loved the change—"I suddenly had a lot of other people to climb with," he said with a laugh—and several of these women seemed to uniquely appreciate him. "Jim was one of the only men who seemed to really treat us as equals," Hechtel told me. "He was just so keen to be out climbing, so it was easier with him than with a lot of other men who had other things on their minds."

One unique influence kept Jim more focused on his climbing than on those other things: his wife in the Valley. In Jim's second spring in Yosemite, Sandy landed a job as the court stenographer for the tiny US district court-house in Yosemite Village. She was given a small cabin just outside the park in the village of El Portal, which meant Jim had a hot shower, a bed, and a warm body waiting for him every night after a climb. Each morning, he'd show up in Camp 4 clean and rested and drag his partners out of the dirt.

Few climbers, though, recall meeting Sandy. They couldn't remember her name or many interactions with her. Steve Arsenault vaguely recollected that she carried beer up to the top of El Cap after they finished the *Salathé*, but he had a hard time conjuring any other times together. Climbers knew that Sandy lived in Yosemite Village, but she rarely made an appearance around Camp 4, while Jim spent all his time there.

It wasn't an arrangement that felt too permanent.

CHAPTER 11

WORK, WHISKY, AND AN UNEXPECTED OFFER

BY THE SUMMER of 1971, Jim had the flow of the climbing life—and, more importantly, the way to pay for it—sorted out. He was spending months at a time in Yosemite without any income, but he was notoriously frugal, life in Yosemite was cheap, and the free accommodation and paychecks from Sandy's court work were a sweet bonus.

And then, when Jim returned for his summer stint in the Tetons that year, a magical addition to the flow—being paid to climb—fell, almost literally, at his feet.

One evening that June, only a few days after Jim had shown up at the Jenny Lake climbers' campground, he was approached by Herb Swedlund, the chief guide at Exum Mountain Guides, the outfit that held the guiding concession in the park. Swedlund explained that one of his team had been injured a few days before, and asked Jim if he might be interested in filling in.

"Herb knew that I'd just done the *Salathé*," Jim explained, "and he felt that somehow qualified me to take people up the Grand. I wasn't so sure about that, but I said yes anyways. It seemed like a great way to get to know these mountains and earn a few dollars."

It's easy to understand Jim's initial hesitation. Yes, he'd had some success on the warm, solid walls of Yosemite, but he still had very little experience in the alpine. He'd really only been on a few peaks, and though his clients wouldn't know it that summer, he'd be working out the kinks and complexities of big mountains—route-finding, storms, questionable rock, snow and ice—on the fly.

Jim was hardly alone in his limitations. That summer, the lead guides at Exum had just started hiring young climbers with hot reputations, signaling that Exum was moving into the new era of climbing. That shift meant several guides in the Exum stable were self-taught and had no certification of any kind.

"It really was the Wild West," Jim said, "and it didn't always work out that well. Exum rightly thought they could sell those reputations, but there were some pretty big egos, and some legendary meltdowns of both guides and clients."

Though Jim could match egos with the best of them, he discovered that summer how much he truly loved introducing appreciative novices to the mountains. Being able to tell a good story and offer a soft hand through hard moments are essential parts of guiding, and Jim had standout skills in both domains. Climbs with him were always full of laughs, and clients never experienced the distance that others saw in him. "He was the most patient and compassionate guide that I ever had," one of his longtime clients told me.

Part of Jim's continuing enjoyment of guiding came from discovering an innovative way to keep the work interesting. "When I first started at Exum," he explained, "most of the guides were just doing the same trade routes over and over again and wouldn't think about pushing their clients. I started finding clients who were as keen as I was and wanted to do things that no one else was guiding."

Rick Black, a businessman from the Midwest, was a fine example. Black was the CEO of a string of successful early tech firms, and he came each year to the Tetons with big ambitions and a good base of talent but without the time to arrange climbs and partners. Jim met Black while the two were on the Jenny Lake ferry, which crosses the lake to the base of the Tetons. Jim was with a client of his own and Black was with another guide, but when the two got to talking about the kinds of climbing that Black aspired to do, Jim had no qualms about stealing Black away.

Black remembered, "Jim seduced me by suggesting that we do the *Northwest Ridge* of the Grand [an eleven-pitch 5.8 that's one of the longest, more continuous moderates in the range]. That turned out to be the greatest thing that ever happened to me. I was in heaven that day, and from then on, whatever he wanted to climb, I was ready to follow."

Black had climbed with many guides, but he said that Jim's talent was singular. "He was just one of the most beautiful climbers, smoother than anyone I'd ever seen. Everything was like a ballet. I think people are fortunate if they ever find someone they can learn as much from as I learned from him."

Jim echoes this sentiment with his own appreciation of Black as a client and friend. "The culmination of our climbing was *The Enclosure* on the Grand Teton, which was considered to be hardest route on the peak at that time. We did the second ascent and the first free ascent. Rick is extremely proud of this climb—as he should be."

Still, most of Jim's work was always going to be with beginners, and as much as he enjoyed those days, he grew increasingly aware that as his mountain sense and skill increased, it was going to be harder for him to accept and accommodate the restraints of guiding. Those repeat days in the Tetons made him faster, and that made it harder for clients to keep up—and for Jim to slow down. "It got pretty bad," he admitted, "especially toward the end of the summer." Like a horse returning to stable, he'd be straining at the reins held by the clients, knowing that he could be home hours earlier if not for them.

Ever restless, Jim had already started to sense that guiding might not be his long-term plan.

AND THEN THERE was the nagging question of how to develop a fuller spectrum of mountain skills. The Tetons were high, but they didn't have much snow and ice. Unless a climber lived in one of the premier ice climbing or mountaineering areas in the Northeast, the Rockies, or the Cascades, there were few places for Americans to polish alpine abilities. As a consequence, through the 1960s, lags in opportunity, equipment, technique, and knowledge kept American ice climbing relatively stagnant.

But those barriers started to shift when Yvon Chouinard came home from a revelatory trip to Europe at the turn of the new decade. A key player in 1960s Yosemite, Chouinard was always an ardent student of gear and technique. In 1970, he traveled to the Alps to see how Europeans were climbing mountains, and then he continued on to Scotland to learn what was fueling the Scots' development of the hardest ice climbs in the world.

Both legs of the trip were transformational. Chouinard shared some of his new ideas about climbing tool design with visionaries in France and Scotland, and he built some of their European thinking into the ice axes that he was manufacturing in his Great Pacific Iron Works smithy in Ventura, California.

Chouinard was also intrigued by the formalized descriptions of ice climbing technique that he heard in the Alps. The French seemed to have words to describe every conceivable foot and axe position, and to Chouinard's ears that articulation was key if Americans hoped to get better on ice. He came back to the United States an eager acolyte, ready to spread the word about what he'd come to call the "French Method."

Chouinard held his first course on the French Method in the Tetons in the summer of 1971, and—once again showing up at a turning point of climbing history by happenstance, like an alpine Forrest Gump—Jim was there. He and Ross Johnson sat in with a small group of NPS climbing rangers who eagerly gathered around Chouinard as the master invoked the holy incantations of the French Method: *Pied à plat. Piolet ramasse. Piolet canne.*

While the exotic terminology never really caught on—in part because the French labels overcomplicated natural practice, in part because Americans aren't too inclined to listen to others tell them about a better way of doing anything—Jim was taken by both Chouinard and the idea of expanding his own skill set.

"Yvon had such an interesting presence," Jim said. "He's shy, really soft-spoken, and through the whole thing I don't think he made eye contact with anyone. He just kind of talked to the ground as he walked us through the descriptions of the systems that he insisted we *had* to learn.

"I'm pretty sure that none of us remembered a single name of the techniques, but we sure all remembered Yvon. There was something about him and the way that he came across that was just so compelling.

"I think his combination of French, Austrian, and Scottish techniques, using the best parts of each, was really his gift to the development of modern ice climbing. It allowed American climbers, who were not bound by tradition, to [eventually] leapfrog in ice climbing."

Jim was keen to try out the ideas that Chouinard had shared, but par for the Donini course, instead of looking for easy ground as a practice area, Jim decided that a big, hard climb would be the best way to test the new skills. The day after the class finished, Jim grabbed Ross Johnson and launched up the *Black Ice Couloir*, an eight-pitch mixed gully on the Grand Teton's north side that was a North American testpiece at the time. Few parties had done the route, which was notorious for a long, complex approach and stretches of lean alpine ice barraged by rockfall.

Jim, however, remembered the climb being "no big deal."

"It was a bit challenging in places, and it was certainly harder than anything I'd done on ice to that point, but I just thought it wasn't as big a deal as its reputation suggested. After all, we were two novices on ice, with the very primitive tools of the time, and *we* got up it," he said.

Still, the ascent was another breakthrough, helping Jim see that he was capable of a high level of performance in yet another area of the climbing game. More importantly, it connected him with Chouinard, who was impressed with the achievement and would figure prominently in the rest of Jim's life.

After Jim and Ross came off the route, Chouinard sidled up to Jim in a Jackson bar and suggested that if he enjoyed the climb, he might think of going to Scotland to try ice climbing on Ben Nevis. He said that the climbing and the scene were both wonderful, and he offered to set Jim up with some of the best Scottish climbers.

Jim committed on the spot—not just to go but to go for the entire coming winter, snatching the chance to spend months in the birthplace of modern ice climbing, learning from the masters, trying the hardest climbs in the world, and carrying a letter of marque from one of the American greats.

He'd just have to convince his wife and a couple of partners to come along.

WHAT CHOUINARD HADN'T mentioned was the weather—and the winter of 1971–72 suffered atrocious conditions even by Scottish standards. For five weeks, from the middle of December 1971 until the end of January 1972, up in the highlands and down by the sea, it rained relentlessly. It was a sharp, constant, driven deluge, but—with rancid irony—not cold enough to freeze into climbable ice. Still, while the rain scoured the early season snow off Ben Nevis, it didn't wash away Jim's excitement.

"We were having a great time," he said. He'd come to Glasgow with Sandy, Ross, and John Grahn, who'd been on the escapade to Montana and Mount Robson four years before. They rented a car and wound north to Fort William, the tiny port town at the foot of Ben Nevis. They were in the thrall of their first trip overseas, and that helped them ignore the weather: everything was odd and special, and the fog and rain and the short, dark days just seemed part of the exotic package.

The locals that Chouinard connected them with were eager, they said, to "take the Yanks out and show them *real* ice climbing"—that is, the terrifying version of ice that Scots considered real. Every night the locals would gather around the wide-eyed Americans in the ancient Jacobite Lounge in Fort William and set the stage: Scottish climbing, they warned, included perpetual fog, ephemeral veins of frozen mist, clumps of turf that you'd hook with a prayer, crampons sparking off glassy rock.

But day after sodden day, the rain continued, and no climbing happened. That, Jim suggests, was perhaps fortunate. Compared to the men that Chouinard set them up with, Jim and his friends were beginners. The climbers who gathered at the pub were the grandees of Scottish climbing, and it would have been hard for anyone in the world to keep up with that crowd climbing—or, for that matter, in the other critical metric of Scottish climbing: drinking.

When the weather finally turned nearly six weeks after they arrived, a sudden freeze created surprisingly good conditions and inspired Jim to be far more ambitious than his hosts anticipated. Instead of starting on a moderate climb, Jim chose one of the most fabled lines in the world: *Point Five Gully*.

First climbed in 1959 in a six-day siege in terrible weather, the six-pitch route up a tight slot on the Observatory Buttress of Ben Nevis was widely considered the hardest ice climb in the world at the time. The notion of self-admitted novices taking on *Point Five* as a first Scottish climb made no sense to anyone but Jim. "We were there, it looked great, and I thought, *Why not?*"

Fat ice conditions helped, but it was still a huge accomplishment to get up the route. "When the Scots found out, they were stunned," Jim said. "People prepared for years to do *Point Five* then, and it had an aura, even among really talented climbers.

"I think," he added, "we were the ones who opened that route up to normal people. When we showed that *Point Five* could be climbed by mortals, Brits started driving north right away to give it a go, and the mystique disappeared for good."

Though they only had a few weeks left on their trip, the good weather continued and the men kept up their run. They climbed the other hard classic of the range, *Zero Gully*, a few days later, then raced up some of the easier lines that the Scots had on their list. Their trip to Scotland had suddenly become a surprisingly successful adventure.

In all the stories that I heard from Jim about the weeks in Scotland, I didn't hear Sandy's name mentioned once—an absence that reflected the next big change in Jim's life. He explained: "I realized when we were over there that I'd just drifted out of love, and while that was happening, she was drifting *into* love with Ross."

When they got home, Ross and Sandy asked to speak to Jim together, and when they all sat down, Sandy told Jim that she wanted end their relationship and be with Ross. "Honestly," said Jim, "it was a relief and I was really happy for them, and happy to be able to get out of the marriage without hurting Sandy. They were married soon, went on to spend the rest of their lives together, and I stayed really good friends with both of them."

But just as Jim often mocks himself in his climbing stories, chasing laughs rather than revelations, the way that he more typically tells the story of the end of his first marriage isn't flattering. The first time he told me about the split, he described it, with apparent comic intent, as a "transaction" between him and Ross, as though he'd horse-traded his wife away.

Jim's sister, Sandy Yanosov, was appalled by that account when she first heard it—and still was when we talked about the divorce fifty years later. "Who *does* something like that?" she asked in frustration.

When I told her the more generous (and more accurate) version, that Sandy was actually the one who approached Jim with the offer, she swore that he'd never told her that. But the alternate truth didn't do much to quell a sister's frustration, or her puzzlement. "Well, then who the hell doesn't explain something like that better to his family?" she said. "Either way, [Sandy] was a really sweet girl who just didn't deserve to be treated like that. I'm just not sure I've ever understood my brother."

Whatever was said or actually happened, it was natural for a sister to hope that a divorce would cause Jim to critically assess his life. From her point of view, he needed to settle down and focus on the things that she believed gave foundation to a life: a secure job, a nice home, a wife, children, something bigger than himself. Though she had no real sense what Jim was accomplishing in the climbing world, or exactly what this climbing thing even was, Sandy was quite certain that it wasn't worth the risks he was taking, and it wasn't the kind of thing that a man approaching thirty should still be doing. It was time, she said, for her brother to grow up.

That was hardly Jim's plan. Though he hadn't been particularly constrained by his marriage, he was even freer now, and he had all kinds of ideas about how to celebrate that freedom.

Only a few weeks after returning from Scotland and helping his wife pack up and move in with his best friend, Jim hopped in his green-and-white Volkswagen bus and headed back to Yosemite.

CHAPTER 12

DAYS IN EDEN: THE YOSEMITE YEARS, PART TWO

IT WAS TIME to push harder, to really see and further stretch his boundaries. Jim wanted to up his game and do things that he couldn't do before, that hadn't been done, that other people couldn't do.

By the spring of 1972, Jim had a growing sense that, for him, Yosemite wasn't the end unto itself, the way it so happily was for others in Camp 4. He was starting to feel a rising certainty that the great climbs of the Valley were preparation for something bigger, harder, of a very different character. He understood that he wanted to improve not just so he'd become a better *Yosemite* climber but also so he could take his improving skills into remote places that would measure him fully.

When Jim drove back into the Valley after Scotland, he saw a shift in the players in Camp 4, one that would play a key role in getting him into those bigger ranges. "When I first came to Yosemite," Jim explained, "almost everyone there was from California, but by my third year, it seemed like everyone from *everywhere* wanted to be in the Valley." The big walls and the classics from the Golden Age were part of the draw, but by 1972, word was also out about the shorter technical testpieces being established by the new generation. Climbers started coming not just from other parts of North America, but from Europe as well.

Jim was often the first local that visitors met, and his gregariousness paid off in some of the most important partnerships of his life—first with strong climbers from the Northeast, and then a swelling stream of Brits through the 1970s.

Two of the Easterners became fast friends and superb partners. St. Louis native Steve Wunsch was one of the most talented American climbers of the new generation and was just beginning his ascendancy when he met Jim in the Valley. Wunsch's talent was evident from the first moment they roped up. He was fantastically flexible, and he had an uncanny ability to find protection where others couldn't and make the kinds of moves that others wouldn't. People swore that Wunsch was the first person they'd ever seen throw a heel hook or stack fingers in cracks, and they spoke with admiration about the man's fierce adherence to a purist's ethic of ascent: always from the ground up, with no pre-inspection; always in control, even on the runouts that some of his routes were famous for. Wunsch was also a masterful guitarist, a student of arcane philosophy, and a brilliant mathematician who'd gone to Princeton and would later build a career that would introduce electronic trading to the world of finance. All of these qualities interested Jim as much as the climbing did.

Jim's other partner from the East, John Bragg, climbed extensively with Wunsch in the Gunks. Like Wunsch, Bragg's résumé included important first ascents across the country, and like Wunsch, Bragg had an Ivy League pedigree, having just finished a degree at Harvard.

Lanky and enormously strong, with striking blue eyes and a helmet of blond curls, Bragg was a commanding figure who had a huge influence on American climbing. Bragg had a glowering intensity, much like Jim himself, but he lacked Jim's ready capacity to shift into a sunnier gear. As a consequence, Bragg was sometimes hard to read—even for people who knew him well. In our conversations, Bragg graciously acknowledged that he knew people sometimes struggled with him, and he said that he'd also struggled to understand others, too. He said that it had been a revelation when he was diagnosed later in life as being on the autism spectrum. When I shared Bragg's disclosure with Jim, he said, "Actually, that explains a lot. People could really misunderstand the way John acted, when he was just shy. I got along with him well from the start, but not everyone did."

Wunsch, Bragg, and Donini's Yosemite stories are tightly interwoven. They were a top-end Eastern coalition that would come every season, often climbing together from 1972 on, putting up new lines and ticking off the latest testpieces. Between them, they created forty new climbs in the Valley and racked up the first free ascents of a number of others. Roger Breedlove, a climber from the era who has taken on the daunting task of mapping the history of Yosemite first ascents, showed that the Wunsch-Bragg-Donini partnership was one of the most prolific in Valley history, and he said that Jim's tally of eleven first ascents in 1973 ranks as one of the most productive single years that *anyone* has ever had in Yosemite.

The relationships between the three men extended well beyond Yosemite, too: Wunsch and Jim remained fast friends until Wunsch's death from cancer in 2019, and not long after their Yosemite era finished, Bragg and Donini would partner up for one of the most important climbs in either of their lives: the groundbreaking 1976 ascent of Torre Egger in Patagonia.

THE BRITISH CLIMBERS who invaded Yosemite in the early 1970s were just as talented, but there was another element to them that appealed to Jim just as much: their antics and excesses.

Jim's initial connection with the Brits came when Rab Carrington showed up one day at Jim's site in Camp 4. The gifted Scot had just arrived in Yosemite with Alan Rouse, a climber from Liverpool. Both men were superb free climbers, and Jim encouraged them to try some of the new short, technical climbs he'd established, but Rouse insisted that their first Yosemite climb had to be one of the Valley's iconic big walls. The next day, barely halfway up the first pitch of Half Dome's *Northwest Face*—pitch one of their entire three-month trip to America—Rouse pulled an aid piece, fell, and badly broke his leg, leaving Carrington hunting for partners. Jim happily stepped up.

Other Brits followed, and their commitments to both climbing and carousing were clear. None of the Brits exemplified both better than Pete Minks, a Liverpudlian who styled himself after Don Whillans, the bête noire of the British scene. Like Whillans, Minks made his reputation on long, hard Alps routes, including a very impressive one-day solo of the *Walker Spur* on Les Grandes Jorasses. Equally in the Whillans mold, Minks was a rough-edged, ready-to-scrap lad from a working-class family who was always ready to take the piss—especially out of American climbers and their pretensions. "If you thought you'd done something special, Minksy would sort you out pretty quick," Jim said with a laugh.

In 1973, Minks persuaded Jim to put aside his distaste for big-wall climbing and commit to an ascent of *The Nose* on El Cap. By this time, Jim's systems were far more advanced than when he'd plodded up the *Salathé Wall* two years before, and he and Minks managed the first two-day ascent of the huge route. "Minksy was fast from all the climbing he'd done in the Alps," Jim explained, "and decided it should be nothing to get up *The Nose* in two days—but, as always, he showed up at my tent completely hungover and quite late. Despite that, we were really quick, and made it to Camp IV with lots of time to spare. We free climbed a lot of the route—including Boot Flake, which had never been freed at that point. If we'd wanted to, we might have even been able to finish the climb that day, but there was a slow party above us, it started to drizzle, and Minks wanted to spend the night on the wall."

Up at Camp IV, when they settled in for a T-shirt bivy, Minks pulled out a joint and a flask of bourbon and started to wax ineloquently about how much he loved California. "I love America," he slurred in the dark. "I love the climbing, I love the drugs, and I really love the women."

Jim laughed. Why hurry a moment as good as this?

BY THE END of the fall season of 1973, Jim had found his stride. He was climbing, especially cracks, as well as anyone else. He felt free to work and play in whatever balance he wanted. He had a stable of top-shelf partners who could give him a chance of success anywhere that he might hope to climb, and he was more than ready to go with those partners and look beyond the confines of Yosemite and America.

All he needed was a plan—or an invitation.

CHAPTER 13

AN OBSCENE JOURNEY TO AN UNSEEN MOUNTAIN

IT BEGAN, THEY think, with a letter. Or perhaps a phone call. No one really remembers how the whole adventure creaked to life, but the Brits who knew Donini in Yosemite also knew about his Volkswagen van, and that green-and-white 1968 microbus became a big part of *their* plan to go to Patagonia and climb the massive, virgin east face of Cerro Fitz Roy. To have Jim along with the van would be a welcome plus.

In 1973, a climb in Patagonia was a bold ambition. The great rock spires that spike the border between Chile and Argentina were just beginning to rise into the consciousness of climbers, but they already had a fearsome reputation. Few routes on any of the enormous walls had been done, and stories of the rare ascents described very hard technical climbing and perhaps the worst weather of any mountains in the world. There were no easy lines to any summit, and men had died just getting to the bases of the walls.

But these are peaks that spear the imagination, as close to perfect as mountains get: claws of flawless tan stone, punching out of the Argentine plain, draped in shrouds of rime, riven with fine cracks that run unbroken for thousands of feet.

In those days, the closest international airport was 1,500 miles away, and the tourist towns of modern Patagonia didn't exist. No matter how you got there, Patagonia obliged an epic journey. Hence the reach out to Jim: "Why don't you and your bus join us?" the five Brits said. "We'll ship our gear to Argentina by sea, then meet you in New York and we'll all drive to Patagonia. It'll be a *cracking good* time."

Just a little research convinced Jim the scheme was ridiculous. "It's over 10,000 goddamn miles of driving," he remembered thinking. "There will be six men in a VW van. There's this thing called the Darién Gap. It will cost hundreds of dollars to get a Carnet de Passage, and you'd need an insurance bond that cost three thousand. They didn't know what they were talking about."

But the plan did have a fabled precedent: In 1968, five men *did* take a van from the United States to Patagonia, and they *did* climb Fitz Roy. The self-styled "Fun Hogs"—Californians Yvon Chouinard, Doug Tompkins, Dick Dorworth, Chris Jones, and Lito Tejada-Flores—drove to Panama, shipped their van across the Darién, surfed and skied their way down South America over three and half months, and then made the third ascent of the mountain, via a very big route in very bad conditions. Inspired by that trip, the Brits presumptuously concluded that Jim's van was the best remedy for their lack of money and surfeit of free time.

Jim agreed to go because the towers were just too magical to miss, but he put his foot down about driving. When the men arrived in New York, he laid out an alternate plan: none of them could afford a plane ticket to Argentina, but they could take the van to Miami, get cheap flights to Colombia, and figure out the rest of the journey from there.

The Brits grumbled, but they were soon back in their usual rowdy spirits. Jim relished the idea of going to Patagonia with these men. He adored the ones he knew. He'd done that one-bivouac ascent of *The Nose* with the endlessly entertaining Pete Minks. He'd climbed great free routes in Yosemite with Rab Carrington. He liked and admired Al Rouse. Jim loved the way that all the Brits refused to take climbing too seriously, and he admired their willingness to push in the mountains. These were his people.

Jim also trusted their word on the two men he hadn't met. John Barker was a bit older, closer to Jim's age, an ex-cop whom Jim felt could provide balance to the mad tendencies of the younger climbers. The last member, Mike Geddes, was a Scot who'd done an impressive string of ice climbs in Scotland as well as big routes in the Alps.

Jim had been around enough Brits to know this trip was going to be an adventure of debauchery as much as of climbing, and that feeling was confirmed before the first night together was over. The team decided that it would be good to climb together before starting the long drive, so Jim suggested they head north from New York to the white conglomerate crags of the Shawangunks and the bars of the nearby college town of New Paltz.

"The game," Rab told me, "was on."

Arriving in New Paltz late in the day, Jim guided the crew to the Homestead, a pub that was a favorite of climbers. It took no time before the Brits were up on their feet bellowing bawdy drinking songs. The owner eventually came over, offering free pitchers of beer if they'd sit down and stop singing.

"Not surprisingly," John Barker remembered, "free beer did not turn out to be the solution." When a few members of the team got up on the tables to dance, the police were called, and the men scrambled to find another pub. Three bars later, there was no way anyone could drive back to the campsite at the foot of the cliffs, and so the six climbers slept in a ditch on the outskirts of town.

(A complicated aside here: stories like this pour out of Jim. He has endless tales from the hours away from the crags spent getting drunk and "trying every drug there was." He tells the stories with laughter, shaking his head at the ridiculous situations he found himself in, amazed that he survived. And to be fair to him, most of his partners have similar stories; Dionysian madness was just part of the adventure.

Still, given the terrible price that several people close to Jim would eventually pay for their own abuse and addictions, there's a discomforting rustling behind the curtain of hilarity in those stories. After all, these people who suffered so badly were doing the same things that his stories celebrate, and it ruined or took their lives and brought terrible, lasting despair into Jim's own life.

Despite that darkness, Jim still tells the stories. They are, after all, what happened, and they're often funny tales that celebrate the mad liberties of the adventure life. But the troubling and sad irony of the celebration isn't lost on him.)

The next morning, jet-lagged and tyrannically hungover, the ragged bunch stumbled up to the crags. Jim proposed they do *Arrow*, a two-pitch route that had an easy first pitch well within the abilities of everyone, despite their condition. They voted to solo as a group rather than bother with ropes, because, said John Barker, "That's the kind of decisions this lot made."

Jim didn't tell the team, however, that it was the *second* pitch that made the climb interesting. It might have only been graded 5.8, but everyone had hammering headaches, Gunks climbs are scandalously undergraded, and the crux of *Arrow* is its very last move, which is reachy, thin, and polished.

By his own admission, John Barker was the weakest rock climber on the team, and by some still-drunken logic, that fact convinced everyone that he should go first in the conga line. He started up the gentle beginning, and everyone else followed close behind, trying to avoid stepping on each other's hands and heads. Minks brought up the rear, with a sequined purse he'd stolen from a woman the night before tied around his waist—the theft warranted, he insisted, so he could carry the cassette deck that was now bellowing Pink Floyd's *Dark Side of the Moon*. Irritated and terrified parties on nearby climbs couldn't believe what they were seeing and hearing.

By the time Barker reached the crux edging move 200 very exposed feet up the wall, the peril was abundantly clear: he was completely stretched out, desperate to find purchase for his fingertips, and all five men were lined up immediately below, watching his legs quiver and mocking him. "I'm glad I didn't fall off there," Barker told me, "or half of British climbing would have been wiped out!"

Barker finally flopped, nauseated, atop the climb, and everyone else joined him. The tenuous success only convinced the men that they were on the right path. They kept on soloing through that day and the next, the madness capped off when Minks, hungover still, soloed up *Roseland*, a notoriously undergraded 5.9 on the Near Trapps crag, with the tape deck in the purse still blaring Pink Floyd. "I'm sure that the locals had never seen anything like it," Jim laughed. "Nor had I . . ."

The van headed south the next day, and Jim decided to stop in New Jersey and risk exposing his parents to the rabble. Betty, always the consummate host, cooked up an extravaganza of Italian food and completely won the men over.

Everyone stayed surprisingly well-mannered at the Doninis and continued through to Florida without exposing America to any further harm . . . until Miami. There they received the news that their flight to Colombia would be delayed for days because Hurricane Ellen had shut down travel across the Caribbean. The boys were set loose on the city. The memories are a blur. They strayed one evening over to the University of Miami and ended up at a fraternity party. Minks danced naked on the bar, then launched headlong down a buffet table, food flying off in his wake. Furniture was thrown off a balcony. Cops were called yet again. They snuck into the Orange Bowl stadium and slept under the stands. Minks had all his money stolen when he tried to buy weed—to take *to* Colombia.

"I was just waiting to get arrested," Jim remembered, "but the rest of them couldn't have cared less. It was all just what you did in America—and, for that matter, what they did every time they went to the Alps . . ."

When the flight to South America finally took off, things only got worse. The men began an epic journey down the continent, starting with a bus from Barranquilla to Bogotá, filled with black-shrouded mourners heading to the funeral—of the corpse riding in a coffin on the roof.

Bogotá, however, was shut down by riots, and the men spent days in a godforsaken hostel, waiting for public transit to start running again and watching what little money they had evaporate. When they finally got back on the road, they drove night and day for 4,300 miles with Minks's *Dark Side of Moon* their only soundtrack. They watched the hours click by with agonizing slowness—but they were completely unaware how ludicrous any concern about their time spent traveling would soon prove to be.

"THE THING THAT you really need if you're going to get up big mountains," Jim said, "isn't skill or fearlessness or toughness: it's patience. You have to be able to sit and wait, to settle in and let things unfold as they will."

When the team arrived in Buenos Aires more than a month after leaving New York, they assumed that their patience would now be rewarded: they would get their gear, decipher a way to cover the last 1,500 miles to Cerro Fitz Roy, and at last tackle the mountain they'd been dreaming about.

Instead, when they headed down to the port in the Argentine capital, they discovered that their gear hadn't even left England. For years, dockworkers in Liverpool had been staging rotating strikes, and the crates and duffels of the British Fitz Roy expedition had been left in limbo by one of those months-long walkouts.

Having come all this way, the team was hardly going to give up, so they settled into the old colonial city much as they might hunker down in a storm-bound tent. Some moved in with a wealthy plastic surgeon named Eduardo Rodriguez, who had offered the floor of his apartment to a few Patagonian teams over the years. Others arranged to stay with Hector Vieytes, a kind and gregarious man who had a contract making sleeping bags for the Argentine military and loved showing off his city.

Early in their time in Buenos Aires, another British climber showed up. Mick Coffey was the advance man for a large British-American expedition to Torre Egger, a peak that would soon figure prominently in Jim's own story. Jim connected with Coffey immediately. "He was a really endearing guy who was incredible to hit the town with. He was one of the funniest people I've ever met, and women *loved* him. You could just follow Mick around and you'd be guaranteed to have a great night," Donini said.

Even with such a fun crew, there were only so many nights out that one could have. As days of waiting dragged into weeks, the plan started to lose steam, and the team drifted lower. They drank more. They smoked pot. They took lovers, including Geddes taking up with Eduardo Rodriguez's wife in full view of their host. "That was really uncool," Jim said. Rouse, meanwhile, aimed younger and took up with Eduardo's eighteen-year-old daughter. Even less cool.

Near the end of December, Jim's patience ran out. He wanted to be climbing. He needed days with more purpose. There was still no sign of the gear, and he was starting to feel that they'd never get to Patagonia. He told the others that his trip was done. They all had one last great party, then Jim got a flight home. He landed back in New York nearly eight weeks after that mad night in the Shawangunks, wondering what lessons to take from the whole strange adventure. The experience hardly suggested that he'd fall in love with Patagonia or that he'd ever bother to climb overseas again.

FOR THE REST of the team, the clock was ticking. It was well into January, with the Patagonian summer season already fading fast, before the men got the news that the gear was coming into port. But a few days later, their months in Buenos Aires came to a difficult turn. After the team collected the gear and somehow got Eduardo to loan them his Jeep for the drive south, a cousin of Eduardo's and a friend named Enrico took the men out for a celebratory party at a lake on the grounds of a local country club. John Barker was doing backwards somersaults off a diving board with a bottle of wine in each hand when he saw club security approaching. Enrico went up to the guards to tell him that he was a member of the club and had brought these friends in with permission, but before he got a word out, one of the guards pulled a gun and shot him.

That sudden violence was typical of the time—there was a lot of random gunfire during the stay in Buenos Aires—but firsthand, it was terrifying. The men rushed Enrico to the hospital in the Jeep. They all gave blood, and Enrico nearly died. The team, shaken, left for Fitz Roy only a few days later.

In the end, the affair fizzled to a close. It was far too late in the season, and the weather was abysmal in the towers. In March, the team returned to Buenos Aires, where they made separate plans to head home. Geddes flew home, but the other three had adventures more in keeping with the madness of the whole trip.

Rouse went back to Bogotá to chase down a woman he'd met in the lockdown. John Barker started north on buses, but on the third day of his journey through Argentina, near the Bolivian border, local cops grabbed him and threw him in jail, for reasons he still doesn't understand. For three days, he was kept in a dungeon, beaten with truncheons, then finally stood up against a wall pockmarked with bullet holes. Cops with rifles lined up across from him, and then the head man turned to the apparent firing squad . . . and they all burst out laughing, saying something in Spanish that Barker could only guess was "We sure had you going there, didn't we?" before hustling him across the border into Bolivia.

Barker couldn't get to the Quito airport fast enough, and he was overjoyed when he found there was a plane for Miami boarding just a few minutes after he arrived. He was in the United States by the evening, and within a few days he was sitting in Betty Donini's kitchen, eating a huge plate of pasta. "The lovely woman had said, 'You boys can come back any time you want,'" Barker explained. "I took her at her word."

Rab Carrington's continuing story was just as subject to the whims of fate, though it was far more positive. Rab had neither a partner nor a job waiting at home, so he stayed in Buenos Aires, a decision that changed the course of his life: To earn money, he started working with Hector Vieytes in his sleeping bag business, learning how to design and sew outdoor gear. He was still sewing in Buenos Aires when Jim came back to Patagonia the following year, and when Carrington finally returned to the United Kingdom in 1975, he took his new skills and started what would become one of the top outdoor gear companies, Rab Equipment. "None of that would have happened," Carrington said, "without that bloody mad trip . . ."

As strange as their journey was, for many of the team it was a launching point for greater things in the mountains—including returns to Patagonia. Jim was back in 1974. Carrington came back again in 1977 with Al Rouse, for a brilliant trip during which the pair made first ascents on both Aguja Guillaumet and Aguja Poincenot.

Patagonia, as they'd all come to believe, actually was *worth* the wait.

CHAPTER 14

TOWERS OF PATIENCE

"OF COURSE I was going to go back," Jim said of his return to Patagonia for the 1974–75 climbing season. "I'd gone all that way and hadn't even seen these mountains, but every day I was in Buenos Aires, they were all we heard and thought about."

Jim felt that the first trip south taught him some valuable lessons for future success in Patagonia: fly instead of traveling overland, keep a shorter rein on your gear, go with a smaller team. He turned to his other Yosemite partners, and after months of waffling, John Bragg finally committed.

The pair agreed that any objective would be worthy. There were scores of unclimbed, high-quality walls on the remarkable Chaltén massif, especially on the three biggest peaks: bulky Fitz Roy (3,405 meters) on the eastern hem of the Torre Glacier and, across the valley, Torre Egger (2,850 meters) and the sky-spearing Cerro Torre (3,100 meters), arguably the most compelling mountain in the world.

But a narrow focus on those highest peaks ignores the beauty and the challenge of the countless other summits in the Torre cirque. Anywhere else on the planet, spectacular towers like the *agujas* (needles) Desmochada, Saint-Exupéry, Guillaumet, and Poincenot on the Fitz Roy side and Cerro Standhardt on the Torre Group would be kings themselves, as would many of the lesser spires in adjacent valleys in the massif. But in Patagonia, metrics of scale, beauty, and difficulty are all shifted in an instant.

Bragg's delayed sign-up meant that he was short on funds, and so he was obliged to travel overland down South America, repeating Jim's trip from the previous year. But at least he wouldn't be alone: when Bragg started telling people he was going, he heard that Mick Coffey and his girlfriend were also heading south, so he decided to join them for the caravan of planes, trains, and buses to Buenos Aires. Jim knew a separation from Bragg could potentially delay their climbing trip, but there was no way he was going to suffer the overland journey again. He left Bragg in Coffey's hands, shipped the climbing gear, and got ready to fly to Buenos Aires in early November 1974.

A last-minute add-on meant that Jim wasn't going to be traveling alone either. Larry Bruce, another Camp 4 regular, told Jim he was interested in at least seeing the towers, if not climbing them. "I was a pretty good rock climber," Bruce told me, "but I didn't have the mountain skills that [Jim] did. I just thought I'd go along and see if I could get up something smaller."

When Jim and Larry arrived in Argentina, they found that the political situation in the Argentine capital had deteriorated dramatically in the past year. Rab Carrington was still learning his craft with Hector Vieytes, and he told chilling stories about how bad things had been. There was constant gunfire, protestors were beaten in public, and Rab himself had been briefly detained at gunpoint.

When the gear arrived sooner than expected, Jim decided that he and Larry could head out to the towers and see what conditions were like. He rationalized that Bragg should be able to find him in the climbers' base camp—even though that camp was 1,500 miles away and he had no idea where Bragg might be.

Jim and Larry took a bus south to Río Gallegos, a filthy industrial outpost near the Atlantic coast, then hitched a ride toward the towers with the Argentine postal service. It was a common climbers' trick: every ten days, a mail truck made the 300-mile journey from Río Gallegos to the gendarmerie and ranger station that would eventually become the town now called El Chaltén, and climbers often got a lift and arranged resupplies of food with the mailman.

The two-day drive west finally brought Jim to the foot of peaks he'd been thinking about for so long. It was hard to imagine a more complete mountain scene. There were turquoise lakes pocked with small icebergs, great sweeps of glacial ice and moraine, spires of incomprehensible scale and beauty. There was much to do: figure out the best location for a base camp, as close as possible to the glaciers but still sheltered in the forest; sort out the approach to the peaks; carry a load or two up the glacier.

But Jim and Larry barely caught a glimpse of rock, let alone any summits, after the first day. The wind was constant, strong enough to lift them off their feet and toss them sideways, and the rain could cut skin.

The east face of Torre Egger, with Col of Conquest on the left and Punta Herron on the right (Photo by Jim Donini)

As the days dragged on without a sign of Bragg, Jim and Larry started to consider climbing something themselves, but the opportunity never came. The conditions stayed terrible, and it wasn't long before their food supplies started to dwindle.

They decided to hike out, meet the mailman at the garrison fifteen miles down the road, and at least try to find Bragg.

There was no mailman and no Bragg at the outpost. Jim and Larry waited for two hungry weeks, then decided that something had happened to the mail and resigned themselves to walking out to the closest village. Tres Lagos was seventy-five miles down the road, but they were out of food and there seemed no other option. As the men started their long trudge east, bitter irony unfolded behind them: the storms finally ended and a shark-tooth silhouette of spires shimmered against clear sapphire skies.

But fortune repaid their commitment to the walk. After ten miles, they caught sight of a Volkswagen bus grinding along the far shore of a large, flooded lowland. When they got to the van, Jim was stunned to discover that he knew the two men inside. He stuck his head in and cried, "Well, well, if it isn't Brian Wyvill and Ben Campbell-Kelly!"

Jim knew the young British climbers from Yosemite, where they'd recently made the fifth ascent of the *North America Wall* on El Cap. Wyvill and Campbell-Kelly had their sights set on Cerro Standhardt, a 2,700-meter virgin summit at the northern end of the Torre chain. A bit blockier than its neighbors, a bit lower, and with less ice guarding its upper reaches, Standhardt seemed a reasonable objective as a first Patagonian peak. Jim started a conversation about combining forces.

The best news from Wyvill and Campbell-Kelly was that they were carrying more than enough food for two teams. Everyone sprang into action gathering logs to get the van across the swamp and en route back to the spires.

FOR A FEW days, it seemed like the tide had turned. Bragg and Mick Coffey finally showed up, and a plan for a climb was devised. All six men climbed up a windless glacier and quickly sorted out a steep and heavily crevassed slope that led to the col between Standhardt and the adjacent tower, Aguja Bifida. From the col, a long, rising snow ledge bisected the face and gave access to a series of major features that rose to Standhardt's summit ridge. They chose the most obvious weakness: a deep chimney that appeared to offer some protection from the inevitable wind. Believing they could reach the summit with just a few days' climbing above the ledge, everyone retreated to prepare for a summit bid, happy to have found a route that seemed safe and wouldn't require a siege with fixed lines.

But, Jim soon saw, "Patagonia makes you pay for optimism." The storms came back with sharper fangs. The winds pummeled the climbers, and the rime ice that usually shrouds just the tops of the peaks reached down to their camp.

As the weeks dragged on, food rations started to thin out again, until the men came up with a novel, if somewhat perverse, remedy. They descended to the Pampas and spent the better part of a day chasing down a flock of sheep. They finally caught and killed one, and then just as they began to roast chunks of meat they'd hacked off, the shepherd showed up. As Larry Bruce explained, "He could have killed us for what we'd done, but he accepted a rope as a trade for the sheep and then helped us cook it properly."

Near the end of December, Bruce decided he'd had enough and left, but just a few days later there was a hint of a more lasting change in the weather. On December 26, the first blue skies in months pushed everyone into action, but not together: Bragg announced that before heading up Standhardt, he wanted to try to solo Aguja Poincenot. It was a culmination of a frustration that had been growing for Bragg since he'd first arrived in camp. John increasingly felt that Jim seemed more interested in climbing with the Brits, and so he headed off to Poincenot feeling, he said, "a bit hurt."

Jim and the Brits went back toward Standhardt, and although a quick return of poor weather kiboshed everyone's plans, the Standhardt team had an eventful day: on the way up the glacier, they stumbled into one of the most notorious sagas of climbing.

On the ice below Cerro Torre, as the men were starting a traverse toward Standhardt, something unusual caught Jim's eye. "I couldn't believe it, but out in the middle of glacier, I saw a fox," he recalled. When he got closer, he realized the fox was poking around in deteriorating human remains. He saw a leather boot, mummified flesh on a piece of leg bone, and, under a rotting sweater nearby, portions of a rib cage. There was also an old cable-laid rope tied in a confusing pattern.

Just a cursory look told the men whose remains these must be. Sixteen years before, in 1959, Austrian alpinist Toni Egger had been involved in one of the most heralded climbs of the twentieth century: an alleged ascent of Cerro Torre with renowned Italian climber Cesare Maestri.

When Maestri told the world that he and Egger had climbed the northeast ridge of that remarkable mountain, everyone understood that it was a stunning accomplishment. No peak of that severity had been climbed before; indeed, Cerro Torre had been called unclimbable by many of the best alpinists of the era. The ascent signaled a huge leap in standards, but Maestri had made a career of climbs that others had called impossible.

Maestri came to Patagonia with an impressive team. Toni Egger was less well known than Maestri, but he was an excellent climber in his own right, having made breakthrough ascents in the Alps and the Andes. Cesarino Fava, the third member of the team, was likewise quietly accomplished.

From the outset, the threesome found the climbing on Cerro Torre even harder than expected, but they still made progress. Much of that success, Maestri would later say, was due to Egger's prowess, especially on ice. Egger led virtually the entire lower section, which was difficult enough to convince Fava to drop out. Fava went down to a snow cave at the base, and Egger and Maestri continued up into the clouds.

The story of the rest of the climb has been argued for decades. Fava waited in the snow cave for six days, then finally went looking for his friends. He found Maestri crawling on the glacier, alone and near his limit. All Maestri could manage was a feeble lament: "Toni, Toni, Toni . . ." Egger was nowhere to be seen.

Once away from the mountain, Maestri filled in the tale. In his detailed but sometimes contradictory account, he and Egger had reached the high col between Cerro Torre and the adjacent tower (which Maestri would eventually name Torre Egger, to honor his lost friend) after some terribly difficult climbing, but then they found a surprisingly easy path to the summit, thanks to an unexpected shell of ice that had frozen around the tower. On the way down from their magnificent success, tragedy struck: during a rappel Egger was torn from the wall by an avalanche, and fell to his death.

Almost immediately, influential climbers began to question Maestri's account. There were naysayers who simply doubted that anyone could climb such a hard route, and inconsistencies in Maestri's account—particularly the easily climbable shield of ice that had never been seen before or since—further inflamed the issue.

The discovery of Egger's remains by Jim and his team only complicated the matter. The location of Egger's body on the glacier seemed wrong. Though glaciers do move things on their surfaces, it seemed that Egger's remains had traveled *too far*. The location of his body raised valid questions about whether Egger had actually fallen where Maestri said he had.

More confusing still was the system of knots on Egger's rope; it just didn't seem to be a rappelling setup. The knots suggested Egger had fallen while heading *up*, not down, and this raised difficult questions about how he'd died.

Jim's initial stance on the discovery of Egger's remains was to support Maestri. "I always want to believe climbers," Jim explained. "Honest accounting of what we do in the mountains is a critical part of climbing; without faith that people are being truthful, a lot of things start to fall apart."

Out on the glacier, the men covered the remains, and as Jim looked up at the huge golden tower that rose to the right of the Col of Conquest, he hatched a plan: he would return to Patagonia and honor Egger's memory by climbing the tower named after him.

As the men turned back to camp, clouds started to brew yet again.

IN THE END, a combination of weather and an unfortunate choice of route finally ended the siege of Standhardt more than six weeks after the discovery of Egger's remains.

They'd still been suffering rain and snow down in the forest, and now time had run out. The men climbed back up to the headwall for one final go on January 6, dragging along a clunky metal-and-nylon box shelter that the Brits had jerry-rigged at home. "We should have known better," Jim said. They shouldn't have considered stuffing the four of them into that homemade shelter for two. They should have realized that the chimney above the traverse ledge was wide and black for good reason: weather pounded the top of the tower and beat the fragile basalt of the chimney ugly.

When the team finally started up the chimney, they began to appreciate their mistakes. Thawing ice was tumbling down, and when the temperatures warmed, rocks followed. "I looked to the left and right and saw all this beautiful, clean, dry granite," says Bragg, "and then I looked up our chimney and wondered what the hell we were doing." But they simply didn't have enough gear to take on the big, bald walls around them; it was the chimney or nothing.

Though the skies were clear, the chimney was cold and filled with iced rubble. The foursome made progress over the course of two days, but on January 9, only 150 feet below the summit ridge, it became obvious it would be pointless to head any higher. Savage winds raked the ridge, and the men knew that even if they finished the chimney, there was no way they could climb beyond.

At 6 p.m., they started retreating. If they needed any confirmation of the wisdom of their decision, it came that night, when wind-driven rain poured through the walls of the shelter and started to rip it apart. In the early hours of the next morning, they abandoned the disintegrating box and watched it fly off into the gale. The climb, and the season, were done.

Nearly four months after leaving home, Jim, John, and the Brits said their goodbyes to each other and to Patagonia. It had been a long, hard stretch, but all four swore they weren't done with the magical place.

Campbell-Kelly and Wyvill would return twice to the east face of Cerro Torre, and within the year, Bragg and Jim would get their chance to live out Jim's promise to Toni Egger—but another, very unexpected turn would come first.

WHEN JANET OAKLEY HUNTER returned to work as a park naturalist that summer in the Tetons, she had everyone's attention. She was tall, blonde, and had striking blue eyes. "I had never seen a more beautiful woman," Jim said, and he knew others felt that way, too: Janet had been coming to the Tetons for a few summers now, and the other guides had told Jim about her. "As soon as she walked in any room, every man wanted to be with her." How could they not? Everyone told me how unabashedly fun, flirtatious, and magnetic this woman was.

A scion of both wealth and political heft, Janet came from the equivalent of royalty in America. Her father, Allan Oakley Hunter, had been elected to Congress for two terms, as the Republican representative of the Ninth and then Twelfth Congressional Districts of California. In 1970, Richard Nixon appointed him chairman of the Federal National Mortgage Association (better known as Fannie Mae). Hunter ran the huge bureaucracy until 1981, and he surfed the highest waves of the Republican Party all through his life.

Like many young people of similar background at the time, Hunter's youngest daughter had strayed a bit from those conservative roots. She had a degree in natural resource conservation, and she loved the alternative lifestyle, and the nature, that surrounded her in the Tetons. The summers that she'd spent in the park also connected Janet to the climbing world. As she told me, "I had climbed Mount Moran with [park ranger] Ralph Tingey; fished the Grand Canyon of the Yellowstone; and rock climbed with Jeff Foote, bouldered with Steve Wunsch, and climbed the Middle Teton with [Yosemite legend] Chuck Pratt."

Not long after Janet arrived in Jackson that year, she came to a casual slideshow that Jim was giving about the trip to Standhardt. She was captivated by this striking man with the mad beard and outlandish stories, and the attraction was mutual and instant. They went to Baja, and a few wild weeks convinced Jim that Janet was up for anything. If she could sleep in a sandpit on the runway of a Mexican airport, as they did one tequila-soaked night, she'd do fine anywhere he'd want to go. They traveled north to Yosemite, where she made quite an impact on the Camp 4 crew. "We'd see Donini with this goddess," one of Jim's Yosemite friends said, "and we'd think, 'Holy shit, what's happening in the universe?!'" If Jim's first wife, Sandy, had been invisible in Yosemite, Janet was anything but. Everybody remembered her.

THROUGH THE SUMMER and fall with Janet, Torre Egger remained on Jim's mind. He and Bragg were already planning to return that winter of 1975–76, and, despite Bragg's initial protestations, Jim convinced him that Janet would be a valuable addition to the team. She was instrumental in securing funding for the trip. Through some Washington connections, Janet arranged a meeting between Jim and the editor of *National Geographic* with the hope that an article about the climb could recoup some of the costs.

Committing to Egger was a big thing. At that point, only one team—the very strong British-American expedition that Mick Coffey had been a member of in 1974—had tried the peak. They hadn't made much progress, and they suggested that Torre Egger might well be the most unattainable summit in Patagonia. *All the better*, Jim thought.

The scale of Patagonia suggested that having another climber along to share the work would be a good idea. Jim and Bragg settled on inviting Jay Wilson, a friend from Jackson, Wyoming, who had an impressive résumé as a skier and climber. Wilson was the most naturally gifted athlete of the three—which was saying a great deal—and though he lacked alpine wall experience, he was fiercely strong, eager for adventure, and easygoing.

Adding people was contagious; suddenly Jay Wilson's sister, Jane, was also coming, as was his brother Sherman, and then Sherman's girlfriend, Maureen. To Jim, it happily felt like they were creating a mini–Camp 4, a posse of easy-living friends that it would be great to have along. Bragg had a different view: "To be honest, I was pissed. I didn't want all these other people with us, especially couples."

In November, the horde descended on Buenos Aires.

FOR THE THIRD season in a row, the political situation in Argentina had deteriorated even further, which once again complicated getting the gear out of customs. It took weeks—and Janet's father's political connections—to finally grease the bureaucratic wheels. With all the extra characters along on the trip, it was more than a month before the group established their village of tents and lean-tos in the beech woods below the towers.

Bragg came up with the plan to reprise the 1959 Italian route up to the Col of Conquest between Cerro Torre and Torre Egger, then work their way up the very blank south face of Torre Egger to the top. The strategy dropped the climbers right back into the Maestri mystery.

By mid-December, the team was back in an all-too-familiar Patagonian routine. It sleeted and howled, but they still got a little work done. Short

Jim in damp conditions on Torre Egger, three pitches above Col of Conquest (**Photo by John Bragg**)

windows of good weather let them fix pitches up the lower wall, following Maestri's line toward one of the most obvious features on the face, a big triangular snowfield about one-third of the way up to the col.

"It was like a trip through climbing history," Jim said. The face below the snowfield climbed a prominent dihedral system laced with relics of the 1959 climb—rotting wooden wedges, disintegrating cable-laid ropes. The climbing was impressively difficult, but, predictably, the harder thing was the continuously atrocious weather. The men climbed a couple of days, but for most of December and virtually all of January, they sheltered in camp, increasingly frustrated. In various combinations, their friends in camp would run out for respite from the storms, but the climbers stayed, bound to the unlikely chance that the weather might clear at any minute.

A measure of relief—at least for those in the party who were happy to have new blood in camp—came when a big New Zealand team, aiming for the route that the 1974 British-American crew had tried on Torre Egger, showed up in early December and established a base only fifteen minutes away. From Jim's vantage, it was great to have the Kiwis' energy infusion. They were raucous, always ready for a party, happy to share stories and meals.

Again, John was less thrilled. "I come to the mountains for solitude and climbing," he said, "and now we had a team that was shooting for the first ascent of the same peak, and in the last thirty days we'd only climbed a hundred feet."

The shine of the New Zealanders was disastrously scuffed at the end of the first week of the new year when the youngest member of their team, nineteen-year-old Phil Herron, fell into a hidden crevasse and perished before he could be extracted. A week later, deflated by Herron's death, the Kiwi team left the mountain.

Not long after, troubles peaked in the American camp too. One afternoon, Bragg, increasingly fed up with the crowd in camp and the lack of climbing, complained again, and he and Jim ended up at each other's throats, Jim ready to throw John to the ground—though they eventually moved apart without coming to blows. The brief scuffle, Jim says, was completely out of character with the rest of their relationship, and he still speaks about it with regret decades later, but in the moment it signaled the toll the whole trip was taking on everyone. It was time to get up Egger or go home. It was January 20, and it wouldn't be long before the season was over.

The three climbers packed again for the tower, and the rest of base camp followed the Kiwis out to civilization.

FROM THE START, the climbers were challenged. They discovered that their gear at the base was buried under twenty feet of new snow, and it took a long day to dig it out. Once they started up the face, the rime that had been plastered all over the wall for the past month calved off in sheets that surfed down through the air in frightening swoops. The cracks of the dihedral, which had offered such good climbing before, streamed with meltwater.

Then storms rolled back in, sending the men scurrying back to the forest. One week became two, then three. Hope evaporated in the damp cold.

In mid-February, a high-pressure bubble opened the skies and the team launched. On this final sortie up Torre Egger, the men reached their high-point quickly, and they soon came upon a big cache of gear left behind by the 1959 team. The path through the breadcrumbs of Maestri's climb was puzzling and disturbing in equal measure. Up to the snowfield, they found gear everywhere, passing scores of scattered pieces of wood, steel, and rope. Then, on the pitch that led to the gear cache, they came upon a setup with no obvious purpose: a rope was clove-hitched into every second or third piece, and two severed strands of rope, which seemed identical to the ropes they'd found by Egger's body, hung from an overhanging block.

The section they were now in, from the equipment cache to the Col of Conquest, was the most troubling: not only did they find no gear at all after finding so much below, the climbing was now completely inconsistent with Maestri's account. This was especially true of the long traverse into the col. From *below* it looked impossibly blank, as Maestri had claimed, but when Jim got up to the traverse, he spotted a hidden ramp that ran over easy terrain—the easiest ground of the entire climb—right up to the saddle.

It was clear that Maestri's description of the route past the equipment dump was based on what would have been *imagined* from below, not what one encountered on the route. "From even fifty feet below," Jim said, "the ramp was completely invisible, but once you were there it was huge."

"I knew right then and there," Jim said, "that not only had Maestri not climbed Cerro Torre in 1959, he hadn't even gotten to the Col of Conquest. His highpoint was the goddamned equipment dump, only a thousand feet up."

I asked Jim how that landed for him, especially given how much he admired Maestri. "It just seemed so stupid. He'd done so many good climbs, and it was ridiculous to throw away his whole reputation on a lie that was sure to get discovered," he said. Jim knew how arrogant Maestri could be, but he said that it would take a special kind of conceit for Maestri to believe that his deception would never come to light because no one would ever be able to repeat the route to the col and challenge his account.

THE AMERICANS' CLIMB above the col to Torre Egger's summit was far more in keeping with the fairest of climbing practices, impeccable in both style and commitment. The steep, smooth face took every trick and ounce of strength they had. Leads took hours, with complicated mixes of sketchy free climbing and hard aid that linked barely useable features.

As they climbed higher, mist wrapped around the spire and condensed into a carapace of ice. It started to drizzle, and the challenge rose dramatically as the temperature dropped. They decided to fix their ropes and descend to the safety of the col.

They sat one last day in the bivouac, then committed to finishing what they came to do. They pushed their ascenders up ice-coated ropes, carefully navigated the snow mushrooms that clad the summit, and then late in the day on February 22, 1976, dug through the last of the mushrooms and became the first people to stand atop Torre Egger. There was no celebration: clouds churned, the wind was too loud for words, and there was no view. Jim clipped into the rope to begin the long descent, with no sense of how much the moment would shift his life.

CHAPTER 15

LIFE OF A SALESMAN

THE ASCENT OF Torre Egger was a tidemark in Patagonian climbing. It was a breakthrough in technical difficulty, up to the hardest-to-reach summit on the continent, carried out in good style by a small team with admirable commitment to the demands of the range.

But it was equally so a watermark in Jim's life, both as a climber and beyond.

Jim understood that he had now entered into a different realm, where more things were possible, where bigger and bolder dreams seemed reasonable, and where people would be watching him in a different way. When he returned from Patagonia, Jim started asking himself what his next big climbing objective would be, but he also wondered what similarly bold steps he might take in the rest of his life.

At first, there was a lull: in 1976, it took time for word about an expedition to percolate out into the world, so recognition for the climb, and any changes that followed, took a while. In the interim, he'd been gone a long time. He needed to reconnect with family and friends. He needed to pay for the trip and get settled back into life. He needed to write the article on the climb for *National Geographic*. He wanted to spend time with Janet away from wind and cold, so they followed the travelers' trail through South America for a month, chasing the sun and getting used to each other again without a mountain in the way.

Back in America, still tired from the sufferings of Patagonia, Jim convinced himself that the best way to recover from all that hard climbing was to go do some more hard climbing, so he and Janet hit the road, starting in the Gunks and eventually heading toward Yosemite. Valley days, he figured, would help him build back the energy he'd need for all the changes he imagined were on the horizon.

He had no idea how far his imagination was about to be stretched.

"I WOULDN'T SAY that I always wanted children," Jim said, "at least not in the way that people mean that today, when they talk of having children as fulfilling a life's purpose. Back then, especially for men, it was just what was *expected*: you'd get married, you'd have a kid or two, you'd find a job to support your family."

It was daunting when Janet told him that spring that she was pregnant. Though they'd talked about having a family, the couple had hardly been leading a life conducive to raising one. "But we were getting along great," Jim said, "and my natural tendency is to think how I can do it all, so I was in. I really thought it would just be another grand adventure."

It was clear to Jim, though, that he didn't want a child to affect his *mountain* adventures, and he believed Janet agreed. He recalled, "Both of us saw that it made sense for me to continue going on climbing trips, and even expeditions. We knew that big climbs could keep opening doors for me, and we certainly understood that it would be part of me staying happy."

Janet supported all that when we spoke. She was overjoyed to be pregnant, she said, and she knew Jim needed to climb. She thought she could manage. She believed Jim would do everything he could to stay safe in the mountains, and she felt he had it in him to be a good and committed father when he was home.

At least in retrospect, Jim acknowledged that his side of the equation was self-centered. "As men climbing then, we didn't worry as much as we probably should have about the impacts of our choices on the people around us. Many of us left women and children behind without accounting for how hard that was for them, and a terrible number of us never came back."

Their wedding, in early July 1976, was a lavish affair with a hundred guests held in Wilson, Wyoming, with the Grand Teton lording over the bustle and climbers in muslin, beads, and headbands mixing with the Republican elite invited by Janet's family. That fall, with Janet well into her pregnancy, the couple moved to Longmont, Colorado, still uncertain of the life they were trying to shape. They didn't know how permanent Colorado would be, or when Jim might head off on another expedition, or how they'd pay for life with new child. For a time, they relied on food stamps.

On January 10, 1977, their daughter, Sage Hunter Donini, was born—in their home, on their antique brass bed. Jim crowed to everyone, "It was the most incredible thing that I'd ever been part of. Here was this person who was a part of me . . . I couldn't believe how lucky I was."

All these changes highlighted that it was time for Jim to look for something other than guiding to structure—and fund—his life.

In the spring of 1977, fate rolled the dice in his favor once again.

THERE WAS A revolution afoot in America: People were falling back in love with nature. The outdoor community was growing, trails and parks were filling, and Americans were more eager than ever to hear about adventures and to have their own.

Key for Jim, a few visionaries were starting to understand that adventure, and in particular adventure gear, could be a *business*. This was a radical shift. Well into the 1970s, the outdoor retail industry in the United States—at least for more technical gear—consisted of a few niche manufacturers selling a limited product line through scattered stores. There simply weren't enough people skiing, hiking, paddling, or climbing to support production on a larger scale.

But the small size of the industry did have an upside: the gear business was very tight, with the manufacturers not only knowing one another but also working collaboratively. Greg Thomsen, who started a backpack and sleeping bag company called Wilderness Experience with his brother Jim at the time, explained the connections this way: "In those days, the outdoor world was a much more fraternal connection of companies that were completely open to sharing innovations with one another. When someone came up with a cool design idea, you could go spend months in their factory to learn how to do a similar thing with the gear you were making. We were all making stuff because we needed better gear to do the things *we* all wanted to do."

Getting the gear out to people was a different matter. Few designers had experience or interest in sales, and the wide spread of shops across the country made distribution a challenge. It was a problem looking for a solution, and that's where Jim stumbled into a role.

"One of the things that I really liked to do after a trip, and which no one else seemed to want to do," Jim explained, "was to write to the gear companies and tell them what worked and what didn't." One recipient of a letter was Wilderness Experience, the company that made the sleeping bag Jim had used on Torre Egger. The Thomsen brothers recognized a keen eye in Jim's input and saw a chance to capitalize both on Jim's growing reputation and an evolving sales and distribution model.

The Thomsens had a connection to Marty Stilling, a climber from the Midwest who'd recognized a problem in the way that gear came to retailers. Stilling explained, "The salesmen who came to the hippie shops from gear companies like CampTrails [sleeping bags] and Eureka [tents and backpacks] wore white shirts and ties and honestly looked ridiculous."

Stilling felt that outdoor athletes would be better ambassadors. This was a bit like hiring Formula One drivers as car salesmen, but the plan worked magic. The climbers, skiers, and paddlers that Stilling brought on in the early days of his marketing agency, Round Table, were a much better cultural match with the outdoor stores, and they helped sales boom.

When Stilling offered Jim a job on the Thomsens' recommendation, everyone saw it was a mutually ideal fit. "I loved the work," Jim said. He loved telling his stories. He could go into a store and spend all afternoon talking about some climb he'd done, and that would be enough to sell product.

Once again in the right place at the right time, Jim stepped into the industry just when the market was exploding. Focusing on the Intermountain West, Jim moved his family to Salt Lake City, Utah, and established himself as a traveling salesman. During the big sales seasons of the spring and fall, he'd be on the road, moving from store to store, finding creative ways to climb with friends and clients across his territory. He'd still pick up occasional guiding work, especially with those special clients who'd become more like partners. He might be away from his family during those push seasons, but then he'd be home for extended stretches as husband and father, and this seemed to suit him and Janet equally. "I was quite attuned to Jim, and his expedition[s]," Janet wrote in an email. "Summers [in the Tetons] with baby Sage were terrific . . . and I ran with a tight group of supportive climbers."

By the end of 1977, Jim felt he'd found the life that might give him the best of all possible worlds.

MEANWHILE, THERE WAS another change building in Jim's life, rooted in a more distant past. Since he was a teenager, Jim had been puzzled by his brother, wondering how and why his twin could be so different.

To Jim, with his growing faith that taking on big challenges was the best source of fulfillment in a life, Bill seemed to have given up, which was saddening and frustrating. Jim felt he had some important lessons to share with his brother, but he didn't know how to get through to this very different man.

But that spring, Bill was suddenly ready to hear those same lessons from their father. Change bubbled to the surface in a random moment. Bill brought his family to join his parents at the Jersey Shore, and Ugo suggested that Bill join him on the beach for a run. Ugo was still running all the time, and he suggested that running would be good for Bill. Bill didn't want to be shown up by his seventy-two-year-old father, but he couldn't keep up, not even from the first few steps.

Jim said that something clicked in his brother's head that morning, sparking a major transformation that made Bill seem a bit more Donini-like. Within a couple of years, he was not just running in marathons but *winning* them, with a personal best time of 2:26. "His transformation was remarkable." Jim said. "I guess we were more brothers than I'd realized; it appears that Donini genes can lead to obsession."

By the end of that year, so many things seemed to have settled down: Jim had a family. He had a career that gave him purpose and freedom. With the changes in Bill, he'd resolved one of the more puzzling relationships of his life.

And he was on the cusp of a grand adventure that would shape his future more than any other had.

CHAPTER 16

LATOK I: THE MAGNIFICENT FAILURE

This is the Shackleton story of the vertical world . . .
—*Thomas Huber*

IN 1977, UTAH climber George Lowe turned a page in a book and found a picture that stopped him in his tracks.

The black-and-white photograph that so captured Lowe's imagination was a touch blurry, fogged in the middle and washed out at the edges, but it's still easy to understand why it was so compelling.

In the background of the image, there are two regal rock towers topped by crowns of snow, painted with the gossamer haze of summits that are far, far up in the sky. An experienced eye will recognize the higher of the two peaks as Baintha Brakk (the Ogre), a fantastically difficult peak in the Pakistan Karakoram that was the scene of one of the most dramatic stories of modern alpinism, when Britain's Doug Scott had to literally crawl down the mountain with two broken legs during the 1977 first ascent of the 23,900-foot monster.

But it's the mountain in the left foreground that's even more commanding—a spine of black rock that cleaves the glacier at its foot and soars unbroken to a sharp summit a mile and a half above. A climber bold enough can imagine a line right up the slender north ridge; it would obviously be a climb that would stay on very difficult ground at a very high altitude for a very long time, and it would be a fantastic accomplishment in the 1970s—or any era.

It would also be a perfect target for a climber of George Lowe's skill and interest. Lowe, from a legendary family of Utah climbers, had been on a run in the past few years, completing a string of outstanding ascents in Alaska and on big, dangerous walls in the Canadian Rockies. He was ready for the next natural step—a high, difficult, virgin peak in the much bigger ranges of Asia—and he had some friends and family who he knew would be very interested in this photograph.

THE MAN WHO took the photo was a kindred soul not just for George Lowe but for most of the new wave of alpine climbers emerging around the world in the 1970s. Through the 1930s, Britain's Eric Shipton pioneered a revolutionary approach to Himalayan climbing that emphasized the *purity* of ascent, through hard climbs in remote areas, carried out by small teams, with summits reached by the fairest means possible. Shipton's longtime partner, Bill Tilman, famously captured the adventurous spirit of their remarkable trips when he wrote that "any expedition worth doing can be planned on the back of an envelope."

Shipton's Himalayan journeys began with explorations of the north side of Everest, then moved into even more remote ranges—first the Garhwal Himalaya of India, then expeditions in 1937 and 1939 that mapped the exceptionally complex terrain of the central Karakoram Range, the magnificent collection of mammoth peaks that straddles the present-day borders of Afghanistan, China, India, Pakistan, and Tajikistan.

Shipton left a tantalizing collection of stories and pictures for future generations, including the picture that captured George Lowe's attention, taken during a months' long assay in 1939 of a striking subrange of peaks west of K2. Shipton circumnavigated this group, the Panmah Muztagh, and took the picture on the upper reaches of the broad, flat Choktoi Glacier.

Locals called the sharp black mountain "Latok" (properly pronounced *Lah-talk*, not *Lay-talk*—as you'll sometimes hear, including from Jim). In the local Balti dialect, the name means Valley (*La*) Mountain (*tok*)—a literal, but perfect, capture of the essence of this remarkable peak that roars straight up out of the glacial floor. Shipton and his surveyors took the name to designate not just the highest peak with the dominant rock ridge, which they called Latok I, but also four other distinct satellite summits that they numbered Latok II through V.

Shipton's image was arresting enough to catch the imagination of several generations of climbers, but it was years before any of them ventured to the Latoks. At first, expeditions were fixated on the much higher peaks nearby, especially the four 8,000-meter peaks of the Karakoram. Then, from the early 1960s to mid-1970s, political tensions between India and Pakistan shut down access.

But when Pakistan reopened in 1974, suitors were ready. In 1975, two Japanese teams came, but they made little progress on the west flanks of Latok I. The following year, another Japanese team attempted the steep, striking couloir that rises between Latok I and Latok III on the west side, reaching 18,700 feet before serac fall killed a team member.

In early 1977, tragedy struck again. A talented team of British climbers gained the west ridge of Latok II, but the expedition ended when the trip leader disappeared in a crevasse. Two months later, an Italian team finally managed the first ascent in the group when they summitted Latok II.

The next year, two teams came to the Latoks. The first to arrive was British, with several members from the same tight Sheffield climbing community that had suffered the fatality the previous year. They hoped to finish the west ridge of Latok II, but this time catastrophe struck before they even saw the mountain. On just the second day of the approach trek, a member was killed by rockfall in the Braldu River gorge. The trip fell apart.

While the Sheffield crew was retreating, a much smaller expedition was starting their trek on the far side of the range, heading toward the grand prize of the Latoks, the north ridge of Latok I. The extraordinary effort of this American team would establish the ridge as one of the most exalted, and elusive, prizes of alpinism.

THE FOURSOME THAT arrived in Islamabad, Pakistan, in June 1978, on their way to Latok I was one of the strongest American climbing teams ever assembled.

George Lowe was on his years-long roll of climbs that were as severe as anything climbed on the planet at the time. In 1977, he'd completed two very hard routes back-to-back in the Alaska Range: the *North Face* of Mount

Hunter and the *Infinite Spur* on Mount Foraker. It was all the more impressive that Lowe did these groundbreaking climbs while starting a family and finishing a PhD in physics.

At twenty-five, Michael Kennedy was the youngest member of the team. A smart and tough young wolf, he was just beginning his own outstanding career in the big ranges, but he had already been George Lowe's partner on both Alaskan climbs.

George's cousin Jeff Lowe, one of a trio of very talented Lowe brothers from Ogden, Utah, would arguably be the strongest member of *any* climbing team of the era. Manically driven and fiercely talented, Jeff was several steps along a path that would see him widely recognized as the finest alpinist of his generation.

Shipton's picture was enough to hook all three men. "One look and you realize what a perfect line this is," Kennedy said. "It's huge, it's remote, it's going to be serious and hard, but it's a ridge so it's protected from hazards." Most important to the climbers was the sense of adventure in attempting a peak that was, said Kennedy, "utterly unknown."

Kennedy and the Lowes believed that a mountain this beautiful deserved to be climbed the *right* way. Recent ascents by British climbers of huge walls in India's Garhwal Himalaya epitomized the evolving ethos of alpinism that Shipton, as well as Donini's Italian heroes, had embraced: Don't attack a mountain with a big team and an attitude of conquest; honor the mountain with fairer rules. Climb light and clean. Don't lace your objective with fixed ropes, but instead move from bottom to top in a continuous push. Keep the team small, with no locals endangered after the approach.

Kennedy and the Lowes recognized that the right team for a climb of this scale would be four people, not three; facing nearly 8,000 feet of difficult climbing, it would be better to divide loads, keep people fresher and stronger, and have more brains to look at challenges. It took them only a few minutes to go through the list of climbers capable of climbing Latok the way they wanted, and Jim's name was at the top of that list. Though none of them had done much climbing with Donini, aside from some sunny rock routes or short ice climbs, they knew his emerging reputation.

Jim joked that he was clearly the B-Team, but George countered by saying, "It was actually only a few days from when I asked Jeff and Michael to when we invited Jim. And honestly," he added with a laugh, "if *Donini* is on a B-Team, who the hell is the A-Team?"

George Lowe, Michael Kennedy, and Jeff Lowe at Camp I on Latok I **(Photo by Jim Donini)**

IN HIS TRAILER one desert evening four decades after Latok, Jim pulled out his iPad to show me photographs of the trip. He began with a grumbling apology: he has reams of photographs from his many expeditions, but he's never really gotten around to organizing them. So he started randomly, partway up the peak, a striking shot of three climbers traversing below an enormous wave of corniced snow. "Those traverses were really tenuous and went on forever. And, in a few places," he said, pointing to a large gap in a cornice, "when we came back across them again, there were huge chunks missing. You sure didn't want to be there when those *went* missing . . ."

The next slide was a ghostly portrait of Jim, slumped in a snow cave, glowering, exhausted, near the end of the expedition, his eyes as hollow as a battle-beaten soldier's. He made a passing comment—"You see what a starvation diet will do to someone with my metabolic rate. It took me six months to recover"—before he moved on to another random picture.

This time, the image was of his three partners up on the first bivouac, on a perch of rock with enormous drops to either side. They're shirtless. "It was incredible how hot it was those first days," Jim said. Michael and Jeff look a little feral after the long walk in and a hard day's climbing. Jeff sits in the forefront, with his signature handlebar mustache and his long, blond hair tied back with a leopard-print bandanna. Michael has a beard that's heading wild and a glare up at the wall that says it all. George is still somehow clean-shaven and neat. Behind them, a sea of unclimbed and unnamed 6,000- to 7,000-meter peaks fades into the dusky desert horizon of Xinjiang, China.

Jim was about to jump to yet another random image. I had to ask him to take me back to the beginning of the story.

"BEFORE GEORGE CALLED," Jim began, "I'd never even heard about Latok." He hadn't really thought about going to the Himalaya either—"I thought expedition climbing was already over"—but the call from Lowe and the first glance at the picture changed that. "I was so stoked," said Jim. "It was one of the most obvious lines that I'd ever seen, and it completely met my need for challenge and exploration.

"And to be invited by these three, that was incredible. There was no one that I could imagine would be better for a climb like this."

He agreed to join the team without a moment's hesitation, despite the reality that he was committing to months away from home, with a daughter who would be barely eighteen months old when he left.

It's a difficult dance for adventurers—stepping away from their everyday lives and committing to the distance and perils of expeditions, going off to have an experience that their partners, their children, their families won't share—and perhaps can't understand. The choice to step out the door with no certainty of return can be incredibly selfish, and with hindsight, Jim acknowledged that uncomfortable truth. "When I was deep into my obsession with remote alpine peaks," he said, "I suspect that people around me might have been giving only reluctant support. I think that in those days a lot of us had blinders on when considering the effect of our choices on our families."

But in the moment, Jim believed that Janet was fully on board. They both told me they talked through the challenges and possible consequences of the

Latok trip, and they agreed that even if going to Pakistan didn't make sense in a conventional way, it did in the mountain world. Janet assured him that with the support of family and friends, she'd be fine.

Still, when it came to the final decision to go, this was an expedition of its time carried out by men of their time. Each inhabited two very separate worlds: the one they lived at home, and the one of the mountains, which could be all consuming and didn't always welcome the intrusion of the domestic. More often than not, when men like these headed into the mountains, they left the rest of their lives far behind.

PAKISTAN WAS THE first taste of the strange madness of Asia for Jim, Michael, and Jeff. The team landed in withering heat in Islamabad on June 10, 1978, and stumbled through frustrating permit delays and ritual protocols in the bowels of the vast city.

When their bags finally cleared customs a week later, a flight northeast to the launching pad of Skardu brought relief from the heat, but not the chaos. Somehow, all the team's equipment disappeared, and it took five days of berating airline officials before the bags were found in Rawalpindi.

The pause gave the men the chance to take stock of one another. George was the sober, methodical, planful one, the master of the route. Michael was the organized one who sorted out the food and logistics. Jim was in charge of the gear. And Jeff was in his happiest place: the energizer, perpetually psyched, already talking about the next big plans.

Then there were the doctors: George's dad, George Lowe Jr., had come along for the approach march, and he'd brought his friend Ralph Richards. Both men were physicians and very strong despite being in their sixties. Jim remembered that they all gelled immediately. "We were all getting along great, with lots of laughs and lots of chances to meet the locals and get steeped in the idiosyncrasies of Pakistan," he said.

The delays were due in part to the Latok team's commitment to minimalism. They were a small team that would neither be adding much to the local economy nor generating much attention for Pakistan, so they simply weren't a bureaucratic priority. By the time the gear finally arrived, other teams heading into bigger mountains had hired many of the better porters in Skardu, but the tiny team's size meant they hardly needed any support staff. The Americans shouldered loads just as big as those carried by the small team of Balti porters and finally headed into the mountains.

THE DUST, THE heat, the dubious water and food—they all took their toll. Latok I was only a forty-mile trek from Skardu, but the team had to navigate the tortured path of the Indus River, then the roaring, gray Braldu, then the desolate Panmah Glacier, to access the moraine-streaked Choktoi. "It felt," George Lowe recalled, "like we had walked off the edge of the world."

They had. This was a barren land of rocks and dirty ice, with big elevation gains and losses required to avoid landslides and dangerous water. To varying degrees it beat everyone up, but Jeff suffered the most. Usually a powerhouse, he was visibly knocked down by a fever that took him to the edge of delirium. Everyone was thankful they had doctors along.

Whatever suffering they endured, it all seemed worth it when the team turned the elbow at the north limit of the Choktoi Glacier and finally looked into the tight hollow of peaks at its western end, the massive north ridge of Latok I soaring far into the sky. "I'd seen very big walls in Patagonia," said Jim, "but this was on entirely a different scale."

That afternoon, they set up a spartan base camp at 15,000 feet. After a couple of days helping the team get ready, the doctors said their goodbyes and left with the porters. The two base camp staff—the Liason Officer and the cook—settled in for a wait of uncertain length, and the four climbers cast off up the peak.

STYLE MATTERED. JEFF Lowe was the strongest advocate for a true alpine-style ascent—using no fixed ropes, no retreats to base, and constant movement of the camps up the wall—but the others believed that the scale of Latok meant that they'd stand a better chance, perhaps their *only* chance, if they climbed "capsule style," shuttling fixed camps up the wall.

They already knew they'd be coming down the same way they went up. The photograph of the route, and especially the view from base camp, told them there was no other sensible or safe way off the mountain. They also saw that the cornices high on the route meant that they should carry ropes to fix just a few spots—they didn't want to have to reclimb these dangerous traverses on the descent. Still, a commitment to capsule style was hardly a capitulation: they'd all be climbing, not just fixing ropes from bottom to top and yarding up the ropes, as expeditions on other mountains were still doing.

The plan was to stay on the ridge itself whenever possible, but it was soon clear that it would be more efficient—and, at times, necessary for safety—to leave the ridge. That was true from the very first day, when the men elected to climb a gully left of the ridge, a decision that let them gain height quickly and, more importantly, avoid the dangerously hot sun. The high-altitude rays broiled the men and triggered nearly constant serac fall. When they finally reached their first bivouac site, Jim said, "It was so warm that we didn't even bother to set up our tents. We just dug out platforms and slept out in the open."

When I asked about the technical challenges of the climb, I got predictably modest answers: Sure, there were hard sections, but nothing that hard. It was merely big, rather than difficult. The hardest and most dangerous stretches were avoided by traversing.

Photographs from the ascent and comments by other climbers who attempted the route in the years that followed, though, suggest such modesty was misleading. This was a very, very big climb, with more than ninety technical pitches of rock, ice, and snow that demanded exceptional route-finding.

There was joy in this route when you were on the sharp end, but heavy loads made following tedious. And then there was the weather. Some 3,500 feet up the wall, the first of several storms boiled up out of the valley and pinned the men down for days, changing the feel of the ascent. There'd be no more climbing in T-shirts. Instead, as George wrote in his journal, "We'd spend day after day in the tents listening as the north face boomed and bellowed all around us. Conditions were obviously getting pretty interesting up there."

But then it cleared and the men moved again, blessed by another stretch of sunny days. At the end of the second week, they were finally at the long section of heavily corniced ridge at the middle of the climb that worried them in the pictures. "That was some pretty stout climbing there, and we were damn lucky that it hadn't stayed warm," George recalled.

Above, both the climbing and the bivy sites started to get leaner. The sheer volume of climbing, the conditions, and the altitude started to add up, and everyone was visibly wearing down. But the men still made impressive progress over the next week and were now staring up at what they believed would be the last big obstacle: a headwall of white-veined black rock that appeared to lead to easier snow and the summit. Jeff and Jim started digging a cave, while Michael and George led up the difficult wall, then fixed a rope for the next morning's climb, which might well take them to the top.

"All of us suddenly thought that we could make it," Michael said. "We believed we had maybe 600 feet of easy snow to the summit . . . but that was before we saw the storm rolling in from the west."

It was a torment of a storm that hammered the tiny snow cave and sucked the remaining life out of everyone. They all suffered, but everyone's attention was on Jeff, who had a fierce headache and a wracking cough. The following day, their twentieth on the climb, a foot of snow fell outside the cave, and the men elected to wait one last time for better conditions.

When they woke the next morning, the storm had abated a little, but the situation was clear. They had almost no food left. If they were going to summit, it had to be now. Despite how poorly he was doing, Jeff rallied and said that he felt strong enough to follow the others up.

Michael and George jumared back up the final pitch of the headwall and started up the snowslope, but it was clear almost immediately that Jeff could go no farther and needed everyone's help to get back to the snow cave. That was it. No one would be going higher. Getting their friend down became their whole purpose. "We had really pushed the envelope," Jim said, "certainly more than was prudent. But on that ledge, at that time, we didn't have to say one word . . . we just started down."

Although the men are quick to dismiss the nobility of their decision to abandon the attempt so close to the top, history has been more generous, calling the descent from Latok I one of the most selfless and expertly executed acts in mountain history. Conditions were part of that appraisal. A storm bulldozed back up the valley, pinning the men in the cave again, with increasingly dangerous implications. Jeff worsened dramatically.

And that's where Donini stepped in. Michael was effusive while remembering what he saw: "Jim can come across as such a hardcore bastard, but he was like a mother caring for a child when he took charge of Jeff. It was phenomenal to watch. He had a real gentle touch, and without a word you understood that you could just step aside. Jim knew exactly what to do."

After five storm-walloped days in the cave, they finally started descending for the last time. They divided Jeff's load, and foot by foot, the three shepherded their friend down the endless rappels and the traverses over huge chasms.

On the second morning of the descent, everyone woke with fears about Jeff's condition. He was covered in frost, his head resting on Jim's shoulder. "I was sure," Jim explained, "that I was waking up next to a corpse."

But when George called over to ask how Jeff was doing, it was the corpse who shivered to life and said, "Oh, I'm fine."

Even with Jeff improving, the rest of the descent was still epic. Everyone was at their limit, and it took another five days before the men took their last, fumbling steps on the Choktoi, came around a boulder, and surprised the hell out of their liaison officer and cook, who were in the last stages of abandoning base camp. There were shouts and hugs and cries of gratitude, and the Baltis proclaimed it a miracle. After all, the climbers had been gone for twenty-six days—ten days longer than planned. There had been terrible storms. There had been no sign of headlamps on the wall for ten nights. All hope seemed lost. Then, just as the food at base camp ran out, the climbers, who looked like ghosts of the men the Baltis knew, reappeared.

Clearly, they said, Allah had intervened.

ALL THESE YEARS later, I asked Michael, George, Jeff, and Jim if they'd understood the significance of the achievement and how it would be received. "Not really when we were up there," said Michael. "When you're on something that big and that long, you can lose any realistic sense of what you're facing. You just do the work, and it's hard to compare it to anything else."

George added, "But we did know that we'd done some hard, complicated climbing, and knew that we'd come really close to the edge. I'd say we had maybe a forty percent chance of actually making it down alive when Jeff got sick and the storm was happening, maybe even thirty percent, so I understand why people talk about it the way that they do."

Unlike some historic climbs that lose cachet when modern advances rub the shine off the original accomplishments, the reputation of the north ridge of Latok I and the legend of the American team have only grown with time. Since 1978, thirty-nine expeditions, which have included some of the very best climbers of several eras, have tried the ridge or variations on either side of it, and not only has the entire ridge likely never been climbed, the American highpoint has only been reached once.

Jim and his partners are quick to insist that the lack of success by later teams is due to luck and not because the 1978 team were better climbers.

"Everything has to be right on that climb," George said. "A little more snow or a little less snow, and it's a very different climb." It's important to note, too, that all the attempts since 1978 have been in pure alpine style versus the modified capsule style used by the American team. An alpine-style ascent of such a big route is—as the Americans appreciated—a far more serious commitment.

It took until 2018 for Latok I to be climbed by any route from the north. That summer, a strong team—Briton Tom Livingstone and Slovenians Luka Stražar and Aleš Cesen—had eyes on the summit rather than on an unwavering commitment to the ridge proper. They found a creative solution in a traverse right of the ridge at 6,300 meters, which allowed them to reach the col between Latoks I and II, and thence to the summit of Latok I from the south side of the peak. It was a fantastic ascent, but the prize of the entire ridge to the summit still awaits.

Despite the hardship of the 1978 climb, Latok only whetted the appetites of everyone on the team. All four followed up with hugely influential climbs—George on the *Kangshung Face* on Everest and the *North Ridge* of K2; Michael on the *Northeast Buttress* of Thalay Sagar, the *Northeast Face* of Ama Dablam, and the *Wall of Shadows* on Alaska's Mount Hunter; Jeff on Kwangde Ri and Tawoche in the Nepal Himalaya, the Trango Tower in the Karakoram, and a stunning solo of a new route on the Eiger Nordwand; and Jim, in the pages that follow.

All of the men remained lifelong friends and, with the exception of Jeff, have continued to climb well into their seventies. In 2000, Jeff was diagnosed with a motor-neuron disease similar to ALS, and he spent the next eighteen years battling progressive incapacitation, climbing while he still could and remaining very much a leader in the climbing community. He passed away in August 2018 and was rightly heralded as one of the very best climbers of the modern era.

CHAPTER 17

THE SADNESS OF VALLEYS, PART ONE

RETURNING TO THE world after an experience like Latok can be a trying journey in its own right. Leaving a mountain behind can bring an unforeseen mix of relief and regret. All the planning and dreaming is over. The power and purpose felt daily on the mountain is so much harder to find at home, yet life at home seems so much more real and sensible. The intense experiences that filled every day for months become little more than strange and distant memories, especially when you return to a world that has gone on without you and can't seem to understand—or is indifferent to—what you've seen and done and felt.

When Jim came home from Latok, all of those things were true, but—as is often the case for the returning adventurer—there wasn't much time to work them all out. He needed to hit the ground running, though even in a literal sense that was challenging—he could hardly walk. Four weeks in wet leather boots on the climb had left him with severe trench foot that took months to settle down.

The community response to the climb was much more immediate than it had been for Torre Egger, and that carried its own weight—but for Jim that was a weight of opportunity: people were effusive in their admiration for the climb, and doors opened.

But there were some unexpected, if understandable, changes at home. It had not been as easy for Janet to be alone with a toddler as either of them had hoped. Jim had been gone for more than two months, and the isolation and unknowns took a toll. Janet told me that she found herself suffering tension headaches and bouts of sadness, worsened by enduring them alone. She didn't have the words to describe what she was going through ("I thought it was perhaps unique to me, and that I ought not talk about it," Janet explained) and said she wasn't sure that Jim would have had any better capacity to understand or fix things than she did herself. From what she'd seen, men of the time didn't talk about things like depression, weaknesses, or vulnerabilities, and she thought that was even more true in the mountain community, where there was often just one answer offered as the panacea for the struggles of life: a good, hard adventure.

By the time Jim returned to their new home in Salt Lake City and settled back into his work, Janet had already found an outlet for those stresses. Since she was a teenager, people had been telling her she could be a model, and she decided to follow that path. She took a course, signed on with the prestigious McCarty Talent Agency, and soon had regular bookings, including extensive work for several outdoor manufacturers, including REI, Eddie Bauer, and Helly Hansen.

All that added challenges for the couple that were amplified by Jim's nearly constant sales travel and paid appearances to tell the stories of Egger and Latok. His work for Round Table took him on the road every week for much of the year and gave him all kinds of freedom—and Latok brought him consistent applause. He traveled from shop to shop, trade show to trade show, presentation to presentation, and it was hard not to get caught up in the growing myth of himself. He loved the life, and he was busy enough that the answer to the perpetually asked question "What's your next big mountain?" was simply "Work."

In 1979, Jim's success at the sales game was rewarded with a much more lucrative territory, the Northwest, which included the biggest fish in the outdoor pond: REI. The change of region impelled a fourth move in less than three years for the family. They'd gone from Guide's Hill in the Tetons to Longmont, then to Salt Lake City, and now they settled in Leavenworth, Washington, a pretty tourist town surrounded by the eastern slopes of the Cascades. For Jim, Leavenworth offered a fine mix of mountain living, easy access to Seattle, and an abundance of granite crags and peaks. He was successful and ambitious enough that he decided to run two parallel businesses: his sales work and a new mountain-guiding outfit, Leavenworth Alpine Guides.

As exciting as all of these moving parts were for Jim, he believed they created tensions at home. Others around the couple were also seeing warning signs in small difficulties, much like dimples in a snow-covered glacier can hint at yawning crevasses below. Jim said that he was finding home a less welcoming place and was starting to tire of his wife's dissatisfaction—though once again with the grace of hindsight, he acknowledged, "In truth, I suppose that I was the root of her dissatisfaction."

Janet had her own strong perspectives. In our conversations, she was critical of both Jim and the world that swirled around him. She framed him as increasingly attentive only to his own needs, with his weekday work trips often rolling into weekend climbing trips that kept him away longer than he'd promised.

Looking back at that time, Jim suggested, "I do appreciate that I probably was far too absorbed in what I was doing and not as present as I should have been with my family. I missed a lot of signs of looming problems both with my wife and my family. My personal selfishness, which I didn't recognize at the time, surely contributed to their problems and, for that, I am truly sorry.

"If only I could have seen then what was going to follow . . ."

EARLY IN 1979, a gentling factor entered the mix. The couple decided to have a second child, and on October 3, their son, Montana, was born.

He was a beautiful boy, but by the spring, clouds gathered on the horizon. Janet slipped into a postpartum depression. In those difficult times, Jim was entirely out of his depth—unable to understand the changes in his wife, unsure where to turn for help, still obliged to travel for work. "It was the most helpless I'd ever felt," he said, "and I really don't like feeling helpless."

Things came to a head that May. Jim was away again on business in the Tetons, and Janet reached the end of her rope. At the bottom of her despair, in the middle of a very difficult day, she cut her wrists.

Jim rushed home and stumbled into the rift that's always there when suicide cracks open a family. It's impossible to overstate how profoundly a suicide, an attempt, or even the threat of the act can alter the trajectory of a family story. Once the possibility of self-harm surfaces, every conversation that follows is colored by it. There are painful, long-lasting—and sometimes permanent—changes in a home.

After Janet's attempt, Jim finally understood that things had been far worse than he knew. He no longer had certainty that he could go away again without great consequences. He had no idea how to treat his wife, talk to her, or help her. And he was *angry*. In his mountain world, you push through your challenges. If storms come, you don't quit, you try harder. But he also saw that his "mountain way" perhaps had little merit in the less black-and-white world of the valleys. There, just toughing out troubles might not always be the right way.

Janet rallied impressively in the months after the attempt. After a brief hospital stay, she got help from friends and professionals, stepped right back into caring for the children, and didn't miss a beat as a parent, while Jim was back on the road almost right away.

In the end—as it often is—time was the cure. Two active, happy children became a solid anchor. Janet shone, Jim said, when his father passed away from prostate cancer that fall. Her resilience helped the couple rebound, and they came to an agreement: they would both ask for and do whatever it took to make the marriage work.

With greater faith that things had settled, and with a growing need to step away from the strains of the past year, Jim made his ask for a chance to get back on a big mountain.

CHAPTER 18

SIGUNIANG: THE UGLY AMERICANS

MOUNTAINS *CAN BRING* out the best in us. They can lift us up to accomplish extraordinary feats, bond us for life to ropemates, bring us to our knees in awe, spark renewed appreciation for the lives we've left behind. But just as easily, mountains can show us the worst of ourselves: they don't tolerate hubris, and they're happy to rain disaster on the vain, the unprepared, the overcommitted, and the uncommitted.

After Latok, Jim could have justifiably expected his next expedition to be just as inspiring, just as life-affirming and life-altering. He'd surely banked some good karma, gained valuable experience, learned what was important in himself and his partners, and come to understand his strengths and his limits. He understood what kind of climbing he wanted to be doing and believed he'd figured out the formula those climbs would demand. By any reckoning, he should have been able to find a next project with all the right ingredients.

Siguniang was none of those things.

WHEN WE SPOKE, Jim began the story of the great peak in Sichuan Province in southwestern China with a sigh. "I should have seen what was coming," he said, "especially that day in Bozeman when we did that slideshow and got interviewed on the radio." He paused. "Don't get me wrong—I probably still would have gone, because you don't turn down a chance to go to a mountain like that—but that one night should have set off some louder alarms in my head. It was *insane*.

"Hell," he said with a shake of his head, "that whole trip was."

In the late summer of 1981, the four men who'd soon be heading to the striking 20,510-foot granite peak were deep in the thickets of last-minute preparations when they were offered the opportunity to do a slideshow at Montana State University. Their names would surely attract a good crowd at the outdoorsy campus: Jim had his tales of Latok and Torre Egger. Kim Schmitz was already established as one of the premier US climbers, having made the first ascents of the Great Trango Tower and the magnificent east face of Uli Biaho Tower in the Karakoram in the late 1970s. And Bozeman locals Jim Kanzler and Jack Tackle had just made a bold attempt on the massive Isis Face on Denali earlier in 1981. Having the four of them together guaranteed a full house, and the student radio station was thrilled to conduct a live pre-show interview.

What the hosts of the event didn't anticipate was how the subversive counterculture of climbing and the stresses of preparing for the trip and presenting to a crowd were going to combine that night. Jim and Jack were already in Bozeman and were able to come to the radio studio relaxed, but Kanzler and Schmitz had just finished several full-on days of guiding in the Tetons to help pay for Siguniang, and they had to race up to Montana to get to the show on time.

When they arrived at the station just minutes before the show was set to begin, it was clear that they had been celebrating the end of their guiding season on the drive. "Kanzler and Schmitz just reeked of booze," Jim explained, "and the poor host didn't know what the hell to think when Schmitz pulled pills out of his pocket and started hammering them with a coffee cup, then snorted the powder just as the show went *live*.

"Somehow, the young woman got through her introduction, but when she tried to engage us by saying, 'You must be excited to go to China . . . ,' Schmitz interrupted her with a growl and slurred, 'China is a fucking *shithole*,' and Kanzler roared with laughter.

"You could see the blood drain out of her face. Schmitz kept on snorting those pills, and Jack and I tried to do most of the talking from then on."

In the 1980s, it was hardly unusual to attend a climbing community event and see a drunk, or high, presenter. There were (and to an extent, still are) legendary stories of well-known climbers who'd had a few too many drinks stumbling onstage and launching into over-the-top tales lapped up by howling audiences who were often just as intoxicated themselves.

That night in Bozeman—filled with fantastic images of groundbreaking climbs, but also slurred stories and more snorts, that had the audience roaring—became one of those legends.

Years later, Jack Tackle shook his head as he explained some less understood, and less humorous, backstory to the moment: A year earlier, Kim Schmitz had broken his back in an avalanche in China, and by the time he came to the show in Bozeman, he was well into what would become a lifelong struggle to control the terrible residual pain with opiates—which was what he was pounding and snorting. Jim Kanzler, meanwhile, was fighting some personal demons that had shadowed most of his adult life. They were both exceptional climbers and found great acclaim for that, but both had other sides to their stories that the applauding fans never got to know, which could make an expedition, or a public show, difficult. "I loved these guys," Jack said, "but that wasn't always easy."

"You've got to understand," Jack went on, "that we were going into a pretty complicated place in a pretty complicated time on the other side of the world, and this was how we showed up. Donini and I just sat there and wondered what the hell we'd gotten ourselves into . . ."

IN 1981, CHINA *was* a complicated place to climb, and the stunning mountains of Sichuan Province were as complicated as any on the planet. The Héngduàn Shānmài range of southwestern Sichuan, a twisted warren of hundreds of peaks and valleys on the eastern hem of the Himalaya, was still one of the most compelling unknowns on any climber's map. These are magnificent mountains, but when Jim and his team arrived, many of the peaks had never been photographed, let alone climbed, and very few mountaineers had even heard of the area.

For much of the mid-twentieth century, Chinese authorities forbade access to the range. The Héngduàn was too close to the political troubles of the Tibetan Autonomous Region to the west and the contested border with the Indian state of Arunachal Pradesh to the south, and the Chinese government had little incentive to let foreign climbers near the range.

But on either side of that forbidden period, Americans were in these mountains.

The first American expedition into the region produced a surprisingly successful ascent in another challenging time. In 1932, four Harvard students—Terris Moore, Jack Young, Arthur Emmons, and Richard Burdsall—set out from Boston to climb one of the Sichuan giants. Their journey was a far more complex undertaking than expected. The men spent two months traveling by sea from Boston, then landed in Shanghai just as Japanese forces began a monthlong bombing campaign against the coastal city.

The team was pressed into searches for survivors, and when the siege finally ended in February 1932, they began a three-month journey toward Sichuan, through a countryside ravaged by the early years of Mao's civil war. The Americans were hoping to find and climb Minya Konka, a peak rumored to be not just the giant of the range but perhaps the tallest mountain in the world. Moore had first read about the peak in a book by two of Teddy Roosevelt's sons, Theodore III and Kermit, which documented a hunting expedition searching for giant pandas in 1929. The back of the book featured a small sketch of a snow peak that the Roosevelts called "Minya Koonka" with a handwritten note that said the mountain was 30,000 feet high. That claim was more than enough incentive for Moore to invite three friends to help him find this summit higher than Everest.

Over the spring and summer of 1932, the team surveyed Minya Konka and determined that the peak was actually much lower than the Roosevelts had suggested. Still, even at their revised height of 24,891 feet (now officially revised to 24,790 feet), Minya Konka was the highest peak in China proper, and the eventual climb of the mountain's northwest ridge took them to the summit of the highest mountain climbed by Americans for another quarter century.

The second American trip to the range came forty-eight years later, when China finally reopened the Sichuan peaks for exploration after decades of revolution, strife, and secrecy. When the doors cracked in 1980, two US expeditions were given permission to climb the peak that was now called Gongga Shan.

One expedition held a permit for a repeat of the *Northwest Ridge* and included three very strong climbers who would figure prominently at various points in Donini's life—Yvon Chouinard, Rick Ridgeway, and Kim Schmitz.

Though the *Northwest Ridge* was a modest objective given the team's talent, it was soon obvious that technical difficulty wasn't the crux of the climb. Not far above Camp I, on just the fourth day of climbing, an avalanche ripped Ridgeway, Chouinard, Schmitz, and a fourth team member, Jonathan Wright, off a low-angle slope and over a cliff band. Chouinard broke ribs, Schmitz fractured several vertebrae, and Wright died. The expedition ended, and getting the men home was a marathon of red tape, endurance, and pain, especially for Schmitz, who had to travel on horseback for days with a broken back barely supported by a sleeping pad tied around his torso.

The accident was little more than bad timing, but it sparked larger consequences: the Chinese authorities were not pleased that the first expedition allowed back into the area had resulted in a fatality, and they considered restricting access again.

The Chinese would have been even less happy had they known that one team member, a Tetons guide named Jack Turner, had gone exploring without authorization while the expedition was being evacuated. Turner had been captivated by the ocean of peaks visible off on the horizon from Camp I on Gongga Shan, and he decided to see them closer up.

Turner disappeared into the area and was thrilled by what he found, particularly when he trekked north out of the village of Rilongzhen, to the northeast of Gongga Shan, and entered a narrow valley dominated by a spectacular massif with four distinct summits. Locals told him that these were the peaks of Siguniang, "The Four Sisters Mountain," and said that the highest summit with an impressive ridgeline on its north face was Yāomèi Fēng, "The Mountain of the Youngest Sister."

Turner snapped a picture of the beautiful 20,506-foot peak and vowed he'd return. He went home to Wyoming and applied for a permit to climb that ridge.

"JACK TURNER LOOKED at that picture for a long time, then realized that Siguniang was probably beyond his skill level," Jim said. "Then one day, he sent the picture to me, and that was all I needed."

Turner had photographed an incredibly compelling wall of granite, nearly 8,000 feet high. An obvious crest that looked like it would offer both good rock and protection from overhead hazards soared right up the middle of the huge face, reaching almost to the summit. Best of all, base camp was only a day's walk from Rilongzhen.

To Jim, the colossal line seemed like a perfect objective: big, but relatively safe; hard, but feasible. Better still, the peak was unclimbed. Turner was happy to pass over the permit—as long as Jim satisfied one request: all members of the team had to be Exum guides.

The first choice was easy: Kim Schmitz was one of the finest, toughest, and most experienced climbers Jim had ever met. His climbs in the Karakoram were huge advances in standards that brought big-wall skills to the higher ranges. He was justly famous for his fierce drive, jarring intensity, and masterful technical proficiency. "Schmitz," Jim says, "could aid an A4 pitch as fast as anyone else could climb a pitch of 5.7." Jim hadn't climbed much with the man, but he felt that Schmitz's reputation among the hardcore was word enough.

Jim had a more complex decision to make when Schmitz suggested Jim Kanzler as a second candidate. Donini knew Kanzler was an exceptional mountaineer and could be a lot of fun, "but he could also come across as a real ass—arrogant, sarcastic, sharp, and bitter. Even though I'd never had problems with him personally, I trusted the people who warned me about him, and that gave me pause."

Jim knew Kanzler had something of a troubling backstory and thought that might explain some of the man's tensions with the world. Kanzler came from a family deeply connected to—but also haunted by—the mountains of Montana. Kanzler's father, Hal, was a legendary character in Montana mountain life in the 1960s. A skier, climber, and engineer from Butte, Hal nurtured a love of the outdoors in his two sons, but he also wrestled with alcohol and other demons and finally shot himself in the chest when Jim Kanzler was nineteen. Hal's dramatic death deeply affected both his sons—but especially Jim, who'd found his father's body right after the trigger was pulled.

Two years after Hal Kanzler's suicide, during the Christmas holidays of 1969, an avalanche swept the younger of the Kanzler boys, Jerry, off the north face of Glacier National Park's Mount Cleveland. Jerry died at eighteen with four of his closest friends.

The loss of so many young climbers in one accident shook American mountaineering, and Jim Kanzler, barely twenty-one, was devastated. But the two terrible heartbreaks only served to fuel his commitment to climbing harder. By the time Donini met him at Exum, Kanzler had a reputation for formidable talent and an unbridled willingness to push his limits—but also for volatility. As Jim was soon to discover, Kanzler had inherited his family's vulnerability to addiction and self-immolation—not great qualities in a partner on a big climb.

Jim's final selection didn't comply with Jack Turner's insistence on only including Exum guides, but it was the easiest choice of all. Jack Tackle was the youngest member by almost a decade and had the least big-trip experience, but he was a shooting star. Jack owned a gear shop that Jim sold to in Bozeman, Montana, and he'd climbed hard routes at home and in Alaska. Always in a flat cap, Jack sported a burly handlebar mustache and spoke with a slow, deep, calming drawl that made him easy to like and trust.

The final member of the Siguniang crew—Greg Thomsen, co-owner of the Wilderness Experience gear company—wouldn't climb on the trip, but his willingness to take on the onerous tasks of organizing fundraising, permissions, logistics, and gear made him an invaluable addition. Thomsen had been doing business in China for a few years, and it was a special advantage to have someone on the team who understood how challenging it could be to navigate the crevasses of Chinese culture and bureaucracy.

When the team finally gathered at Thomsen's Los Angeles home for last-minute preparations before their journey east, Thomsen understood right away that this was going to be an expedition with more complexities than usual—and not just due to China's infamous red tape. He explained: "Schmitz told me that I needed to go see my doctor to get narcotics for the first-aid kit. He said that his terrible experience getting out from Minya Konka the previous year taught him that you really didn't want to be in a situation like that without the right drugs.

"But then he explained just what those 'right drugs' were. 'Greg,' he said, 'you need to get us plenty of Percodan and vials of injectable morphine.'

"I thought that was ridiculous, but went to my doctor anyways. He looked at me like I had just ordered a kilo of heroin, and I think that the only reason that he actually wrote me the prescription was that the request was so absurd that he thought it had to be genuine!"

And so it began.

ON OUR ZOOM calls, Donini, Tackle, and Thomsen all groaned about the International Date Line.

"I don't know what the hell happened," Jim said, "but we all seemed to forget how that worked."

Tackle rolled his eyes and glared at Jim. "Well, our *leader*, who was holding all our tickets, forgot how it worked, anyways."

Thomsen added his own side of the story: "The ridiculous thing was that I had been to China a bunch of times at that point, so I knew all about the time change, but it didn't even *register* with me. We landed in Tokyo for a layover, and it just never occurred to any of us to check the *date* of our connecting flight.

After the long flight from LA, a twenty-seven-hour layover in a city as exciting and exotic as Tokyo seemed a fair reward. They'd get a chance to walk around after sitting on the plane for thirteen hours and enjoy one last taste of the ordered world before heading into the chaos they'd been warned to expect in China. So they cut loose, reveled in Japan, and got to know each other better as a team. They showed up at Haneda Airport twenty-four hours later, very responsibly allowing three hours before their plane left for Shanghai.

Except they had actually missed their flight by a day, which in 1981 was no small thing. It was still the era of fixed paper tickets; changing a flight was complex, and there were few airlines that would take a no-show as seriously as the state-run Civil Aviation Administration of China, especially when the wayward passengers were rough-looking Americans on an expedition closely monitored by the government.

It took hours to issue new tickets, and for all those hours, the new flight, filled with Chinese citizens, sat on the runway waiting for the Americans. "When we finally came on board, everyone glared at us," said Jim. "And then, when we finally landed in Shanghai, they made sure we weren't going anywhere. They let everyone else off, but we were surrounded by guards with machine guns until we took off again, with no one else on board, heading to Beijing."

IN THE FRENZIED capital, every step was watched by state police, every minute of their time scripted by their hosts from the Chinese Mountaineering Association (CMA). The CMA certainly helped make things happen—navigating bureaucratic and linguistic barriers would have been a nightmare without them—but the chaperones added their own twists, not the least of which were social obligations that always included the ritual of *gānbēi*.

"That's how they measure you in China," Jim explained. "Every meal involves the endless toasting they call *gānbēi* [literally, 'dry cup'], and you have to prove you can keep up."

Tackle added, "But they're toasting with Maotai [a fearsomely potent drink made of fermented sorghum], and they're experts at drinking that foul stuff, so you'll never keep up.

"But God knows all of us, especially Schmitz and Kanzler, tried."

After two nights of endless toasts, the team flew to Chengdu, the Sichuan capital, and then finally began their drive into the mountains. The truck trip was only 160 miles long but took three days filled with landslides, tows, and other mysterious delays. When the team finally reached the village of Rilongzhen, they were stunned—twice.

The first shock was how primitive the conditions were. The food, the water, and the health of the townsfolk were all medieval, and that sparked fears in the team—which would turn out to be justified—about impacts on their own health. A more aggravating twist came when locals told the Americans that a Japanese team had made the first ascent of Siguniang a week earlier. Though the Japanese had climbed the peak from the south, leaving the prize of the much harder north face unclaimed, the Americans were furious that the CMA had let another team onto the mountain.

"We'd paid extra for a virgin peak," Jim said, "and the CMA didn't say a thing about there being another team," but the CMA representatives wouldn't reduce the peak fee and suggested the Americans were simply overreacting.

The Americans felt some release when they left Rilongzhen and headed up the winding Changping Valley. It finally felt like they were on a Himalayan trip, sharing the trail with yaks, the great north wall of Siguniang looming at the head of the valley. The approach took just one day, despite some slow going through swampy sections. It was, after all, only twelve miles to their base camp, with barely 2,000 feet of elevation gain.

From their base camp, the mountain looked even more enticing than it had in Jack Turner's photograph—though it was now clear the ridge they planned to follow didn't quite reach the summit, but instead faded into the main face at a snowfield at about 20,000 feet.

Once they started up, the route was everything they'd hoped: steep, solid rock in a fabulous position, good ledges for camps just when they needed them. The only hitch, Tackle explained, was that the rock was *more* perfect than they'd expected. "We honestly thought there'd be a lot more mixed climbing, so all we brought to climb in was our big white plastic boots. We were so pissed that we didn't have rock shoes with us."

For the first few days, the conditions stayed impeccable, and the team reached a good campsite at a col just above 18,000 feet on just their third day on the wall. It seemed as though they might be able to summit in just one or two more days' climbing, but the following morning, a storm brought high winds and a drop in temperature. The men fixed some lines and headed back to their advanced base camp to wait out the weather.

"Jack and I were really psyched to get back up on the climb," Jim said. "We had the hard part done. From our high camp, it seemed like it would be maybe a few rock pitches to the easy summit snowfield.

"But I realized something was really off when I found Schmitz the next day, sitting outside his tent with glassy eyes and this ridiculous grin."

Schmitz and Kanzler had been chewing their way through the medical kit and were quickly losing interest in the climb, despite how well it had been going. Schmitz told Tackle that his back was bad, and that he'd already taken eight Percodan that morning. It was less clear what pain Kanzler was trying to medicate, but he was matching Schmitz pill for pill.

When the storm faded after a couple of days, the team headed back up the ridge, but Schmitz and Kanzler were crawling and it took the men four days to reach their high camp at the col. Still, Jim and Jack were certain that they'd soon be on top of Siguniang.

Instead, the following morning brought one of the sourest anticlimaxes in big-mountain history. Not long after dawn, with only a light snow falling and the temperatures more enticing than they had been the last time at the col, Tackle and Donini were ready to head up to establish a final camp on the upper snowfield. But the first words they heard from the other tent were a bellow from Kanzler: "Down! We're going *down!*"

Jim and Jack struggled to comprehend. "What the fuck does he mean, *down?*" Jim asked. "Why would we go down?"

Jim tried to talk directly to Schmitz, but Kanzler just kept yelling over him, "*Down!*"

"That was it," Jack explained. "Jim lost it. He went over to the other tent, unzipped the door, and started yelling. Then he dragged Kanzler, in his sleeping bag, out of the tent and pulled him up to his knees, screaming at him that there was no way that we were going down when we were so close to the top."

Kanzler cowered as Jim shook him by the collar on the tiny ledge with massive exposure below. Kanzler finally said, "Throw me off. Throw me off now. I'd rather die fast than slow."

"I didn't know what the fuck he was talking about," Jim remembered. "No one was going to 'die' here. We had about four pitches of moderately difficult mixed climbing to do, then it would be easy to the top. We all knew that."

But the drama of that mad moment—two strung-out partners who had no interest in the climb, anger boiling over in a precarious place, a waning capacity to stay focused given the conflict and the drugs—sucked the life out of the climb.

"You always want partners who have the same level of commitment as you do," Jim underscored, "nothing more, nothing less."

"It was obvious that none of us wanted to be up there together anymore," Jack added, "and we didn't have the equipment to split up the resources and climb separately. So that was it. We packed up and started down."

It's difficult to conjure how acrid that retreat must have been. Four people seething at one another, enduring forty-plus shared rappel stations in bitter silence, down to a base camp that no one wanted to stay in.

While the short exit out of the valley a few days later was a blessing in one sense—at least they didn't have a marathon trek together—the tensions were still high when the sullen men hiked back to their bleak hotel rooms in Rilongzhen.

Thomsen decided that someone had to make an effort to nudge the team toward reconciliation, so he suggested that Tackle and Schmitz share a room that night. (Thomsen laughed when he recalled that there was no way that he was going to propose that Donini and Kanzler be locked up together.)

But reconciliation wasn't the first thing on Tackle's or Schmitz's minds, either. "Kim and I got into it as soon as our door closed," Jack remembered. "He said something, I said something back, soon we're pushing each other, and then I see something in his eyes that tells me that if I don't push back with all I've got, he's going to kill me. I gave him one really hard shove, and he goes flying backwards. There's this coat hook on the wall, and that hook caught Kim right where he'd broken his back the previous year. He melted to the floor, writhing in pain.

"I went running over to him, apologized, and that was it. We were done. It was like we were two fifth-grade kids who just needed a scrap at recess to get it out of our systems. That was the moment when we formed a really great friendship that lasted from then on."

The Donini-Kanzler feud wasn't so easily remedied. The two men barely spoke during the long ride back to Chengdu, nor on the final leg to Beijing, where the CMA once again had special events arranged despite the failed attempt. Things came to a dramatic head at a party that the CMA had arranged at a posh hotel a couple of nights before the team was to fly home.

The hotel's dining room was a huge hall with glass tables and koi ponds surrounding a big, recessed dance floor. CMA dignitaries and party officials shared a table with the team, and other groups sat at tables nearby.

None of the Americans felt like celebrating. As one *gānbēi* flowed into the next, Schmitz fell asleep in his seat, and Kanzler stumbled drunkenly over to the fishpond. Donini grabbed the too-perfect opportunity to vent his frustrations about the past few weeks. "I didn't care where we were, or who we were with, or what the consequences might be, I just couldn't help myself," he recalled. He stood up, walked up behind Kanzler, and booted him full force into the pond. Kanzler went underwater, and then came up furious, ready for the battle that had been simmering for days.

But instead of engaging directly, Kanzler swerved at the last minute and picked up one of the huge glass dining tables and threw it toward Jim. The table tipped sideways midair and then hit the dance floor, where it shattered, spraying thousands of pieces of glass across the room.

The room went completely silent, and then security guards appeared with chilling efficiency, sweeping the Americans into the bowels of the hotel. "It was pretty obvious that we'd screwed up pretty badly," said Jack. "We sat down there for quite a while before this American 'businessman'—or whatever he actually was—showed up out of nowhere and told us that he'd managed to work something out with the police. He said that we could go back to our hotel if we were willing to pay for the table. Then, before we drove off in a cab that he'd arranged, he said in a pretty serious tone, 'You guys have just set Chinese-American relationships back a long, long ways,' and then slammed the door."

While that nerve-wracking experience should have been enough to encourage everyone to just head back to their rooms and sleep off the

Maotais, the team decided instead to go out for a few more drinks. The men dodged their overseers in the lobby, then flagged down a taxi. They somehow managed to convey that they wanted to go to whatever might pass for a disco in 1980s Beijing.

Things got worse when the team pushed into the club recommended by the driver. The disco, complete with spinning mirror ball, was empty, but when Schmitz spotted an aquarium he saw an opportunity to spice up the evening. He walked over and grabbed a fish, sticking it in his palm as he went to shake the hand of the bar's owner. Schmitz thought this was hilarious; the owner, less so. Security forces materialized again and, without a word, hustled the Americans into a waiting truck.

Back at the hotel, other officials explained with clear displeasure that the men needed to go pack, as they would be heading immediately to the airport, two days before their scheduled departure.

And with that, the strange and bitter adventure of Siguniang was over— save for one last scratch from the CMA's talons. Perhaps because the team had crossed a boundary with the brawl, perhaps because they'd missed their flight weeks before, or perhaps because, as Jack Tackle suggested, the CMA was simply looking to extract as much foreign currency as possible, when the team got to airport, they were told that there was one last step: they'd have to "go through protocol," a final reckoning of the costs incurred by the expedition, which in this case added hundreds of dollars in unexpected tariffs, including a $1,000 glass table.

Everyone was furious at the blatant grift, but they started pulling money and traveler's checks out of their pockets. They were beyond done with China, and with each other, and at that point they'd do anything to go home.

HOME, IT TURNED out, wasn't exactly what they'd been hoping it would be. And China, they came to understand, wasn't so easy to leave behind.

China had managed to work its way inside three of the men in literal ways: After they returned home, Thomsen, Tackle, and Schmitz all started to suffer physical ailments. Tackle had a parasite that took him more than a year to overcome. Thomsen developed hepatitis that was similarly resistant to treatment. And Schmitz was hospitalized with severe pancreatitis.

Personal changes after the expedition were also dramatic. Jack came home to an empty house and a petition for a divorce, and Jim and Janet

Brothers reunited (bottom to top): Kim Schmitz, Jim Donini, and Jack Tackle, 2003 (Photo by Angela Donini)

decided it was time for a change at the Doninis'; they packed up their home, yet again, and moved to Seattle just a few months after the return from Asia.

Siguniang was a far bigger turning point in the lives of both Kim Schmitz and Jim Kanzler.

Despite the many positive sides to Kanzler's story—he continued to have an exceptional reputation as a guide; continued to be a big character in the Montana mountain scene; was a mentor to many ski patrollers, guides, and forecasters; and was a leading avalanche forecaster early in the history of that uncertain science—the currents of instability, temper, and addiction that ran through the expedition in China continued in waves through the rest of Kanzler's life, On April 18, 2011, Kanzler gave in to those currents and shot himself in the heart, just as his father had. He left behind a son and two grandchildren.

Schmitz's story after Siguniang was also filled with anguish. In 1983, he suffered yet another accident, one that likely would have killed just about any other man. Guiding a young client on Symmetry Spire in the Tetons, Schmitz told the client not to touch the rope while he ran out an easy pitch. For some reason, the client pulled the line and Schmitz fell eighty feet directly onto the belay ledge, pulverizing the tibiae and fibulae in both legs. Tackle visited Schmitz in the hospital and told me, "It looked like someone had taped grenades to both his calves and pulled the pins."

In the years that followed, Schmitz went through thirty rounds of surgery, several near-fatal blood infections, and colon cancer. This all left him a shadow of the incredibly forceful man he'd once been, but he beat every prognosis and continued to work as a rock guide well into his sixties.

But opiates were a constant plague. Jack, Jim, and Greg shared many stories about their years of struggles to help their friend. Jim told me, "You always took pity on Kim because he was such a lovable guy. We all knew he could never stop the pills, and none of us knew how to do anything other than be there for him."

In September 2016, Schmitz was doing as well as he had in years, but returning home after a paddle down one of his favorite rivers, the Middle Fork of the Salmon in Idaho, he rolled his car. Schmitz dragged himself out, found a majestic tree where he could sit and see the mountains and the river, and died.

Despite all that followed Siguniang, Tackle said, "I actually look back on that trip fondly. It was a disaster, but we were all hooked together forever because of what happened."

The Chinese themselves shifted the narrative, too. In 1992, representatives from the CMA came to the States and publicly exonerated the American expedition when they proclaimed that everything that had happened was simply proof of the team's "adventurous spirits."

For Jim, the most lasting impact of Siguniang was the way it clarified how he wanted to approach future climbs: "No more big teams. No more people that I don't know. When I go onto a big route, it's going to be with just one other person that I know I can trust."

It was a lesson that he'd heed to acclaim and ignore at his peril for years to come.

CHAPTER 19

CITY WAYS

FOR A TIME, the new, more urban life was good. "Seattle," Janet said, "seemed an antidote for the longer absences I was enduring." And the move seemed to suit Jim, too. It had been a long time since he'd lived in a city, and there were many things he liked about the place. It was rich and varied, and with Puget Sound at hand, water adventures were added to the mix.

Those years after Siguniang saw the most conventional life that Jim had experienced since childhood. The family moved into a home north of the city on the shores of Lake Washington in the very established suburb of Lake Forest Park. Now that the kids were a little older, it was easier being a dad. Jim found his niche with them—in the outdoors, on the water around Seattle, on hikes in the Cascades. They slipped into the suburban life: cats and pygmy goats and a pug named Hubert, a Montessori school, voice lessons for Sage, Little League for Montana, tennis, boating. Seattle brought culture and opportunity and a full social calendar. Every climber passing through town crashed on the floor. Janet was modeling again, resumed her involvement in environmental education, and was active at the kids' school. The couple managed to get away together for a few trips—skiing, kayaking, traveling to Belize. "I got so happy," Janet said about those trips, "thrilled when he guided just me!"

And then there was climbing. In spite of all the family and work obligations, Jim said he never slowed down, remaining as keen as ever to climb. When the Vertical Club, America's first climbing gym, opened in Seattle, Jim was member number 003. The crack meccas of Squamish, British Columbia, and Index, Washington, became his new home turf, and he was regularly off on weekend trips that kept his skills honed.

But bigger mountains were still on his mind. He wanted to undo the disappointment of Siguniang, but finding time and the right objective was challenging. The metrics of his goals had changed. He wasn't prepared to be away from home for months at a time. He wanted a remote, untouched mountain. He wanted a cleaner and simpler experience than Siguniang. He wanted to be with people whom he knew had the same motivations, skills, and interests as he did.

It was little surprise, then, that Jim turned down the next big trip that came his way. In 1983, the renowned Colorado climber Bob Craig started pulling together a team to attempt the first ascent of Everest's enormous west ridge from the north, and early in the planning he called Jim. It was a superb technical objective, and the team was going to be talented and familiar—the trip included Jack Tackle and Kim Schmitz—but it didn't take long for Jim to decide that a large-scale assault on Everest wasn't for him. "I was flattered to be asked, and it *was* Everest, but I realized I had no interest in any of the 8,000-meter peaks except alpine style with a small team," said Jim. "I felt that the big expeditions were just not real climbing . . ."

Even if a more suitable trip had come along, Jim would have struggled to commit. By the end of 1983, life at home was ragged again. Arguments were more frequent and tensions more obvious, and it seemed wrong to propose an expedition. Janet told me that she felt many of the difficulties were rooted in the life Jim was leading. He was often away, she said, and was drinking a great deal. She insisted that with alcohol now involved, Jim was increasingly inattentive to the children.

It frustrated Jim to hear this portrayal. He says he doesn't believe he was drinking too much. Instead, he says, he was simply matching the tensions in the home, and living the social life, including the excesses, that everyone in the business was. "The outdoor industry was party central then," he said. "I wasn't drinking any more than anyone else, and I wasn't doing cocaine, like a lot of the others were." He was successful, he said, making money for the family, and didn't know what else his wife expected.

But when I pushed him again later about Janet's comments, Jim owned a bit more of how things may have felt at home: "Work was becoming far more onerous as the industry grew. The competition was more sophisticated and the stresses ramped up on the race to be on top, and that took a toll on me."

And there was another element in the mix: as Janet explains, she felt that their family life often suffered from an inevitable contrast to Jim's beloved mountains. She told me, "He felt wonderful when climbing. He attuned to that vibration, and I believe nothing else compared. In a way, it seemed the children and I failed to stimulate him enough to adjust to domestic life."

That's a perception shared by many spouses of adventurers—books have been written about the sometimes severe impacts an adventure life, with its absences, risks, and self-aggrandizing culture, can have on a family. In retrospect, at least, Jim acknowledged it was a little too true in his case. "Like a lot of alpine climbers," he conceded, "I wasn't always there for my family in the truest sense." Yes, he said, climbing was too often his priority—even if he hadn't been on an expedition in the four years since Siguniang.

In those years, the two halves of the puzzle of Jim's life—the joyful freedoms of the mountains and the more complex world of the valleys—started to more tangibly pull apart, and it was increasingly difficult for him to understand how to knit them back together.

Fortunately, a creative solution appeared on the horizon.

CHAPTER 20

TACKLE, PART ONE

IT WAS JACK TACKLE who proposed the remedy.

Alaska, Jack suggested, would offer everything that Jim was looking for. Huge, virgin climbs. You could be in a base camp at the foot of a new route the same day you left your house. Even on popular routes, climbers often felt like they had the mountain to themselves.

By 1985, Jack was very familiar with Alaska—or at least one route. In 1979, 1980, and again in 1982, Jack indulged an obsession with the massive *Isis Face* on Denali. It had taken Jack three expeditions, including one that required a rescue, to make the first ascent of that wall, and the experience taught him that you can't ever assume you'll succeed in Alaska.

Now, he had another ambitious project in mind. Each time Jack had been up on *Isis*, he'd look south and see an enormous rhombus of good-looking stone on the east face of Mount Hunter. The great plate of rock reminded Jack of the Diamond on Longs Peak in Colorado, and he started calling the similar feature on Hunter the *Diamond Arête*. He suggested an attempt to Jim.

There was a gamble with Jack's proposal, though: the east face of Hunter is very difficult to get into—and out of. It roars up the back of a tight cirque at the head of the Southwest Fork of the Tokositna Glacier and is surrounded by huge rock walls on three sides, and a chaotic spill of an icefall on the fourth. Bush pilots in Talkeetna told Jack that no one had ever landed a plane in that cirque, and even if there was a pilot who could land there, only a completely empty plane could take off again.

Cementing the problem, photographs suggested that descending through the icefall would be near impossible. So if you landed in the cirque, you'd be obliged to make the first ascent of the unknown face, traverse the summit plateau, then descend the other side of the mountain to get home. Jack and

Jim agreed that such a high level of commitment only made the route more appealing.

The men traveled separately to Talkeetna, and Jack laughed remembering Jim's arrival—"keen as always, but not exactly prepared," having left home for a multiweek trip in big mountains without gaiters, gloves, and sunglasses. By pure luck, the tiny trading post in Talkeetna had replacements. The trip could have ended right there in a blowup; instead, because Jack already loved Donini despite his quirks, they just smiled and shopped. That night in Talkeetna, the two men celebrated with moose steaks, admiring Denali and Mount Foraker glowing in the midnight sun.

The next day, the climbers tried to sort out access to the cirque. They figured that someone among the talented and gutsy local pilots had to be willing to challenge the reputation of the landing. They heard the only man with a possibly suitable plane was Cliff Hudson, who had a small and agile (if somewhat antique) Piper Cub.

Hudson, who'd been flying in the range since the 1950s, was game for a try, and on the morning of June 11, 1985, he loaded Jack and half the gear into the Cub. Jim and the remaining kit would come on a second flight.

The step was extreme—particularly for Tackle, who could well be stuck in the cirque on his own if Hudson decided he didn't want to risk that second flight. But it was a spectacularly beautiful day, without a scratch of wind in the sky, and Hudson managed a fine landing on the flat snow right below the wall.

As predicted, taking off, even empty, was another matter. Hudson taxied the plane to a spot right below the base of the east face and set the engine screaming, and he still barely cleared the edge of the icefall when he throttled out of the cirque. Jack settled in to wait for Jim, sitting in one of the most impressive mountain arenas he'd ever seen. The head of the cirque looked like a Gothic cathedral out of a horror film, with soaring walls of black rock only a few hundred yards apart funneling toward the colossal wall the men hoped to climb.

Jim was thrilled when the plane returned to the dirt airstrip without Jack, because that meant the climb was a go, but he was puzzled when Cliff Hudson brushed past, muttering. Hudson headed over to talk to his son, Jay, pointed back at Jim and the pile of gear, and then shuffled off.

Jay Hudson told Jim that he'd be flying the second leg and then had a bit of fun at Jim's expense. Though he was actually very experienced, Jay looked like he was still in high school and played that up. He flew erratically on the way to the glacier, then clattered up through a tight notch in a ridgeline before descending to the glacier, where Jack was a faint dot. Jay furrowed his brow, squinted, and with a feigned tremor in his voice said, "Pops landed *there? Jesus . . .*"

Jim tightened his seatbelt, but Jay managed a perfect soft landing, and as he taxied to a bouncing stop, shot Jim a look that said, "Had you going there, didn't I?" Jim smiled back and said, "Well played . . ." Jay bounced off back down the glacier, and then there was complete silence.

It was barely noon. As Jack had seen, this was an extraordinary place. The route started only half an hour's flat walk from the landing site. Somewhere 7,000 feet above, the glacial cone of the North Peak of Hunter capped the wall. This was going to be quite the climb.

Just as Jack had promised, the simplicity of Alaskan climbing couldn't have been more obvious. The men would be carrying everything they had up and over the mountain, so there was no need for a base camp. All they needed to do, and could do, was climb. Minutes after landing, they carried their packs over to the base and started up.

FROM THE FIRST swing of their axes, the climbing was superb. They guessed that the left edge of the diamond would offer the best climbing and headed across a steep icefield to reach a vertical slot behind the rim of the huge plate. Conditions made for fast travel, and the men were happy to see that the chimney appeared to reach the top of the feature.

But the fine weather of that first afternoon was a ruse. It snowed constantly through their three-day run up the side of the diamond, and spindrift from the slopes above sloughed continuously down their gully, making long belays miserable.

The higher they climbed, the poorer the rock got, and when the rock finally ended the conditions were even worse. The ice above was the bane of the range—gray Alaskan concrete that has been frozen for centuries and makes front-pointing, placing gear, and especially setting up tents hard work.

Five days up the wall, the conditions finally changed in their favor. The hardest climbing was done, the steely ice now covered with perfect sixty-degree snow that allowed them to pick up speed. Through the afternoon, they felt blessed, but they were soon punished for their complacency. As

Jack chopped out a ledge for the night, Jim sorted the ropes. To release some kinks, Jim untied—and then dropped—his end of one rope, only to see *both* ends slither down the slope and then whip off into space.

It took just a second to figure what had happened: wrapped up in his own work, Jack hadn't told Jim that he'd untied, and Jim hadn't told Jack what he was doing. Now, twenty-five pitches up the wall and a long ways to go up, over, and down the mountain, they only had one rope. This meant no more hauling and twice as many rappels—which would oblige sacrificing a lot more gear on the descent.

It was a huge mistake, but through it Jim understood what a partner he'd found in Jack. They were both able to laugh at the simple humanity of the moment. There was no anger, no recrimination, no sense of despair—just an acceptance that they'd have to adjust. They tacitly accepted a shared blame for the miscommunication and trusted each other's ability to accommodate a revised plan.

At least the conditions continued to improve. The last pitches of the face fell fast, and on the sixth day they found a surprisingly easy path through the huge ice cliffs that guard the summit plateau. Thirty-eight pitches up the wall, they finally came to the end of the technical climbing.

But the snow on the plateau was deep, the air brutally cold. For a few hours, they slogged through exhausting, bottomless powder. They'd started the day with a plan to leave their packs just a few hundred feet from the summit, then tag the top and start heading down, but seventy-mile-per-hour winds and poor visibility vetoed that scheme. They forsook the summit without much discussion and started heading down toward their imagined line of descent, the northeast ridge, now embroiled in storm.

"IT WAS A pretty big decision," Jim said, "to commit to unknown terrain, in a whiteout, with bad snow conditions, but it was a lot easier with Tackle at the other end of the rope."

They were descending a long and complicated ridge that had only been climbed once before. In 1971, a Japanese team had fixed almost the entire route over many days and encountered several difficulties, including fifty- to sixty-degree ice gullies, knife-edged ridges, and complex route-finding.

Right from the start, Jim and Jack saw that getting down this side of the peak was going to be just as challenging, and perhaps even more dangerous, than their ascent. For the first few hours, as they traversed from the summit ridge to the northeast ridge proper, they had to focus on staying clear of the frightening black void to their left, but each time they moved to the right, they triggered avalanches that cracked off under their feet and fell away into the fog. By midafternoon, they finally decided conditions were too dangerous and dug a snow cave for the night.

For the next two days, the men could only hope they were on route. Midday on the second day, they finally found a remnant of old rope and decided to stop and orient themselves. They spent hours excavating a cave, but when they took a last look out of its mouth before settling in, they saw the skies had cleared. They packed up all over again.

Uncertainties about the best line down plagued them. They'd choose a path, descend, and then have to climb back up again when they couldn't find anchors. It was easy to misjudge the size and steepness of features, and far too easy to get close to danger. They eventually came to a large snowfield that allowed them to leave the endless ridgeline, but that decision carried its own risks: when they reached the bottom of the snowfield and stepped to the side, the entire slope slid and roared off the lip of the enormous serac beneath. They decided to get off the snow and commit to the steep rock wall below, despite the worrisome obligation to one-piece anchors their choice would entail.

After thirty rappels, and with almost no gear left, the mountain played its last cards. Only a few pitches from the ground, a grapefruit-sized piece of ice falling randomly from the sky above nailed Jack in the head, leaving him unable to move his arms or speak properly for more than thirty minutes.

Jim took over and led three long rappels down to a small ledge above the glacier. There, in another twist of fate, they saw that the final band of rock between them and the ground was a steep, bald chunk of stone a full rope length high, with no cracks for a midway anchor. They were obliged to tie off their entire rope, praying it would reach the bottom. It did, but the gamble left them with only a short length of rope to cross the heavily crevassed glacier that stood between them and the Kahiltna Glacier airstrip. Conditions on the glacier couldn't have been worse, obliging the men to crawl on hands and knees around crevasses, watching with frustration as planes took off and landed all day. It was 1 a.m. before they finally dragged themselves to the edge of the shoveled-out runway gleaming in the midnight sun.

They were overjoyed to be finished, but they were already feeling the inevitable alpinists' curse: they'd been cold and tired and wet and frightened for days, and they had families and friends and warmth to return home to, but they couldn't help but stare up at the other beautiful mountains that rose so magnificent and inviting, right across the runway.

All they wanted was to do it all over again.

CHAPTER 21

TACKLE, PART TWO

THIS WAS THE mountain relationship Jim had been dreaming of. He'd had very good partnerships before—with Bragg and Wunsch, with the Latok team—but this was different. With Jack, he'd discovered the formula for new possibilities: Both men ensured that they found time in their busy lives for their adventures. They made big plans without doubts about each other. They moved fast and well. They laughed and swore and struggled easily. They forgave inevitable road bumps and stupidities.

"I trusted him completely," Jack said. With Jim, he never felt the dangerous edges he'd seen in some other very accomplished climbers. The feeling was mutual. Jim had boundless admiration for Jack's talent, and an even greater respect for Jack's ability to step away from any plan when that plan was wrong. "Sure," he said, "we both have egos like everyone else, but I always felt that we shared the most important attribute in alpinism: a complete commitment to getting back *down* the mountain."

That faith made it easier to feel it was fine to leave home again. At least for a time.

JIM WAS BUSY at work, and he didn't want to take too much time away from Janet and the children, so Jack's next proposal, to climb in the Andes, sounded perfect. It would be good to return to South America, and it would be far easier to get into the heart of the Andes than to go back to Patagonia. Even if they were gone for only a few weeks, they should be able to climb several peaks.

Their prime target was one of the most enticing challenges of the range, the enormous southeast face of Nevado Jirishanca, but they planned to acclimatize for Jirishanca by circumnavigating its home range, Peru's Cordillera Huayhuash, climbing a few lesser peaks along the way. The circumnavigation would be stunning in its own right: it's a hundred-mile circuit around a tight constellation of peaks that includes seven summits above 6,000 meters, and, in 1986, many of the most impressive faces remained unclimbed.

The trip around the Huayhuash was dazzling, following the edge of a serrated chain of spectacular summits that soared up out of turquoise lakes. All three objectives for the trip—the odd basaltic plug of 5,652-meter Puscanturpa Norte, the great red-gray limestone pyramid of 5,644-meter Trapecio, and the finale on Jirishanca—were superb goals in their own rights. Each was going to be a first ascent of a challenging line on a big face.

But there were surprising setbacks. The pair couldn't sort out the maze of cracks and pillars on Puscanturpa; there were just too many dead ends. The climbing on the lower three-quarters of Trapecio was splendid, and they pushed a fine new route up its big southeast face, but poor snow conditions kept them from reaching the summit, and Jim will always tell you that no route is complete without stepping on the top.

And Jirishanca was just damn hard. The peak looked outstanding from a distance, but close up, the rock was poor, the ice tenuous, and, as a consequence, the route circuitous.

Still, the acclimatization from the first two climbs had paid off, and Jim and Jack scratched a new line up the lower two-thirds of the mountain's northeast face. After two nights on the wall, they were done with the technical climbing and were perched just below a long, sharp ridge that led to the summit. They had every reason to believe they'd tag the top the next day, but when they pulled onto the ridgeline they discovered treacherous snow. As close as they were to the summit, climbing any higher was going to be very risky, and conditions seemed unlikely to improve in the time they had left. As disappointing as it was, rappelling was once again the best decision.

They finished the circumnavigation, then headed home.

ONE EVENING AT his home in Ouray, I asked Jim about the Huayhuash, and he struggled to recall details. He didn't have many pictures, had some facts wrong, and, more surprisingly, hardly had any stories. "You know," he finally said, "I think I've forgotten about that trip partly because it was a letdown to be turned back on all three peaks, but more because of what happened afterwards. It was like the whole trip to Peru just got painted over."

Back in Seattle ten long days later after retreating from Jirishanca, Jim was once again thrust into a family crisis. While he was flying, Janet was hospitalized again, this time for depression and a viral illness that left her exhausted. Though she was discharged not long after, it took weeks for her to fully recover, and in the aftermath, Jim was left feeling that the marriage had tilted more toward unhappiness—but not enough for him to really commit to change, at least in the form of professional help. "Jim was quite macho and would never consent to counseling," Janet told me, and so, she felt, the onus for solving problems was mostly on her, but she says she made the most of the opportunity. "The depressive episodes, my healing process and maturation in my thirties formed the bedrock of my strength," she wrote. "I stayed in therapy for years on my own, developing, growing, and creating another psychic template: a more authentic one, [of] spiritual growth, physical strength."

Jim, meanwhile, turned increasingly to the solution that he believed was an equally authentic spiritual and physical path to happiness.

WHEN JIM AND Jack threw their gear into Jim Okonek's plane in Talkeetna in the spring of 1987 and headed west toward the rocky scars of the Kichatna Mountains of Alaska, Jim thought the fabled range would be the perfect place to put the woes of his world into perspective. It would help to clear his head with snow and winds, to suffer a bit, and get out again with Jack in their first trip since the Huayhuash.

The Kichatnas are famous for their suffering. Separated from the bigger and better-known peaks of the Alaska Range by seventy miles of empty tundra, they are subject to bad weather that roars through the tight knot of peaks to the west, hitting the highest and most impressive towers of the range, the Cathedral Spires, with ferocious, infuriating predictability. The few climbers who'd ventured into any of the five finger valleys of the Kichatnas since the first ascents in the mid-1960s always said that these were *hard mountains*: hard to get into, hard to get up, usually hard to see. But if you were willing to wait out storms and disappointment, it was a tremendous place to climb.

One special characteristic of the Kichatnas was catnip for Jim: a lack of information. Climbers establishing routes in the range followed a tradition of writing cursory and even intentionally vague accounts of their ascents, which preserved an ethos of adventure but could cause frustrations for newcomers trying to make plans. That was certainly true for Jim and his series of trips to the range.

On this first foray, Jim and Jack had their sights set on a new route on Kichatna Spire itself, the 8,985-foot incisor of a peak that is the highpoint of the range (and in Jim's judgment, the most difficult summit to reach in North America). They believed that Kichatna's massive east face had been attempted by the Yosemite master Royal Robbins in the late 1960s, and they came up with a plan to complete Robbins's line. But they were chasing a myth: Robbins *had* come to Kichatna in 1969, but the climb he tried was on the other side of the mountain—a reality that wasn't entirely clear in the write-up of the expedition, which left not just Jack and Jim but many climbers talking about this fabled Robbins route that didn't actually exist.

It's certainly easy to see why Robbins could have been interested in the wall. It's an immaculate piece of stone with clean corners that go on forever and an endless selection of fine-looking lines. When Okonek landed Jim and Jack on the head of the Shadows Glacier, untouched granite soared nearly 4,000 feet above.

But the decent weather that allowed them to land disappeared almost as soon as Okonek took off, and Jim and Jack made little progress as it snowed and rained for three weeks. The corners were running with water and were more discontinuous than expected. Between cracks, verglassed traverses across unprotectable slabs slowed the pair to a crawl.

After three futile weeks, hoping that conditions might be better on a lower summit, they turned their attention to Avalanche Peak, a 6,900-foot spire down-glacier that had been climbed in 1966 by the first team that came into the range. By rare fortune, the day that Jim and Jack launched up Avalanche, the skies cleared and they had a stellar time completing the first ascent of the southeast buttress. Jim remembers ten pitches of 5.10a on great rock, which, he insists, almost made up for the endless days in the tent.

While the men were up on Avalanche, they watched in puzzlement as Jim Okonek flew into the valley and landed by their camp. Like the climbers, Okonek had seen the weather window open, and he believed this might be his only chance to make a pickup. Seeing no sign of the men, he took off again, knowing he'd have to come back on the assigned pickup date. If he could.

When Okonek did return two days later, his intuitions about worsening weather proved true. Jack laughed remembering the dicey takeoff. A wind blew hard in the wrong direction, and the Cessna clattered up off the ground just before huge crevasses yawned.

In three weeks, they'd climbed only ten pitches, but to Jim, "it was a great trip."

THE RAIN ON the tent in Alaska had given Jim time to think about how he could gain more control of his life. Perhaps, he thought, it was time to consider changing his work. Perhaps life on commission, with all its uncertainty, all its pressures of time and travel, was more of a problem than he'd been acknowledging. Perhaps a more anchored, stable job would suit his marriage and his family better.

As it always seemed to, opportunity for change, unbidden and unexpected, drifted Jim's way. Not long after Jim's return from Alaska, Yvon Chouinard's booming clothing company, Patagonia, came to him with an offer: Would he be interested in working full time at Patagonia? They had already hired some of the best climbers in the country as sales reps, and, as Chouinard told me, "There's no one who can sell as well as Jim." Donini said yes without hesitation.

The move to Patagonia promised less pressure, but there was a deeper draw for Jim: Chouinard himself, whose vision for the company and powerful sense of the ecological responsibility of the entire outdoor clothing industry were both dramatically reshaping not just *what* Patagonia made but also *how* they made and marketed their gear.

Jim was proud to be working for a company that was trying to make a difference, just as when he'd worked for the startups that changed the outdoor industry in the 1970s. But the new job didn't reduce the tensions in his life; it added to them. Commitment to Patagonia's visionary ideals increased Jim's focus on work, and the daily exposure to so many impressive athletes with big plans only whetted his appetite for more grand adventures of his own. It was increasingly difficult to accommodate the spreading gaps between Jim's successes at work, his joy and reputation in the mountains, and how he felt when he walked through the door at home.

I ASKED TACKLE one afternoon how those pressures showed up. He paused for a moment, measuring what he wanted to share. "Look," he said, "Jim always had this incredible ability to just show up on a mountain, clock in, and perform at a really high level. It worked for a long time.

"And, selfishly, that's the way that we all wanted it. We loved having a partner who could be counted on to step up whenever we needed him to. But at the same time, we all knew he'd been having problems at home, and saw the problems starting to wear him down.

"As climbers, we always hold out hope that a good mountain trip can sort life out. We'd all seen how that can happen, both for ourselves and for our friends.

"Or at least," Jack added with a smile, "that's what we keep telling ourselves."

In 1988, Tackle put forward a plan that he hoped could be a tonic for his friend: Why not try for the second ascent of the *Infinite Spur*? The enormously long—9,000 feet—and complex arête runs up the middle of the chaotic south face of the second highest peak in the Alaska Range, Mount Foraker (17,402 feet). It's a testpiece with a stellar reputation, mixing long sections of necky, knife-edged snow ridges with technical rockbands.

Jim didn't need much convincing: he shared Jack's faith that a big, tough climb could be a good reset. Still, looking back years later, Jim saw that he may have gone to Foraker with the least positive frame of mind he'd carried up any of his climbs. "Honestly," he said, "I didn't care what I was going to do—I just needed to escape, and be away, up on something challenging, with my head thinking about something other than what was going on in the rest of my life." They headed north.

THE CLIMB WAS hard from the start, especially in the conditions of that year, but Jack felt it was the human factor that was the real difficulty. As he told me, "I had absolutely no doubt that we could have gotten up that route if Jim had been *on* his game, but for the first time that I ever saw, he just *wasn't*. We didn't get very far up the ridge before he seemed to hit a wall. It was really hard on him. I was leading every pitch, and he just couldn't find his gears."

On day two above base camp, a blizzard settled over the mountain, offering a pause. Staring up at the ceiling of the tent, the men had an honest talk about Jim's performance, and everything else beyond the mountain. "I figure that I knew him as well as I knew anyone on the planet at that point," said Jack, "and there wasn't anything that we didn't get into."

The pair made plans for climbs to come and tried to fix the problems of the world. They talked about work. Thanks to a recommendation from Jim, Jack had also started at Patagonia, and there was much about the clothing world to discuss. They talked about the way that issues at home can impact plans for adventure, and everything else. Jack had stepchildren, and they talked about taking risks as climbers with family responsibilities. They had friends who'd stopped climbing after having kids, and they talked about how it would feel to give up mountains for their own children.

The storm continued for three days, and it snowed enough to make it clear that continuing up was off the table, but Jack also saw that Jim's head still wasn't straight enough to continue even if the weather had been on their side. They started rappelling.

When they returned home a week later, Jack kept the code of the alpine brotherhood, which includes a tacit agreement that what happens on the mountain stays on the mountain. He wrote a succinct report for the *American Alpine Journal* and simply stated that the weather had forced their retreat.

For a long time, Jack didn't tell anyone that Jim hadn't been able to pull his weight. He'd rather give his brother another chance, hoping they'd find it in a return to Alaska that was already on the calendar.

CHAPTER 22

DEL MAR A LAS TORMENTAS

This place is hell on Earth.
—Yvon Chouinard

BUT PLANS CHANGE. Jim's next venture was neither with Jack nor in Alaska, but instead was a very unexpected return to a familiar haunt with other great friends. Yvon Chouinard and Rick Ridgeway were heading to the remote western side of Patagonia in the late fall of 1988, and they asked Jim to join them.

In theory, their scheme seemed ideal. Jim liked and admired both men, and he hadn't been getting enough time with either of them. The trip would be a real adventure of exploration, and for all of them, that was truly the point. They all loved the thought of stepping off the map into the mysteries of the lesser-known world, chasing the elusive golden mean of adventure: the sweet balance of wildness, beauty, and hardship.

For Yvon and Rick, the chase would be all the sweeter this time, with a plan to blend two passions: sea and summits. The idea was to fly to southern Chile, kayak through the wild waters of the Magellanic fjords, climb a virgin peak, then paddle a different route back to the world.

Chouinard came up with the idea, fed in equal measure by serendipity and drive. He had been working hard for years, had sculpted his company closer to the shape he wanted it to have, and was looking for a reward. By chance, he'd seen a captivating photograph on the cover of a program catalog for EarthWatch, an environmental group that supports citizen science. The picture showed three spears of granite towering far above a sunny sea, and the story inside described a glacial-research expedition into the ragged maze of islands, mountains, and channels that guard the Pacific coastline of Patagonian Chile.

The rock looked good, and Chouinard showed the picture to Ridgeway. "These things were unbelievable," Ridgeway told me. "They looked like miniature Fitz Roys that had never been climbed, and when Yvon said, 'We gotta go do these things,' I said, 'We sure do.'"

The pair agreed that a foursome would be ideal, and the first person they reached out to was Doug Tompkins, who'd been with Chouinard on the Fun Hogs' ascent of Fitz Roy in 1968 and, like Chouinard, had gone on to become a powerhouse in the garment industry, founding both The North Face and Esprit clothing. As was the case with Ridgeway and Chouinard, Tompkins was an experienced kayaker, both on whitewater and open ocean.

Inviting Donini was a natural next step. "Neither one of us had done anything in the mountains with Jim for a while," said Ridgeway, "but if you wanted to get up an alpine rock climb, there was no one better to ask." They knew that Jim had done little paddling but figured he could partner with one of them in a double kayak.

Still, as the planning progressed, Jim found himself wrestling once again with questions about partnership. He had every faith in Chouinard and Ridgeway, but when he started telling people that Tompkins was on the team, he heard more than a few stories about how challenging the man could be.

Jim had to weigh out the uncertainties. After Siguniang, he'd made commitments to himself about only going on big trips with people he knew well. Tompkins was a wild card, but it would be great to have extended time with Chouinard and Ridgeway in such a fantastical place.

Jim tossed the dice and committed.

JIM DOESN'T REMEMBER seeing the photograph that had caught Chouinard and Ridgeway's attention, but that didn't really matter: none of the men really believed its bright promise. All were completely aware what the truer picture of the west coast of Patagonia was. It has some of the worst weather on the planet. The Magellanic fjords are deep claw marks through wild lands scraped by ocean winds, and it rains almost constantly. Travel to the peaks was going to be ugly and hard. The spires were about seventy-five miles from the Chilean outpost of Puerto Natales, and there'd be no contact with the world once the men left port. If anything were to happen, there'd be no hope of a rescue.

Still, everyone agreed this was all an acceptable bargain. "Knowing that everything was only on us just made everything so much more real, so much richer," Jim said. "We were all looking forward to being out there, unreachable. That was a rare privilege in our lives at that point."

After the trip started to coalesce, Chouinard found out that another American, Jack Miller, had been in the area a few years earlier. Miller confirmed expectations about the weather: in his months of travel through the fjords, he'd never seen *any* mountains, let alone the three target spires that Chouinard now understood were called Los Cerros La Paz. Clearly, that name, "The Towers of Peace," did not refer to the weather that veiled and flailed the spires.

Ridgeway headed down to Chile to arrange logistics, visiting the Instituto Geográfica Militar in Santiago on Jack Miller's advice. "They didn't have maps," Ridgeway said, "but they had these black-and-white aerial photographs with exquisitely fine detail."

The aerial shots helped Ridgeway draft a plan. They'd hire a local fishing boat to take them south to the base of their peaks on the eastern shore of the tight and tall Fiordo de las Montañas. The team would attempt the peaks, then kayak north along the fjord to a point where there was an intriguing possibility: the La Paz group sat on a long, north-south peninsula with a narrow waist, and Ridgeway believed that the team could paddle up to the waist and portage over to the east coast, potentially saving about forty miles of circuitous kayaking. It seemed a brilliant shortcut.

THE TEAM JOINED Ridgeway in Punta Arenas, Chile, in late October, all of them itching to get out on the water. They made their way down rugged roads to Puerto Natales, where they drank like locals; ate like they were about to endure a month of camp food; took measure of one another; and toasted to sun, summits, and laughs.

The trip through the fjords, though, was a cold jolt of reality. For two days, the small fishing boat thrashed through big waves, lashing winds, and horizontal sleet, and it was lost on no one that they'd have to paddle back through the same seas a month later. By the time the team was dropped off at a small, rocky beach along the endless gray coastline, they hadn't had even a moment's glimpse of a vertical world above them. The team unloaded their gear, the boat cast off, and Chouinard said, "Well, boys, I guess we just cut the cord."

The next morning, the men ignored the rain and tested their paddling systems. Chouinard and Ridgeway set out in their single Feathercrafts; Jim joined Tompkins in the double.

Jim saw right away that the pairing was going to have its complications, rooted in a joust of formidable egos and a feeling by Tompkins that Jim was an interloper in the tight threesome he had with Chouinard and Ridgeway. "As soon as we got into the kayak," Jim said, "Tompkins started telling me what I was doing wrong. I wanted to tell him to go fuck himself in the first five minutes . . ."

Chouinard chuckled when I asked him about the tension, saying, "Oh yeah, Doug could be a force of nature and get on people's nerves. He knew he was always right, and everyone else wrong, and he never had any problem pointing that out. Donini wasn't having any of it."

Still, the paddle that morning offered at least a glimmer of hope. For a few brief moments, the mountains dropped their shroud, and the team saw the trio of peaks far above them, beautifully seductive. The men paddled back to shore, keen to navigate the steep approach slopes.

Instead, it rained and snowed. The wind wailed. The four settled into the familiar misery of a Patagonian wait, with weather that Chouinard remembers as far crueler than anything he'd experienced on the eastern side of the range—or anywhere. It was a weighty evaluation coming from a man who'd spent months stuck in storms during the Fun Hogs' ascent of Fitz Roy.

After three weeks, even Jim's much-heralded base camp patience was threadbare: "It was driving me nuts to just be sitting there, so I started pushing to at least carry loads up the hill, thinking we might be able to see something above the clouds."

Tompkins took up the gauntlet, and Jim recalled another ego clash as the two fought their way up the slope above camp, leapfrogging through ugly brush up to the saddle, cursing under their breath, neither willing to cede the lead. They finally collapsed at the top and waited in vinegary silence for Ridgeway and Chouinard. Without many words, the four of them dumped the gear at the fog-bound saddle and retreated down to another sodden week of storm.

By the third week of November, it seemed obvious that the climb was not going to happen, and the men addressed some hard realities. They faced a long paddle back to Puerto Natales, and there was no guarantee that the portage was going to work. As tedious as the days in base camp had been, the idea of paddling out into the storm in a cold kayak hardly held more appeal. The trip was going to be brutal, but there was no alternative.

On November 25, the men headed back up to the saddle to fetch their gear. But one of them left camp that morning with an eye on the clearing storm.

"NOT TRYING IS never an option with Donini," Phil Gleason had said of his time with Jim in Yosemite. "You always give it everything you have. You never leave the ground thinking that you're not going to succeed, and you don't start up with a list of excuses that give you an out."

Jim insists that it really is that simple, even in a situation as improbable as the one they faced that cold morning in Patagonia. "There was no way that I was going to leave without at least touching the mountain," he said.

The result was predictable to anyone who knows the man. The foursome reached the saddle after the long slog back up through the brush, and Jim suggested they at least get up the steep glacier below the towers and have a look around.

The storm hadn't cleared at all. The wind was bellowing, and by the time they reached the rock, rain was coming *up* from below. But the summit occasionally emerged out of the swirling fog—and *occasionally* was enough for Donini. He pulled out a rope, asked for a belay, and started across toward the highest tower (a 1,190-meter spire that would eventually be named Aguja Oeste). He paused for a moment, stuck in a single piece of gear—"Not to protect the climbing," Ridgeway clarified, "but to stop the rope from ripping him off the wall."

Jim huddled at the base of the tower, screaming into the wind for someone to follow. Ridgeway and Tompkins looked at each other, shivering with their hoods drawn tight, and shook their heads: *No.* Chouinard shrugged his shoulders and said, "Aw, hell, I'll tie in. We won't get anywhere anyways."

In Jim and Rick's telling, Chouinard's choice to head up was at least partly informed by his turning fifty, a sort of "I can still do this" moment. But Chouinard brushed off that hypothesis with a huff. "That's crap," he told me. "I wasn't going to make a stupid decision just because I had a birthday."

Ridgeway offered a similar assessment of Jim's choice to start the climb: "Jim had had a series of failures on expeditions recently, and he told me that he wanted to 'break his streak.'" Ridgeway was thinking of the trips without summits—Foraker, the Huayhuash, the Kichatnas—but Jim insisted that Ridgeway was also wrong. His alternative calculus was that "I've never considered any of my climbs 'failures,' because there's always something to learn. That day in Patagonia, I started climbing up because we were *there* to climb."

The first pitch turned out to be better than expected and encouraged the pair to continue. Chouinard took the second lead, recalling, "It was god-awful conditions: real 5.10 climbing with rime ice that covered everything and built up on our bodies when we belayed.

"It was way more than either of us were comfortable with, and I'm not sure why, or even how, we continued. But I guess it's fair to say that if Donini wants something, he'll go after it."

The higher they climbed, the worse conditions got. Belays were bitterly cold, but the climbing was too hard to move quickly. Each man found himself dancing a familiar mountain tango with his better judgment: *We must be close. We'll just do another pitch. We can't stop when we've come this far.*

When they finally reached the summit, neither man cared to celebrate. There was nothing to see. The wind was roaring. It was starting to snow and get dark, but they didn't have headlamps because they'd only planned to retrieve their cache.

Chouinard remembered the descent as "a trap for me. I was at my limit, my brain addled from the wind and the cold. I remember building this rappel anchor out of some big blocks near the summit, and when Donini started down, the whole damn thing started to move. The only thing I could do was to step on the ropes with all my weight and pray that I could hold him." Though Chouinard had survived many close calls, this one made a big impression. "I realized right there that I didn't want to be in situations like that anymore, that those days were past me," he said. After a quiet pause, he added, "I sure was fine with that . . ."

Chouinard's lasting appraisal of Jim was cemented that long day: "I've been with a lot of tough climbers, and I had heard stories about how tough Donini was, but I'd never seen anyone like this. He just bit in and took us down."

Yvon Chouinard and Jim enjoy a rare moment of Patagonian sun. (Chouinard collection)

By the time the pair regained the col, they were spent, but they still had to get to camp. It took all night to reach the shoreline, and when they got there, they had to thrash blindly through tidal swamps to their tents.

Back down at base camp, Ridgeway and Tompkins were starting to believe they'd lost their friends. They'd had an epic of their own getting down and were overjoyed when they heard the clatter of gear just after dawn, but their relief was tempered when they saw Donini and Chouinard, soaked, their clothes ripped to ribbons. But the men were down, and they had managed the first ascent of the Cerros La Paz.

And now all they had to do was climb into kayaks and paddle seventy-five miles home.

"**TO NO ONE'S** surprise," Jim said, "the climb was just the beginning." After an edgy paddle up the coast, they found the right spot to begin the carry inland, but the few miles across the neck were a sufferfest. The ascent was difficult enough, but the descent down the much steeper and much more vegetated lee side was the stuff of nightmares. Dragging the boats, the men balanced precariously on top of wet, wind-crippled brush, constantly falling through, praying they wouldn't break a leg.

Back on the water, the foursome hugged the shoreline for safety, but headlands and coves added distance to every day. And then there was the wind. When they didn't suffer the vexations of headwinds, the men feared the temper of the williwaws, microbursts of wind that broadsided the kayaks with sledgehammer force. One particularly bad moment, when Chouinard paddled out of a cove to reconnoiter an upcoming leg, he felt a pulse of wind and was flipped underwater as though slapped by a giant hand. Unable to right the boat, he crawled on top and kicked toward shore, uncertain whether he would make it. He barely reached a rocky beach, where the others got a fire going. "The closest I've ever come . . . ," he said.

The team battled the headwinds along the east coast of the peninsula for five days, and then the water gods finally helped out. Just when the men had to make the largest open crossing of the trip, the wind turned and they were able to raise their paddles as sails and surf wave crests for miles.

They reached Puerto Natales the following day, having climbed a peak that no one had ever heard of and having taken chances that would be hard to explain to anyone who hadn't been there.

CHAPTER 23

TACKLE, PART THREE

THE TOWERS OF Patagonia had been magnificent, the vertical relief of the Latoks stunning, but as Jim saw when he and Tackle first arrived in the Ruth Gorge in Alaska in the spring of 1989, American mountains could be every bit as extraordinary.

As their plane banked north to begin the landing on the Ruth Glacier, massive walls of granite flashed by along both sides of the ice. It felt as though they were flying down Wall Street, except these walls rose five times the height of the skyscrapers of New York.

On the right, Jim traced the ragged profile of the Moose's Tooth, with its clean buttresses, improbably long veins of ice, and four summit cusps. On the left, the other guardian of the gorge was even more impressive: Mount Dickey towered nearly a vertical mile above the ice.

As the plane taxied to a stop, Jim got his first glimpses of three big peaks that would figure prominently in his mountain life: To the south of Dickey, he looked up at the colossal southeast buttress of Mount Bradley, where he'd go on to establish a signature hard mixed route in 1996. North of Dickey, he saw the striking profile of the east face of Mount Barrille, which was the prime objective for this trip. And three peaks south, the daunting relief of 9,100-foot Mount Wake, which he and Jack had optimistically framed as a "warm-up" for the route on Barrille.

They were intrigued by the big, unclimbed east face of Wake and hoped to climb one of the two prominent buttresses that cup the face like the paws of the Great Sphinx of Giza. The pair thought the northernmost buttress would offer the best line, and they started up a steep mix of granite, ice seams, and snow early the next morning.

The ground fell away quickly. The climbers were fast and fluid, and they sorted out the line easily. After twenty hours of continuous climbing, they'd ascended over 3,400 feet and felt that they'd broken the back of the route. Above them, it looked as though they'd be able to kick steps up a small face, then follow a corniced ridgeline 600 feet to the summit. They guessed there was only an hour or two of easy climbing left.

They were tired, though, and when they came to a flat spot, they decided to stop and use the tent they were carrying.

Sometime during the half light of the Arctic night, it started to snow.

THEY WOKE IN the morning to deep snow piling up around the tent and, worse, on the slope above, so they decided to wait a day, hoping the snow would stop and consolidate. Neither of those things happened. Instead, the storm continued, much more snow fell, and wind entered the mix, polishing the surface of the slope into a dangerous slab.

On the third morning, the men realized they were going to have to move despite the conditions. Jim set off, kicking deep steps into the face while Jack belayed warily. Fifty feet up, the inevitable happened: Jim kicked, and a fracture 12 inches deep and 200 feet wide propagated out from his boot, roaring down the slope just inches from Jack and exploding over the edge of the 3,000-foot north face.

A new reality was distressingly clear: continuing up was unsafe, and they needed to get down. The only question was *how*. They couldn't get to the easier west face without going over the top of the mountain, and even if they could, with all the new snow, that far side of the peak might well be even more hazardous than the slope they were on. And they couldn't go back down the way they'd come, because their route up had included several rappels down overhanging gendarmes that couldn't be reversed.

Their best option—their *only* option—was to follow the path of the avalanche, straight down into the unknown maw of the north face. It was madness, but it was all they had.

When they reached the edge of the wall, they saw how complete their commitment was going to be. They'd never be able to come back up once they made even the first rappel. They'd have to use every bit of gear they had—and that was going to require some wiles. Creativity began with the first anchor: at the lip, Jack buried his cheap plastic avalanche shovel, looped the rappel line over the T-shaped handle, and prayed. Against the odds, the shovel held. Jim followed.

That's how it went, all day. They pounded snow pickets into pockets of gravel, looped slings around dubious blocks of rock. They had to trust single-point anchors, pitch after pitch, down increasingly steep rock.

Every time one of those dreadful rappel stations creaked or groaned or settled when the first climber went down, the man left at the belay had to ask himself a terrible question: Should *I* stay tied to the anchor, too? As Jack framed the ugly dilemma when he wrote about the climb for the *American Alpine Journal*: "Swift and violent if the piece pulled, or slow and alone if stranded on the wall: Which was the better way to die?"

The first rappeller would set off with no guarantee of a next anchor point, facing the most primitive reality: he found an anchor or they died. But Jim swears these are the moments that he loves best—where the truths and consequences are the sharpest and he truly sees what he's made of. "I wasn't ever afraid that afternoon," he insisted. "I felt *alive* . . ."

Late in the afternoon, Jim came down one of the steepest rappels, and when he got to the belay, Jack shared a troubling fact: they had only one piece of gear left, and the wall overhung a good thirty feet. Jim looked down and laughed. "I bet if we tie the ropes together, they'll reach the bottom!" he said.

There was nothing to do but cross their fingers and find out. Jack pounded in a single razor-thin Bugaboo piton, tied their ropes end to end, and headed down the fully overhanging rock.

Halfway down, Jack was spinning in space far out from the wall, but he saw that Jim's guess had been right—the ropes just touched down onto snow below.

The relief didn't last long. By the time Jack reached the knot joining the two ropes, he realized that he didn't have gear to let him pass the knot. Spinning in midair, his hands frozen and his heavy pack pulling him upside down, Jack started to panic.

With a last-ditch burst of energy, he pulled himself up the rope, grabbed a bight below the knot, and wrapped it around his leg. Barely able to hang on, he lowered his weight onto his leg, then clipped his rappel device into the lower rope, spun to untwist the rope around his leg, and shot down, scarcely able to slow the rappel before hitting the snow 150 feet below.

But he was down. Jack screamed up "Off rappel!" but when he looked around, he realized there was a new problem: they'd underestimated the angle of the slope. From above, the ground looked flat and snowy; he now saw he was actually on hard ice closer to sixty degrees.

He didn't share the unfortunate news. Jim passed the knot with fewer hassles and quickly reached the bottom, then looked at the slope and shrugged; the ice was just one more hurdle in the day. They cut off the forty feet of rope that remained, and then started down the slope, twenty feet at a time.

By the time they reached their tent round the east side of the peak, they had been descending for nineteen cold, frightening hours. They collapsed, and Jack asked, "How many times does this sort of thing have to happen?"

"Well, one less now," Jim said, passing over a bottle of scotch.

I ASKED JIM one afternoon if he ever gets frustrated by the uncertainties of first ascents in the big mountains: misunderstanding features, losing time on dead ends, realizing that a climb just won't go. "Absolutely not," he responded without a blink. "That's mountains at their best."

He raised his and Jack's attempt on *Cobra Pillar* on Mount Barrille, the next item on the menu of that spring's trip, as an illustration. "We both had a really strong sense that it was going to be a great line, but we knew right away that it wasn't going to have an easy solution and we'd probably make mistakes along the way. But that's the fun . . ."

For a few days after Wake, the men were exhausted. It would have been easy to call Wake a win and head home, but the beautiful buttress of rock up-valley on Barrille's east face was too compelling. They wrestled themselves back into action.

The line that they planned to try was so obvious that they named it before they even left the ground. *Cobra Pillar* is a clean, arcing buttress that looks every bit like a huge snake about to strike. From base camp, it was also clear that just reaching the pillar might be every bit as challenging as the climb itself.

They committed to a chain of dihedrals that started at the foot of the wall and appeared to reach the tail of the cobra. The climbing was stiff, with cruxes in the 5.10 to 5.11 range, but Jim was in his version of heaven, which is filled with cracks: there were flaring offwidths, fat chimneys, and long slots that accepted nothing but fingers. But there were also countless blind alleys that had to be sorted out by trial and error in the same weather they had on Wake. Day after day, they'd get rained off or snowed on, and they'd head back to base to wait for better skies.

Over the next two weeks, the men made two more attempts on Barrille in short windows of better weather, but they got shut down at their highpoint, six pitches up, both times by returning storms. After five laps up the bottom of the wall, they finally resigned themselves to ending the trip and hitched a ride back to Talkeetna the next time Okonek flew into the gorge. As Jack pointed out with a roll of his eyes, Barrille had a sense of humor: "We flew out at the beginning of what turned out to be the most bombproof high pressure of the entire season. The sky was blue all the way to Siberia for ten days after we left."

THE NEXT CHAPTER in the *Cobra* story was a brief one. Jack was busy in 1990, so Jim rustled up a much less experienced partner. Still, the trip went surprisingly well, and Jim was even able to push three pitches higher.

The new highpoint touched the edge of a lean, steep slab that looked to be the crux of the climb. It seemed that there was no choice but to traverse across that slab, and that was going to require bolts that Jim wasn't carrying that year. Jim shared the news when he got home, and Jack was all in for a third try.

They came back in June 1991. This time, the weather was exceptional, and when the plane landed, they were thrilled to see that the wall was dry. They raced up to the highpoint and found that the hundred-foot traverse across the slab had more features than expected, letting them reach a crack on the far side with only one bolt.

On the second pitch above the traverse, Jim did one of the most celebrated leads of his life, up a 165-foot-long pitch that included a gaping 5.11 offwidth that could only be protected with five-inch gear—which he didn't have. So, Jim explained, "I put in one four-inch piece low down at the narrowest point of the crack, and then just ran it out, past a high crux up ugly, broken rock." It was, said Jack, "perfect Donini climbing."

Above the offwidth two unbroken, full-length pitches of splitter 5.10a hand crack soared up the wall. The walls on either side of the crack were impeccably clean, and a bivouac site on a big ledge immediately above offered one of the most magnificent positions in the range, with the Moose's Tooth across the gorge and Dickey looming to the south.

When Jack and Jim set up camp for the night, they were joyously certain that they'd solved the route, and they assumed they'd summit the next day. A couple of pitches above, they could see another perfect crack system cleaving a steep face—one last bit of technical terrain that should lead to easier ground, and thence to the peak.

But Barrille wasn't going to let them finish without a fight. The next morning, before they got to sink their claws in the cracks, clouds, snow, and a knife-sharp wind shivered up out of the Ruth Amphitheater. They spent another night on the bivouac ledge.

When the blizzard relented for a moment the next day, they headed back up toward the cracks. These offered superb climbing on immaculate rock, until they ended suddenly at a blank sixty-foot headwall. The wind came back and out came the drill. It was hours before Jim finally pulled over the top of the headwall. It was unfortunate that he'd had to resort to aid, but it seemed a fair concession given how much superb free climbing there'd been on the seventeen pitches below.

Above, the seven pitches to the summit were far more typical of the Ruth, mixing occasional stretches of decent granite with patches of rotting gravel. For the first time, the climb meandered a bit, but still, when they stepped onto the sharp top of Barrille a few hours later, it was clear just what an outstanding climb this was. All the waiting, planning, and previous disappointments had been worth it. "I knew," Jim said, "that the climb, with its easy approach, stellar climbing, and easy and stress-free descent would become popular . . . and it has. Descents in Alaska are usually nail-biting. Barrille was, far and away, the safest descent I have done in Alaska."

They bounded down the glacier-clad west side of the peak. It was time for the second act of the year's plan.

"I WAS REALLY excited to be trying something unknown," Jim said about the moment two days later when he and Jack stood below the massive south face of Mount Foraker.

Perhaps, Jim thought, *mystery* had been the missing ingredient in their last trip to the big mountain, when he hit a wall on the *Infinite Spur*. But this

Jack Tackle under a looming cornice on Mount Foraker in 1988 (Photo by Jim Donini)

time, the recipe seemed just right: the big, long ridgeline on Foraker was untouched. Jack had already named the feature *Viper Ridge* in keeping with the season's snake theme, but also because the big serac that capped the ridge did resemble the hovering, threatening head of a pit viper.

When they'd first discussed their return to Alaska months before, the pair had entertained going back to the *Infinite Spur* to get its coveted second ascent, but then the repeat had been snagged by another party, and neither Jack nor Jim were interested in a mere third ascent. There were too many other new routes to explore, and a very compelling one was this fine-looking rib that rose 6,000 feet above the Southwest Fork of the Kahiltna Glacier and joined the *Southeast Ridge* of Foraker just above 13,000 feet.

The peak kept the stakes high. The men spent seven days on the ridge, but they only climbed three of those. The weather was a constant challenge. They made so little progress at first that their snow caves barely moved higher, and up on the headwall buttress, they ran into the most technical climbing and the worst weather. "It was completely a winter storm when we climbed up that steep wall," Jim said. "That was some day."

When the pair reached the snow ramp that rolls toward the summit above 13,000 feet and faced a day's wallowing through three feet of new, unsettled snow, they asked a sensible question: Was it worth the risk to go 4,000 feet up and down easy ground already climbed several times by other parties on the regular route? *No.*

They started down. It took less than a day to descend what had taken them seven days to get up.

It had been, they agreed, a great trip, bringing out the very best of their partnership and themselves, even if, in Jim's mind, they hadn't actually finished the route on Foraker. They set out for home.

CHAPTER 24

THE SADNESS OF VALLEYS, PART TWO

WHEN JIM TELLS the story of losing his daughter, there's more resignation than despair in the account. The story has gone on far too long for him to believe that it might have turned out differently. Yet still, under the skin that's thickened over the years, there's the frustration of the puzzle of what happened to his girl, and how it all seemed to happen so suddenly.

"Maybe I really was just blind," he said, "but it really just feels like she went from being a bouncy toddler to a really happy young girl, then in no time she was a sweet and smart fourteen-year-old with lots of friends—then she was just *gone*." It's telling, perhaps, that this isn't how Janet remembers the flow of these years with Sage. Yes, their daughter was a sweet child, but then all the warning signs were there for quite some time: truancy, school absences, trying pot with friends. "A 1.5-year period in any adolescent's life is not 'just gone,'" she wrote. Sage, she thinks, was visibly trying to get the attention of her parents—and Jim, Janet insists, wasn't listening.

Perhaps, Jim wonders now, if the belief that it was all invisible isn't just another example of his ability to ignore, and then forget, when hard things start to fall around him.

I asked him to tell me more about Sage before that change happened. The first thing he said was, "You should have heard my daughter sing. She had the most beautiful voice."

Everyone told me about Sage's singing, but there was more. She was a shining child, they said: vibrant, creative, full-spirited. People talked about her poetry. She saw things beyond her years. Even as a child, she was a wise soul. She was good at sports. She was a straight-A student. She had a take-charge personality and was always up to a thousand things.

When I asked him to tell me more about the beginning of the change in his daughter, Jim's first response was to turn the light on himself. "I wonder," he asked with equal parts regret and pain, "if it was hard for her to have me go away like I did. If I should have been there more for her."

Jim's question echoes what some childhood friends of Sage, and their parents, told me: that Sage was more sensitive to Jim's absences than anyone else in the family. "I think," one said, "that she was the one who missed Jim most when he was away." It was different for Montana, they said. Jim would go on expeditions or be away for stretches of work, but when he came back, he was a hero to his son and his son's friends.

"Jim was the 'cool dad,'" another friend said. "He did amazing things that we wished *our* dads did, and when he was around he'd do these great things *with* us that our dads never would. But it was really different, I think, for Sage. She just wanted him to be at home, and she didn't get as much from him when he came back."

To be fair, though, there were factors other than just Jim's mountains at play in his daughter's arc, and a big one was the lure of the streets of Seattle.

Just as Jim was a product of his time, so too was his daughter very much a product of hers. As a young man, Jim had to navigate the restraints of the 1950s, the turmoils of the 1960s, and the heady freedoms of the 1970s; Sage had to find her way through the temptations and troubles that were so in front of teenagers in the 1990s.

As many parents of the time discovered, the consequences of giving into those temptations of the 1990s could be far worse than they were in the 1960s and 1970s. New drugs on the street—especially crack cocaine and crystal methamphetamine—stole lives across the country and hit vulnerable teens with still-developing brains particularly hard.

It's a mystery to Jim just how things with Sage came undone, but he watched her fall fast, far, and hard. The happy choir singer was suddenly angry, the singing stopped, and she started to fade out of the family. She met an older boy—or more accurately, Janet points out, a man, a nineteen-year-old convicted felon—who who was part of the grunge scene in Seattle's University District. Within a matter of months Sage had run away with him, moved into a squat downtown, and was using hard drugs. She was barely fifteen.

The system, Jim said, made it difficult for parents to intervene. "Because Seattle was a very 'progressive' place," he said bitterly, "it wasn't illegal for her to run away, so no matter how old she was, we had no recourse in the courts. It was incredibly frustrating to have so little support."

Out of the blue, help came from surprising source: after years with little contact, Jim's brother, Bill, came out to Seattle with his youngest child, Samantha, moving in for a time with the Doninis. Bill arrived just when Sage was starting to veer off course and offered at least a brief reprieve. "Bill was the friendly giant sort," Janet said. "Our kids adored him, and we loved little Sam, too."

Bill also brought plenty of experience in the ways of the system—both of his older children had troubles with the law as teenagers, and both would go on to spend extended periods in prison through their adult lives. Addictions and mental health issues were a huge part of those problems, and it soon became clear that Sage was facing frighteningly similar issues.

When the problems with Sage reached their first dramatic peak, Janet contacted Sierra Tucson, a renowned addiction treatment center in Arizona, and made arrangements for a forced admission. Jim and Bill drove to where Sage was holed up, found her on the street, and wrestled her into their van. Bill pinned Sage, who was screaming the whole time, in the back seat while Jim sped away.

Jim, Janet, and Bill drove Sage all the way to Tucson and signed her in. This was the first of many such centers in Sage's life, and the start of a lasting pattern: she would do well when she was locked up, but she'd eventually fall when she was back out in the world. In the center, Sage was given the first of many psychiatric diagnoses that she'd receive in her life.

It would become endlessly frustrating for Jim to watch his daughter move through the system, with its constantly shifting approaches to mental health, especially when addictions are involved. "There's no consistency," Jim lamented. "They lock people up, then push them back out onto the streets before they're ready. They promise help, then don't properly fund programs, and they judge people, as if those suffering from mental illness somehow bring it on themselves.

"I truly believe that my daughter had a chance once, and if she'd only been able to be kept in a structured place for longer, she might have gotten her life back . . ."

Jim started sobbing then, thinking back on the pattern set after that first stay in residential treatment. It broke his heart to see his daughter losing her way, again and again, for decades. Pounded under by hard drugs, caught up in the endless hunt for them, she fell into the inevitable path of criminal convictions, incarcerations, and treatment programs. Through it all, she came in and out of Jim's life, sometimes without any contact for months before showing up again, swearing she was committed to change, several times living with Jim for sober stretches.

But those moments never lasted.

IT WAS GOOD for Jim to have his brother around, but he wasn't a lasting balm. A few months after Bill came to Seattle, Jim and Janet finally separated fully, and they started navigating the challenges of shared custody. For a time, the brothers even got a place together, near the children's schools.

It was wonderful, Jim said, "the closest we'd ever been as brothers." To Jim's surprise, Bill even expressed an interest in climbing, and the brothers started cragging around Seattle. Then, the day that he proudly did his first 5.11, at a small climbing area east of Seattle, Bill collapsed on the hike out. He had a terrible headache, and when the pain lasted into the next day, he saw a doctor. Tests showed a tumor in the prefrontal cortex of his brain, but surgeons were convinced the growth would be benign.

It was not. The surgery took far longer than expected, because tendrils of the tumor were reaching into other parts of his brain. The prognosis was grim.

Four months after Jim found his twin lying on the trail out on that day of climbing, Bill was dead. He was forty-nine.

As always, Jim turned to the mountains for solace and solution.

HIGH ON THE beautiful ridge of pristine tan granite, Jim was experiencing firsthand what Eric Shipton had meant when he described the "topographical confusion" of the Karakoram. While the ledge Jim was sitting on was barely a few miles from Latok I on a map, that earlier route that had so affected Jim's life was weeks away on foot. The whole range twisted and turned and wrapped around itself like the tentacles of an octopus.

This peak where Jim now belayed in the summer of 1993, Uzum Brakk, rose high above the long, moraine-striped run of the Biafo Glacier. Every direction Jim turned, the view was unbeatable. He saw razor-edged ridges across the glacier, many unclimbed 6,000-meter peaks deeper in the Karakoram to the north, the very high summits of Baintha Brakk and Baintha Brakk II rising above.

It was brilliant to be back in Pakistan, even better to be sharing it with Jack, and this was a superb objective. Just a hair above 21,000 feet, Uzum Brakk was the highest peak that Jim had attempted in years, and the climbing was fantastic. There were long stretches of unbroken rock, with big, clean corners, long, fine cracks, and excellent face climbing. The summit had never been reached, and the southwest face they were climbing had never been touched. Jim had faith that they'd be on the summit in a couple of days.

The line Jack and Jim were trying rose up an enormous amphitheater of rock flanked by long, sharp ridges. Midwall, a massive icefield loomed over the lower face. The plan was to stay well out of the icefield's firing line by climbing a sixty-degree snowslope to the right. Then they'd follow a faint groove that arced left to an obvious step in the west ridge that should provide an excellent tent site. From there, it looked like good rock led to the summit 7,000 feet above base camp.

On June 15, Jack and Jim left their base at 13,500 feet, and good snow conditions helped them gain elevation quickly. They were 4,000 feet higher in barely a day and a half, but there the weather changed dramatically. On June 17, storms settled on the mountain, and after a day huddled in their tent, the men retreated to base.

It was four days before they could move again, but when they finally started back up, it took another four days to reach their highpoint. This concerned Jack. They needed to be moving twice as fast, but Jack wasn't sure Jim had it in him. It seemed like Jim was hitting a wall, and Jack worried that it was the *Infinite Spur* all over again.

Even twenty years later, that was still hard for Jack to say, and harder for Jim to hear. When we first talked about Uzum Brakk, Jim was surprised by Jack's assessment of his performance. Just as with the *Infinite Spur*, Jim's first description of the eventual retreat from Uzum Brakk was that it happened only because of poor weather.

That was at least partly fair: the weather certainly did turn bad. When Jim woke on the high ledge on the morning of June 25 and looked at his altimeter, he saw that the pressure had fallen nearly 800 meters, signaling the arrival of a massive storm. When he pulled open the tent, he saw the tempest had already begun; all around, dark clouds were churning.

The situation was vexing. Both men guessed they had only 600 feet of moderate rock to the summit ridge, and then easy snow to the top, but the storm insisted they shouldn't even think of going higher.

The point, Jack told me, was that they shouldn't have *had* to think. If they'd been climbing at their normal speed, they would have been up and down this climb long before the clouds gathered. Instead, they were now faced with the only sensible decision, which was to get off the mountain as quickly as they could.

When I asked Jim again about how Uzum Brakk had been for him and explained Jack's take that his state of mind was part of the decision to retreat, Jim softened a bit and owned up—just as he did in our conversations about the *Infinite Spur*. Both times, he conceded, he was carrying heavy burdens— progressively more serious troubles with Sage and more glaring differences with Janet about how to parent. Jim finally nodded to Jack's portrayal of him on Uzum Brakk: "It's hard to see yourself as others see you, especially when things go bad or stress in your life affects your performance." He said that it was only through conversations for this book that he started to understand the bigger picture of several parts of his life and the tolls they'd taken on him—and the people around him.

In Jack's eyes, Uzum Brakk changed their partnership. Though they'd never stop being closest of friends, Jack decided to start looking for other partners for big, hard alpine routes. "You just have to be able to completely trust your partners on those climbs," Jack said with sadness, "and it seemed to me that I just couldn't be certain of that trust anymore with Jim, unless a lot of things changed. There was just too much getting in the way."

There was another component of Jack's thinking that was easier for Jim to hear. Jack said that he realized on Uzum Brakk that he was far more inter- ested in doing technical snow and ice routes while Jim was more focused— and always had been—on big rock routes. In their respective hearts, Jim was a rock climber and Jack always more of an ice man.

Though they never really laid out the shift away from each other in declar- ative terms, and though they've done a huge amount of climbing together on smaller objectives since Uzum Brakk, that mountain changed the course of their climbing.

Jack shifted toward those big ice faces, forming new partnerships that produced landmark climbs in the Yukon, in Alaska, and even back again in Pakistan.

And Jim? In the two years after Uzum Brakk, he changed just about everything in his life.

CHAPTER 25

REINVENTION: CROUCH

HE'D DONE THIS many times now: not just make one change at a time, but sweep the table clean. By the summer of 1995, many parts of his life had shifted. His second divorce was finally underway after several bitter years, and as the conditions of the split were being settled, work came under the microscope again. "I was pretty strung out," Jim said, "and just couldn't navigate the divorce and still do justice to my job with Patagonia."

Jim decided that he needed a full break, and the company was generous in response, paying him out with a year's salary. Even bigger changes came from that freedom. At fifty-one, Jim decided that he wanted to be a full-time climber again and live in a mountain town. Some of Jim's people told me they were concerned by how fully their friend cast his moorings—and especially his children—aside, but Jim insisted it all made sense, not just for him but also for his kids. His reasoning had a familiar tone in the mountain world: that there is an important lesson in following your passion and living your true life. It was hard, Jim acknowledged, to think about moving away from his children, but he wasn't going to be getting much time with them anyway: Sage was eighteen now, increasingly lost to the streets, and rarely in contact with either of her parents, and Montana was in Mexico for the year as a foreign exchange student.

So Jim left his life of fifteen years behind and began to plan out his summer. He'd start by visiting some of the many great climbing areas of the Southwest and then figure out where he wanted to live. Though he was done at Patagonia, he'd have one last bash with his industry friends at the Outdoor Retailer (OR) trade show, the massive gathering of the gear and clothing clan that happened each August in Reno, Nevada. At the very least, Jim figured OR would be a great place to rustle up partners for new adventures.

He headed out, with no idea how many things were about to fall into place.

IT HAD BEEN a great summer, filled with endless climbing, exploring, and freedom. It felt like a return to his old life, without the pressure and drama that he'd had in his marriage and his job. After looking at a few mountain towns, he settled, as so many climbers have, on Boulder, Colorado. The beautiful foothills city was home for some very good friends, and it was an ideal place to be a climber: he was surrounded by the stellar variety of the Front Range, was only a few hours' drive from an endless supply of great ice and alpine climbs, and for the first time could explore the bounty of cracks on the towers and walls of the Southwest's deserts.

By the end of that summer of 1995, Jim was fully back in his flow: he was fit, as strong as ever on rock, and ready for a bigger adventure. He decided the best way to affirm his epiphany about being a rock man at heart was to return to the best rock in the world: the granite of Patagonia.

The fates seemed to applaud the choice. "To my surprise," he said, "when I went to the OR show and started talking about Patagonia, old friends said they were willing to fund that trip. That made it pretty easy to find a partner."

Tom Hargis stepped up. Hargis was another Exum guide, and he'd been a strong member of teams that had climbed serious routes in the Himalaya. He seemed like a great partner for a new route in Patagonia, but in the heat of their preparations, Hargis suddenly said that he could only manage three weeks away.

"I was pissed," Jim said. "I told him there was no way we'd get up anything in Patagonia in three weeks, let alone something new, and that was that. He dropped out barely a month before we were going to leave."

Jim resolved to go on his own. Patagonia was far more accessible and popular now, and he guessed he'd just be able to show up, join a team, and perhaps even convince someone to try something unclimbed.

Fate rolled the dice his way again. Only a few weeks before he was scheduled to head to Argentina, Jim was cragging his way down the east side of the Sierras, and in Bishop, California, he ran into a couple of keen young Germans. When Jim joined them for a day on the fine granite crack climbs in Pine Creek Canyon north of town, he saw that one of the men, twenty-six-year-old Stefan Hiermaier, was strong, fast, and easy to be with.

With an audacious scheme in mind, Jim suggested that Stefan accompany him to Yosemite to try some longer routes. Stefan had no idea that he was auditioning for a much larger role until, at the end of a few days' impressive performance in the Valley, Jim made his pitch: "You want a free trip to Patagonia?"

The German was dumbfounded. "But I've never climbed snow or ice. I've never even worn crampons."

It was time to pull out another Donini-ism. "If you can crack climb," Jim insisted, "you can figure all that out."

"But what would we climb?"

Right in the moment, the plan solidified in Jim's head. "Of course," he told me, "I was really hoping to do something new, but even I knew that might be asking a bit much of someone who's never climbed an alpine route, especially in Patagonia. So I suggested that we just do the *Compressor Route* on Cerro Torre."

Just the *Compressor Route*. Maestri's infamous bolted line might be the easiest way up Cerro Torre, but for someone who had never put on crampons, 4,000 feet of alpine rock and ice on the punishing mountain would be quite the classroom.

Still, Hiermaier said, "Okay . . ."

Jim smiled and recalled, "I knew he would say yes, and that's exactly why I asked him."

THINGS *HAD* CHANGED in Patagonia, Jim soon saw, in so many ways. It was far easier to travel to the towers. El Chaltén was beginning to fill in. There were a few funky hostels now and a bridge across the Río Fitz Roy.

But when he arrived in late November 1995 after nearly twenty years away, little of that mattered. The heart of Patagonia hadn't changed just because there were more roads and more people; the screaming winds, the whipping rain, the clouds clotting the peaks—*those* were the things that mattered. The range still emptied when the weather was bad, and this year the weather was particularly foul. There were only two climbers around— two Americans Jim had never heard of—and they were hunkered down in a hovel of logs and tarps. They'd been waiting out atrociously unstable conditions for weeks and had already made nine futile attempts on the *Compressor Route*.

They made only gruff introductions, but Jim felt an instant connection with one the two men, recognizing the same kind of ineffable, intuitive chemistry that he'd felt with Jack Tackle. His sense that Greg Crouch was a kindred spirit only grew in the weeks that followed.

The first night, the two men learned that they shared a connection that neither found too often in the climbing community: the yoke of time in the military. Greg had gone to West Point and to Ranger School, and he'd ended up a lieutenant. He saw active service as part of Operation Just Cause, which invaded Panama in 1989 and captured Manuel Noriega. But instead of reenlisting, Greg walked away at the end of his service commitment so he could climb full time. He'd fallen in love with rock climbing in the Gunks during his time at West Point, and stints in construction now helped him spend long stretches in places like Patagonia, where he and his partner, Alex Hall, had now been festering since Thanksgiving.

Jim saw right away that he and Crouch shared one of the prized badges of military service: the artful skill of ball-busting. Jim had honed his own version of that talent in the Special Forces, and he'd upped the game when he climbed with Brits. The Brits were experts in the cunning mix of endearment, education, and withering criticism, and they swore that *taking the piss* was an excellent test of how well a partner could deal with the ugly realities of a mountain. At the very least, a tongue was just another tool to sharpen during endless days of storm. From the moment they met, Crouch and Donini were merciless with each other.

Greg, Alex, Stefan, and Jim climbed alongside each other on a few futile forays up onto the glacier in the weeks that followed, and as much as Greg was impressed by Jim's skills, those first days together gave him plenty of fodder for piss-taking. He chortled through examples.

"Donini might be a superb climber," Crouch began, "but he has to *get* to the climbs first. He's the only person I've ever seen who can get lost in the parking lot of the grocery store closest to his own home. That's the whole reason Donini has people like me and Tackle around—so that we can keep him pointed in the right direction."

Once he got to see Jim climbing, Greg said, there was even more piss to be taken: "From the first belay we shared in Patagonia, I saw that Donini builds the most fucked-up anchors of any human being who's ever attempted to climb. It would make me really annoyed, because it's so inefficient when you get to a goat rodeo of an anchor and want to get the next pitch started.

"I've got no idea how he's gotten away with that all these years. He just says shit like, 'Oh, well, haven't had an anchor fail *yet.*' It's unbelievable."

But the connection that Greg felt with Jim—his experience, the stories and the laughs, the shared commitment to a style of climbing, the intuitive sense of what mountains mean in a life—were enough to forgive Jim's idiosyncrasies, even the scary ones. "He will get up absolutely everything," Greg said, "and he's just such a good guy to have along when things get rough, or when you want to be entertained in base camp. But just build anchors yourself!"

The weather continued to be poor, even by Patagonian standards, but people kept arriving. A French team showed up, as well as an Argentine team; a couple of young, talented Swiss climbers; and Charlie Fowler, the great American alpinist.

But conditions didn't get better, and no one got anything done. At the turn of the year, Alex had to head home, but Greg stayed on. He'd made twelve attempts on Cerro Torre now, and in two months, he hadn't been able to get any higher than two rope lengths above the Col of Patience, one-third the way up the wall—but there was no way he was leaving. Crouch burst into Jim and Stefan's tent uninvited and announced, "I'm climbing with you guys now."

When the clouds finally unhooked from the summit a few days later, the three men gunned into action. If Stefan didn't have much experience in the alpine, it didn't show. The team cruised up to the Col of Patience, and above, Jim and Greg led up perfect granite cracks.

Because the weather pattern had been so predictably poor for so long, the men decided not to chance a bivouac; they climbed through the night, hoping they'd be just below the final headwall at dawn.

They were in perfect position when the sky started to lighten, on a stance as magnificent as any in the mountain world. The wall dropped thousands of feet in an unbroken sweep to the glacier. Not far below, the two young Swiss climbers were gaining fast. But sharing the wall was not the chief concern; a new storm, writhing its way over from the ice cap, was.

"But we thought we could make it," Jim said. "The top was so close, and we'd been waiting so long for this chance."

The Swiss caught up a few pitches higher and passed without too many words, disappearing into the fog. It was increasingly obvious how tight the margins were. The sky began to scream, and long feathers of rime ice condensed out of the air, onto rock, hair, clothes. It became impossible to talk, and it was hard to hang onto the wall, even when tied directly into the bolts.

When the winds finally pushed the clouds aside for a moment, Jim saw that they had arrived at the final headwall. A pitch above, he could see the Swiss climbers on what seemed to be the last stretch of rock below the summit mushrooms.

Despite just one day's experience alpine climbing, Stefan volunteered to lead the next rope length, which climbed toward a strangely square blob of ice stuck to the face. Stefan set off and Jim caught up to Greg at the belay below this pitch. "We still might make it, but we're moving so fucking slow!" Jim screamed. They looked up and saw that the Swiss were descending. They'd forsaken the summit mushroom—not because it's not part of the mountain, as Maestri had absurdly insisted, but because they wanted to get the hell down.

When Jim and Greg arrived a few minutes later at Stefan's stance, they realized the "blob" was Maestri's compressor, still bolted to the wall after twenty-one years. Greg muscled up the icicles dripping from the compressor and brought the others up to the perch. The Swiss climbers joined them for an awkward traffic jam that ate up precious minutes, then slid off down their icy ropes.

The Americans were only 140 feet from the top, but they knew this last stretch might well be the hardest to climb, because Maestri, in a fit of remarkable conceit, had chopped many of its bolts when he'd rappelled to prevent anyone from repeating the pitch. When Jim Bridwell did the route's first complete ascent in 1979, he drilled a series of bodyweight rivets to replace the missing bolts, but finding, and then using, Bridwell's tiny aluminum stumps in these conditions was going to be treacherous. A crust of rime was plastered to the face and was thickening by the minute, obscuring every feature, large and small.

Greg got only a few feet above the blob before all three men realized the game was done. The temperature had dropped dramatically, and everyone was wet. The summit was out; just getting down was going to be a battle. Greg looked down at Jim on the belay, and Jim pointed emphatically at his watch. They had thousands of feet of rappelling to do. "Fuck it," said Greg. "It's only a climb."

Stefan didn't know what to think. This seemed like a very dangerous situation, but he believed he was with the very best people. As Greg started down, Stefan leaned in and yelled at Jim, asking him what he thought.

Jim high on Cerro Torre in worsening weather (Photo by Greg Crouch)

"Survival," Jim screamed back, "is not assured!"

That line has become Donini canon, an enigmatic enough capture of the man that many people—Jim included—suggested it as this book's title. Was he just being arch, in the way he often is? Or slyly taking the piss out of his partner? Or expecting a laugh, trying to take the chill of danger out of the moment? Was he genuinely frightened, or simply stating a fact, having coldly calculated that the probabilities of making it to the ground were poor?

All the above, Jim said: "I was shit-scared, but it was also kind of a funny thing to say there, just making the ridiculous danger seem completely matter-of-fact."

The trio began the exacting process of moving down through endless anchors and pulling the ropes without losing them to the wind. When darkness folded over them, they had made little progress down the upper wall, and they rappelled through the rest of the night with their separate worlds narrowed to the circles cast by their dimming headlamps.

When the headlamps finally died, they were forced to bivouac, tied into questionable gear on a sloping ledge 1,500 feet above the glacier. They pulled out flimsy sacks and hunkered down, pretending to sleep through the raging winds.

Dawn brought a new world. The storm was done, and a beautiful, warm orange light filtered over the ice-draped towers. They wanted nothing more than to get off this wall, but they'd been on the go for fifty-three hours and knew it would be too easy to make mistakes. They dropped another nine pitches down to the Col of Patience, then settled in for a longer rest. They had to shake their heads at the weather: if *this* had been the day they'd chosen for the climb, they'd be on their way to the top in warm sun.

"Fucking Patagonia . . . ," Jim said, sure that was word enough.

THOUGH THEY HADN'T made the summit, and though they hadn't been on a new route, Cerro Torre was as much a benchmark for Jim as Latok, or Hunter, or any of his other great climbs. He'd shown himself—and others—that, even in his sixth decade, he was every bit as eager and capable of taking on a huge alpine route as ever. He hadn't lost the drive, or the steel, to be up in hard places.

Most importantly, he believed that he'd found another ideal partner. Crouch was smart, talented, had a wit sharp enough to trim a hedge, and was easy to be with when things were boring or terrifying. When they got down to base after the climb, Jim insisted that they plan to try a new route together somewhere.

If Jim needed further proof of Greg's mettle, it came only a few days after Jim left. Crouch teamed up with Charlie Fowler for another go at the *Compressor Route* and finally reached the summit of Cerro Torre after three months of trying. Jim, Greg said, had made that happen, through a kindness that Crouch still talks about today. Before leaving, Jim gave Greg all the gear Crouch needed for his climb of Cerro Torre: clothes, a rack, a tent—more than $1,000 of personal gear that Jim might well never have seen again and was, according to Crouch, "the only reason I got up Cerro Torre."

"DONINI IS A damn good salesman," Crouch said with a chuckle during a Zoom call one afternoon. He counted out the Donini pitches he'd succumbed to in 1996:

One: "I didn't know that I was even *looking* for a roommate, but there I was in Boulder, living the bachelor life with Donini as soon as we were back from Patagonia—because *he* needed a roommate."

Two: "Climbing in Alaska wasn't on my mind at all. I wanted to either go back to Patagonia or go somewhere with a cultural element. But Jim went on about how Alaska was five times cheaper than Patagonia and a hundred times easier to arrange, and then he said, 'If you're looking for culture, well, there's enough exotic and weird culture in Alaska to last a lifetime.' Next thing I know, there we are, in damned Alaska, sitting in a tent in the rain below this huge peak."

Three: "And when I'd tried to tell Jim that I didn't think I had it in me to do a first ascent on a big mountain, in Alaska or anywhere else, he glared at me and said, 'You're a good climber and you know how to suffer: What the hell else do you think it takes?'"

The new route that Jim had in mind followed a series of steep corners up the massive southeast buttress of Mount Bradley. The 9,104-foot monster sits immediately north of Mount Wake on the west side of the Great Gorge of the Ruth Glacier, and during Jim and Jack's epic descent down the north face of Wake seven years earlier, they'd spent the day staring at the route on Bradley.

It was a daunting prospect. The south flank of Bradley looms above the Wake-Bradley Glacier like an enormous tombstone, with thousands of feet of relief. An Austrian-German team—Andreas Orgler, Heli Neswabba, and Arthur Wutsher—had made the first ascent of the face a year earlier, following its right-hand edge. They'd reported dangerously loose rock, but Jim was convinced a system of corners and face to the left would be safer.

But if this rain kept up, it was going to be hard to climb anything. For two days, they hadn't had a glimpse of the mountain, and they worried that Bradley would be glazed with ice once the skies cleared.

Jim's lightweight plan—they wouldn't carry a portaledge or tent; they'd take a minimum of food and a light aid rack—was noble, but it involved serious consequences if anything went wrong. With such tight margins, ice on the wall could make the climb near impossible.

In the months in Patagonia, Greg had heard countless stories about Donini margins. He knew about the epics on Hunter and Wake and Jim's legendary disappointments on Latok, Siguniang, and Cerro Standhardt. But he'd already woven all these tales into what he thought was the only narrative that mattered: Jim might have failed to reach some summits, and he may have been through some alarming descents, but in each case he had failed magnificently. "Donini," Crouch later wrote, "stands as tall on the strengths of his failures as he does on his successes."

When the skies finally lifted on the third day, the men had reason to fear another epic: the ice that had plastered their faces for days was thawing, and the sound of falling rocks constantly echoed round the tight pocket of their valley.

Jim suggested they start climbing. "It's not that he wasn't concerned," Greg explained, "but he just thought we'd be able to make more informed decisions once we were actually on the wall. Donini has very strong, and usually good, intuitions of how to make choices in moments like that.

"Though," he added with a laugh, "when I think about it, Donini intuitions always do seem to involve going *up*, rather than down!"

As they started up, Jim's instincts proved to have been fair. The weather was good and when they could climb out on the face, the granite was fantastic, as solid as they'd ever seen.

But the corners they were sometimes forced to climb were an entirely different matter. That's where the rocks were whistling down, and where rivers of water melting off the wall were funneling.

Smart route-finding the first day helped them avoid all but a couple of short corners low on the wall, and eleven pitches up they came to a decent bivouac ledge that seemed to be safe from rockfall. The mountains, though, were happy to remind them to check their assumptions: only a few minutes after they set up camp on the ledge, Jim heard a huge explosion and turned to see an enormous cloud of rock, ice, and snow thunder down the north face of Wake, annihilating the rappel line he and Tackle had followed seven years earlier. He fell asleep wondering if their route on Bradley offered any better protection.

The next morning, they faced another ugly hurdle: the wall around them was bald, and there was no choice but to commit to the biggest corner system on the wall. And that, Crouch said, "was a fucking waterfall." For several hours, they were waterboarded as rocks cannonaded past. Jim said it was like "swimming upstream with great white sharks coming at you."

When they finally escaped the crack and headed out onto the sunny face near lunchtime, the pace slowed to a crawl. The rock was superb, but often blank enough to require intricate aid work to avoid placing bolts. Jim stepped up: he used skyhooks for the first time in his life, found tiny nut placements, tied off bad pitons, and chanced big runouts, pitch after pitch.

The third day on the wall, the angle lessened and the climbing accelerated again, with some stretches of stellar free climbing. After twenty-seven pitches, the men found a final, superb bivy ledge, and Jim reveled in sharing it. The experience had already converted Crouch to the Church of First Ascents, but Jim proselytized anyways: "See," he bellowed to the great sweep of the Ruth, "*this* is why we do it! This view! Total commitment! No one else in the history of the whole goddamn world has been where we are!"

The rest of the climb, though, was filled with the other sacred rite of the alpine liturgy: penance. The last ten pitches to the summit were angled even lower, but they required a much higher level of risk tolerance. The rock was atrocious. Twice, huge blocks of stone roared down the mountain from high above and vaporized belay stances the men had just vacated.

None of that tempered Jim's pleasure at being there for his friend's first new route. They reached the top of Bradley with a magnificent sunset lighting up an ocean of peaks piercing orange clouds, and Jim swept his arms wide and proclaimed with Pentecostal enthusiasm, "I present to you . . . the Alaska Range!" Crouch rolled his eyes.

The view was a splendid capstone for the ascent, but, as the men wisely knew, ascent is barely half the battle. Though the initial plan had been to descend a quick gully between Wake and Bradley, conditions dictated otherwise. Instead, they were going to have to slog down the long glacial slopes on Bradley's west side, then circumnavigate not just Bradley but also Dickey and Barrille to return to their tent.

The trip down and around to the Ruth was an epic even by Donini standards: the snow conditions down Bradley and then five miles up the Backside Glacier were horrible, every step was a knee-deep posthole. Eight hours into the march, as they started up the final hurdle of Pittock Pass, Greg saw Donini falter for the first time. Jim dropped his pack, fell to his knees, and started vomiting and then dry heaving, his fingers clawing at his belly. He was utterly spent, dehydrated, and slamming up against a wall. But after just a moment indulging his pain, Jim rose like Lazarus, growled "Fuck," and then shouldered his pack and marched on.

"He's twenty-five years older than me, but until that I moment I'd barely been able to keep up," Greg said. "It was a relief to see that he was actually human." It was another twenty-four hours before the pair reached their tent.

When we talked about Bradley years later, Greg framed the trip glowingly as "this perfect adventure that I'd never have the guts to attempt without Jim's encouragement. He absolutely carried me over the threshold. I really feel like everything came together in a way that I'd never experienced before. Bradley totally showed me what Jim meant about partnership being everything . . ."

Jim knew exactly what Mount Bradley meant: "It showed that the two of us could get up anything."

IT IS ALWAYS jarring to come home from weeks away on a great mountain. The land has color and smell again, you're not always cold or afraid, and there's someone else to talk to other than that too-familiar person jammed into the tent with you. But after Bradley, the contrast was even bigger for both Greg and Jim, who were stepping into very new chapters in their lives.

The chance to write a story for *Climbing* magazine about Bradley gave Greg the opportunity to start on a truer course. He would be a writer, and his first published piece was about Jim. "A Short Trip with the Donini-a-Saurus" was a beautifully crafted paean to partnership and an unabashed homage to the pleasures and idiosyncrasies of climbing with the unique man.

The change for Jim was rediscovered freedom. He gave a few slideshows that year, but thanks to the severance package, what he joyously did, almost every day, was climb. He felt as strong as he'd ever been. He had wonderful new ground to explore and hundreds of excellent partners to choose from.

That summer also offered an opportunity to connect more regularly with a partner from the past. Several years before, Jim's old army buddy, Ross Johnson, had moved to Evergreen, Colorado, just west of Denver, and had opened a restaurant with Jim's first wife, Sandy. Ross was often over at Jim and Greg's condo for extended stretches, and when Ross was there, drinking beer and yelling at baseball on TV, it felt like old times.

But the other side of Jim's life continued through that year, too. The troubles with Sage were always a concern, particularly when Jim didn't know where she was. Sage turned eighteen and received the first of her adult criminal charges for squatting in an abandoned home in Florida. She'd been through multiple treatment programs at that point—several obliged by the courts—but the streets always pulled her back. With tears in his eyes, Jim said, "I think I knew that I had to give up on my daughter, and that was terrible. But I just couldn't see how things could change." He could go months without hearing a word from her, and he feared the inevitable phone call telling him she'd perished on the streets.

All of the shifts—the sweet and the sad—helped put the privilege of Jim's life in Boulder in perspective. He'd had a remarkably fine year climbing, but it wasn't in his nature to sit back and see it as being good *enough*. The climbing season in Patagonia was starting again; why not add another trip to close out the year?

"EVERYBODY TALKS ABOUT how hard it is to make trips like this happen," Greg said. "With Jim, it's never like that at all. There's never any drama. Those years when we were climbing together, I didn't even unpack my duffle bags anymore. It would take me about an hour to get ready for these big, complicated trips. That really was the great thing about climbing with Jim."

The trip back to Patagonia in early November 1996 was a perfect example of the ease. Their only plan was that they would only do first ascents, no matter how constrained they might be by weather, time, or convenience. For the first twenty days in base camp, it was easy to claim the purity of that commitment, because torrential rain fell and no one climbed anything. But when a brief window of blue skies opened, the pledge was tested.

They had their eyes on the first ascent of the striking west ridge of Aguja Innominata, a sky-snagging 2,482-meter spire in the southern half of the Fitz Roy massif. From the glacier below, Innominata appeared to be dwarfed by Poincenot to the north and Saint-Exupéry to the south, which encouraged Jim and Greg to propose it as a warm-up for some other, bigger project to come.

The weather window was short-lived. They got loads up to a camp after a long trudge up boulders and slabs, but they were immediately shut down by another four days of wind, rain, and snow.

When the skies finally opened again, two other very talented climbers—American Doug Byerly and Argentine Rolando Garibotti, who had already established himself as one of the most accomplished climbers in Patagonian history—showed up at the high camp, and the four discussed their parallel objectives. The presence of the other two men and their boundless gusto encouraged Jim and Greg's commitment to climb the west ridge in a single day. They packed accordingly, bringing only a couple of liters of water, eight Snickers bars, and no bivouac gear.

Going so lean wasn't wise. It took thirty-six hours to climb the twenty-four pitches up to the ridgeline, and while there were some fantastic cracks on the way, they were filled with ice that slowed progress. Six pitches from the top, where they joined an existing route, Jim and Greg had to address a disappointing reality: they had essentially completed a huge new line—bigger than most climbs in Yosemite or the Alps—but, out of food and water, they had no safe choice but to forsake the summit and head down.

In his book *Enduring Patagonia*, Greg put their overreach plainly: "Most very committed climbers fail in Patagonia because of bad weather, but we failed on Innominata under a deep blue and windless sky. If we'd brought sleeping bags or a stove, we'd have bagged a Patagonian first ascent, a dream I've held for years. We don't deserve a second chance."

Jim was more forgiving: "I was pissed that we didn't make it, but that just made me more intensely committed to get up whatever we were going to try next."

WHAT CAME NEXT was one of the best climbs that either man had ever been part of.

Rolo Garibotti recommended a spectacular line of brilliant, unclimbed cracks on the enormous north face of Aguja Poincenot, the 3,002-meter spire that towers above Innominata. Because the wall isn't visible from anywhere on the valley floor, only climbers who had gotten to another summit had ever seen the face, and no one had attempted to climb it.

Another weightier reason no one had climbed that face of Poincenot was that getting up to the climb entails one of the longer and more dangerous approaches in the range. From Los Polacos base camp, supplicants have to climb nearly 1,500 meters of mixed terrain, up scree, snow, and icy slabs, and then traverse below an ugly hanging glacier perched between Poincenot and Fitz Roy. "If you didn't have to go under that glacier," Jim said, "that upper face on Poincenot would be one the most popular walls in all of Patagonia . . ."

Jim and Greg decided in the moment that the spectacular wall was worth the risk, but reflecting back years later, Jim acknowledged that crossing below the glacier was one of the more dubious decisions of his alpine career, a prime example of the kind of cold calculation that is difficult to make sense of in the alpine game—not just for non-climbers, but even for the majority of climbers who just won't do such risky routes.

These calculations usually involve some questionable rationalization. When they first crossed under the glacier, there was little debris on the ground, and Jim found himself wondering if they'd perhaps overestimated the danger. But at the same time, it was hard to ignore a contrary certainty: it didn't matter if debris hadn't fallen *yet*; the only thing that mattered was whether it fell the *next* time.

Another even more dangerous calculation came into play once they started up the great sweep of bronzed granite. The rock was so immaculate, the cracks so clean and continuous, that it began to feel in hindsight that *any* level of risk on the approach would have been worth it. The men sailed up nine superb pitches with no dead ends and few objective hazards, reaching a superb perch of a ledge toward dusk. Above, it looked like their crack system continued to the summit.

But then the other troublesome constant in the Patagonian equation showed up yet again: ominous clouds clawed over the top of Fitz Roy. The men got their sleeping bags out just as snow started to fall.

The next morning, they had to wrestle with more reckonings. The storm showed no signs of easing. They had more food than they'd taken up Innominata but didn't have enough to get them through more than a couple days of storm. They had a stove to melt water but didn't have much extra fuel. They had sleeping bags, but they weren't going to stay dry for long.

They agreed to wait on the ledge, but only for one more night. They disappeared into their bags beneath cold clouds, unable to move without bumping into each other.

Halfway through the long afternoon, Jim wriggled his head out and growled, "This is bullshit. This sport sucks. In my next life, I'm playing baseball. Those sons of bitches get paid millions of dollars for playing a kid's game. I bet my ass every time I get on one of these granite tombstones and I don't get paid a goddamned dime. Fuck this . . ." He settled back into his cocoon.

Their second night on the ledge was far colder, and by morning they both shared Jim's sentiment: *Fuck this.* They rappelled with frozen hands and passed underneath the gallows of the hanging glacier for a second time, descending to their camp on the Torre Glacier.

The weather, of course, started to clear as soon as they got to camp. "Patagonia . . . ," Jim grumbled. They committed to another go the next morning.

Not long after dawn, they started up the approach, and the toll of the back-to-back days showed. It took until noon to reach the wall, and this time they had to traverse below the glacier in the heat of the day. By 6 p.m., they were only four pitches up, and they spent the night far below their highpoint.

In the morning, though, the weather was good enough to launch for the summit. Jim dug into the first pitches, making up for lost time. He was up at the storm bivouac within a couple of hours, and then he started up the first truly hard stretch of the climb, the steep and frighteningly wide crack on pitch ten.

"Greg and I each got a 'Medal of Honor' pitch that day," Jim recalled, "and that was mine." In *Enduring Patagonia*, Greg spends three pages describing what it took to psyche himself up for his own lead, ruminating about the dire consequences of an unprotected fall in Patagonia. Jim, on the other hand, was somehow graceful on his even harder lead, levitating up a pitch that Greg wrote would "reduce most modern hotshots to grovels and sniffles."

The rest of the route, up to the summit ridge, was such a fine and absorbing mix of brilliant hand and finger cracks that the pair completely ignored the weather. Up on the ridge, though, when they looked across to the Torre Group and the vast sea of ice beyond, they realized just how dangerously focused they had been. Each of the sharp towers around them seemed to have snagged its own stack of storm-boding lenticular clouds, and a ghoulish wave of fog was rolling across the ice cap.

Still, there was no conversation about calling the game. The summit looked only a few pitches away, and the angle eased off, so they should have been able to move fast. They left one rope and gear at the top of the face and started up the ridge. Looks, however, were deceiving. The climbing was far trickier than expected, and they had neither boots nor crampons—only climbing shoes that were nearly useless on verglas.

Worse, when they finally reached the "summit," they realized it was only a first bump in a much longer ridge serrated with many false summits. The true peak, now fading in and out of the fog, was going to involve traversing across difficult, icy ground.

But they weren't going to repeat the disappointment of Innominata. Greg volunteered to solo back to grab more gear, and Jim sat down to wait.

The temperature plummeted while Jim huddled on the lee side of the ridge, and the thickening storm blackened the sky. It was forty minutes before Greg returned. By then, night had overtaken the plains to the east, 3,000 meters below, and storms in the distance were swallowing entire mountain ranges. The men simul-climbed over ice-slicked rock, reaching the actual top of Poincenot with a faint orange light still diffusing the horizon.

Despite the wind ripping at their hoods, it was Greg's turn to wax romantic: celebrating his first first ascent in Patagonia, Crouch quoted a stanza from Tennyson's "Ulysses"—"Made weak by time and fate, but strong in will . . . ," et cetera—to which Jim supportively replied, "You are so full of shit."

It was time to begin what would surely be a long night of rappelling.

IT WAS. THE storm that threatened never grew claws, but the Patagonian wind snagged and twisted the ropes on almost every pitch, in the worst case obliging the men to reclimb sections of pitches by headlamp. The margins of error got tighter as they got lower. They had to cut one of their jammed ropes. Their rack dwindled as they forfeited piece after piece to the anchors.

At a pale dawn, they reached their sleeping bags at the ledge atop the fourth pitch and, realizing their exhaustion could lead to mistakes, grabbed a few hours' sleep. They finally arrived at the base in the day's building heat.

There was still the hanging glacier to deal with, but after all they'd been through, one last crossing just didn't seem like a thing. Jim went first. He was halfway across the ledge when Greg, who could still see up into the glacial bowl, screamed, "Fuck! *Rock!*"

Jim could do nothing but freeze where he stood. "I had the most surprising sense of calmness," he remembered. "I just knew there was nothing I could do to change the outcome." A rock as big as a car pounded into the ledge between the men, followed by a choking cloud of dust, then silence.

The men stared at each other, miraculously unscathed.

It had been a great year, but it was time for it to end.

"I KNEW THAT I'd eventually have to find work again," Jim explained as he walked me through the surprising turns of 1997, "but I sure didn't expect all the other changes to come."

The three remarkable trips of 1996, with new routes in Alaska and Patagonia, made for one of the most impressive years in Jim's story. Indeed, it would have been a great year for any climber of the time—let alone a fifty-three-year-old.

Still, there were some down-to-earth realities to consider. Jim's severance package had been dented by three consecutive expeditions, and he was starting to see that he missed the stimulation of work. Returning from Argentina just before Christmas brought him full circle. Several companies asked if he'd be willing to do contract work as a gear rep, and Jim started to map out how that work might look: he'd want greater freedom than he'd had with Patagonia and Round Table, and he also wanted time with his son to be a priority. Montana was at an age where Jim was feeling a much stronger and easier connection with him, especially through time spent together on adventures.

The two took the first of several kayaking trips together on the Sea of Cortez, following whales down the coastline of Baja California. "That was one of the best times I ever had with him," said Jim.

It was easy for Jim to knit the pieces of his new life together. He and Greg came up with a plan to return to Alaska in the spring and try yet another new line in the Ruth. People were interested in working with him again, including his Colorado friend Malcolm Daly, whose new business, Trango, was catching fire. And slideshows seemed to fall out of the sky. People loved hearing Donini's stories, and it helped that, in contrast to his peers, many of Jim's tales had just happened the past year, not thirty years before.

Most of the shows happened in predictable venues with an outdoor community, but Jim was starting to get invitations to surprising parts of the country, where he wouldn't have guessed there'd be enough of an audience to fill a room.

One such offer was to give a couple of talks in Texas in 1996 and 1997. The presence of a climbing community around Houston was a telling sign of just how much climbing had changed in the thirty years since Jim first touched rock. Despite being many hours' drive from the nearest crags, by the 1990s Houston was home to several talented climbers, and a slideshow by a climber of Jim's stature would draw a good crowd.

Jim was surprised by the turnout for the Texas events, but, he laughed, "I was more surprised that they led to a wife . . ."

Angela Goodacre was a strong member of the local climbing scene and a quickly developing talent. In just a few years, she'd climbed in the Canadian Rockies and the Wind River Range, had ice climbed with Jeff Lowe in Colorado, and had made a first ascent of a direct variation on a 6,000-meter peak during one of two trips to the Bolivian Andes.

While Jim's name was known to many of the people at the first slideshow, in 1996, it wasn't to Angela, who was in charge of publicity for the talk and had created posters that identified the special guest as "Joe Doninni." By Jim's second visit the following spring, she had his name right but still wasn't particularly impressed by the man: it was clear that he was an interesting person who'd done impressive things around the globe, but her first thought was that "he seemed awfully full of himself." When Jim talked about *Cobra Pillar* in the spring 1997 show, she even heckled him: when he warned the men in the audience that the climb required small fingers, Angela shouted out that it therefore sounded like a better climb for women.

Jim liked everything he saw in this woman taking him on: she was smart, she didn't hesitate to share her opinions, she was single, and as an English expat who had built a high-level professional career in medical research, she had a touch of the exotic about her.

No matter how Angela felt at first, the strange chemistries of life had their way. When Jim was out of the spotlight later that night, Angela saw a softer side to the man. There was a wrap party at her house, and she offered Jim her living room floor to crash on. Out came a bottle of whiskey, then a bed, then a plan for a rendezvous in Boulder, then a wedding three months later.

"What can I say?" Jim laughed. "I'm an alpinist, and when I see a window of opportunity, I take it!"

But there was some climbing to do first. Jim flew back to the Ruth Gorge with Crouch in early May, while Angela and friends headed down to El Potrero Chico, Mexico, to go sport climbing.

DONINI AND CROUCH still bicker like old hens about how their fine route on the south face of the Moose's Tooth, *Shaken, Not Stirred*, came to be. Jim is adamant *he* first saw the thin vein of ice from the summit of Bradley and knew right there it was destined to be a classic; no, Greg insists, *he* saw it from a special vantage out on the Ruth and had to convince Jim it even existed.

Whatever transpired, Jim and Greg left at midnight the day after they arrived in the Ruth, threading their way through a complex and dangerous icefall that led up to a hanging glacier, the Root Canal, and thence to the upper wall that held the line of ice.

When they finally crossed the high glacier and started up the route itself, it climbed like a dream. There were sixteen unbroken pitches of ice, including a five-pitch stretch where the gully was barely more than a couple of shoulders wide. The crux was a short but thought-provoking puzzle of mixed climbing that surmounted a jammed boulder. At 9,400 feet, the couloir topped out between the Middle and West summits of the Tooth. Jim and Greg reveled in the view, opted for the slightly lower west summit, and began a descent down the far side of the peak.

It was obvious to both men that this was going to be a classic of the range, and the prediction held water. *Shaken, Not Stirred* has become one of the most popular technical routes in Alaska, conceivably climbable in two days door-to-door now that climbers can land on the Root Canal.

The pair decided this one outstanding climb was enough and headed out to Talkeetna on the first flight.

WHEN JIM HAD left for Alaska, there was every reason to assume that his plan to try a big, new alpine route would be a far more dangerous endeavor than Angela's sport climbing trip. Exactly the opposite proved true.

So much had happened in the weeks that Jim was out of contact. Angela and her friends had arrived in Mexico, settled into the climbing paradise west of Monterrey, and on May 24, 1997, the day before Jim and Greg climbed Shaken, Not Stirred, she and her friend Tito Carrasco had decided to do a popular moderate, multipitch bolted climb.

One pitch from the top, Tito was leading out from the belay when spontaneous rockfall started strafing the route. Angela slammed herself into the wall, then saw Tito slumped on a bolt only a few feet away. One of his arms was hanging by little more than a strip of skin, and the bleeding was profuse. "I'd heard that sound is the last thing to leave the brain," Angela said, "so I held him and talked to him." Tito was breathing, but over the next long hour as Angela scrambled to bring nearby parties over, he never regained consciousness.

Jim was stunned by the news, but Angela, it seemed, had everything under control. She'd already been home for a week, a service had taken place, she was back at work, and she'd even had a successful interview for a new job.

If anyone was going to understand that compartmentalization, it was Jim. Tito was yet another sad addition to the long list of friends he'd lost to the mountains, and Jim knew the ritual: you try to make sense of the accident—how it fits into the arc of that person's story, why it happened, how to make sure it never happens to you—but you also move on.

Jim and Angela decided to marry quietly in early July on Rick Black's property in the Tetons. They also agreed that Angela should get back in the climbing saddle soon, or she might never get in it again. So on the way to Jackson, they stopped at Vedauwoo, Wyoming, home of infamously toothy offwidth cracks. It was a good release, and, as Angela recalled, "Those cracks ensured that I had to pick a huge bouquet of lilacs to cover up my crack-climbing scars!"

The ceremony was sweet and small, and it took a bit of the sorrowful edge off the recent weeks. The next day, July 4, Jim and Angela hiked toward the

Grand Teton, planning to climb it by the classic *Exum Ridge* after spending a night at the Exum hut. It was a beautiful day, and on the way up to the hut, the newlyweds ran into an old friend from Yosemite, Allan Bard. Bard was a superb climber, skier, and guide, and he was going to be climbing the Grand on July 5 as well, taking a client up the Owen-Spalding route. They spoke for just a bit before Bard and his client moved off toward their camp, while Jim and Angela headed off toward the hut at the Lower Saddle. They hoped that their climb might offer some catharsis after Tito's death and imagined they'd see Bard again atop the Grand the next day.

Neither of those things happened. Though Jim and Angela summitted, the upper half of the *Exum* was icy, and Jim had to be cautious despite the moderate ground. And there was no sign of Bard. Instead, when Jim and Angela got down to the Grand's lower slopes, they were first troubled to see a rescue in progress and then shattered when they discovered that it was actually a recovery—of Bard's body. He'd slipped on easy terrain he'd guided dozens of times and fallen to his death in front of his client.

Angela and Jim were both matter-of-fact when we walked through the many lessons of this difficult chain of events: That Tito would have wanted her to continue climbing. That Allan Bard's accident was a matter of a moment's distraction, and distraction can be controlled. That capitulating to fear or sadness would only be wrong. That incapacitating flashbacks didn't have to follow terrible events. That it all helped them develop a bond not all couples have, even if it came at a dear cost.

"THIS WAS THE time of longer-term settling," Jim said about 1998. "Deciding where we wanted to be for good, doing the work that we wanted to do, living the life that we wanted to lead."

Some fixed contracts kept Jim busy and gave him the chance to travel and climb. Angela had started her new career with a global optics company, and she was on the road nearly all the time too. She had a more planful mind than Jim, which helped make it all work: she created schedules that brought them together for weekends at climbing areas far from home, and she got to know Jim's many connections around the country.

Angela also stepped into the complex terrain of Jim's family and helped navigate it in a new way. Jim had always been emotional and reactive with his daughter, while Angela took a more meticulous approach, burrowing into the hundreds of pages of court documents and treatment records—many of which Jim had never been able to handle looking at—taking extensive notes, clarifying patterns, and helping set more constructive boundaries with Sage.

Through it all, Sage reached out, then evaporated, again and again. She came out of treatment or incarceration, took Jim up on offers to move in or live nearby in a treatment home, but then inevitably tripped out of sobriety.

It was all disheartening, and mountains didn't offer much relief that year. After the remarkable successes that Jim and Greg had had in 1997, they were eager to keep the magic of the partnership going. The first plan was a return to the Kichatnas in June 1998, aiming for a new line on the northwest face of Kichatna Spire, but Jim's luck in the range only worsened. In three weeks, they barely left the snow-hammered tent. Jim called it the "biggest nonevent of my whole climbing career."

Still, during those endless days in the tent, the pair hatched all kinds of ideas of better places they could be climbing, including a return to Patagonia. They agreed that they wanted to head into one of the more remote valleys north of the Torre Group and made tentative plans to head there at the end of the year.

What followed instead was one of the stranger trips of Jim's life. That fall, out of the blue, Jim got a call from Alex Lowe, the ferociously strong and boundlessly energetic face of a new generation of American climbers. The young mountain guide from Bozeman, Montana, had been setting the climbing world on fire, and he asked Jim if he'd be interested in going to Patagonia and, even better, having a trip to Antarctica paid for. Lowe laid out the opportunity: he had a guiding client who wanted to climb in the remote and rarely visited Transantarctic Mountains, and Lowe thought that Jim could come along as a second guide, and then he and Jim could go to Patagonia afterward.

Jim knew that going with Lowe meant that the tentative trip with Crouch might not happen, but as he explained, "I just couldn't say no to a trip with Alex, couldn't miss a funded chance to go to Antarctica, and, if I was lucky, thought I might be able to hook up with Greg later." The opportunity seemed all the richer when it turned out that Angela and Montana could also come to Patagonia at the end of the season and trek around the towers. Jim had always wanted to share the place he loved more than any other with his son.

It seemed like all the stars were lining up magically, but magic is some-times just misdirection. When Jim met Lowe's plane in Punta Arenas, he saw that Alex had a pronounced limp. Alex explained that he'd rolled his ankle playing soccer with his kids just before leaving for the airport, and it had gotten much worse on the flight. It was clear there was no way Alex was going to climb in Antarctica, let alone do a wall in Patagonia. Lowe suggested a new plan: Jim would take the client on his own, and then he could go meet Crouch in El Chaltén. Lowe went home, and Jim kept heading south, sure he could figure out Antarctic guiding when he got there.

But the guiding never happened. The client was having family troubles and flew back to Europe immediately. Jim decided he'd take advantage of the unique opportunity and climb something else, and Conrad Anker, another shining American light who was also at the Antarctic climbers' camp, pro-posed a new route on Mount Epperly, a 14,300-foot summit six miles north of Mount Vinson, the highest peak on the continent. The west side of Epperly is a huge rock rampart, and the ridge that Anker was proposing juts out from the face in jagged, stegosaurus-plate steps.

The climb was long, hard, cold—and an awakening for Jim. He was simply too slow to be safe. "I might have been far ahead of the curve for my age—fifty-five—but on Epperly I saw I wasn't quite the man I had been before." He and Anker bailed halfway up the route.

The experience on Epperly triggered a recalibration in Jim's climbing. He certainly went on to do hard climbs again—including returns to Patagonia—but Epperly saw him begin to focus more on the joys of exploration, with difficulty (and speed) becoming increasingly incidental in the recipe of his climbs. Whether intentional or not, this shift ultimately allowed Jim to stay happily and remarkably active for far longer than many of his peers.

DELAYS GETTING OFF Antarctica meant that Jim never connected with Crouch in Patagonia, but he ended the trip with one of the best experiences he'd ever had with his son. Angela and Montana joined him in Punta Arenas; the three traveled by Jeep to El Chaltén, where they enjoyed spectacular weather for a hike through the towers. "It was wonderful to spend time with both of them in a place that meant so much to me," said Jim.

Jim pulled up an image from the trek: nineteen-year-old Montana, a handsome boy, standing shirtless on a crest of snow under a cobalt blue sky, hand on hip, the golden rock of Fitz Roy towering above. It's among Jim's favorite pictures from any of his trips to the mountains.

"That's the way I'll always remember him," Jim said.

WHEN JIM RETURNED from the trip south, he had no idea what would come next. No one had come forward with any climbing suggestions yet for 1999, so he focused on work instead.

It was a happy surprise, then, when Malcolm Daly grabbed his arm at the trade show and suggested what would turn into the ill-fated trip to Thunder Mountain. Of course, Jim said, he would go. Angela was easily supportive: she had a busy work schedule and she'd be happy to have an even more fulfilled husband back at the end of the trip.

The accident on Thunder tilted the plane of Jim's life. The deaths of Tito and Allan Bard, the non-climb in the Kichatnas, the disappointment of Epperly—Jim had dealt with a lot of the harder parts of the climbing life in the past year, but none of these matched the gravity of what happened with Malcolm. This was a reckoning of a completely different order, regauging not just the meaning, weight, and consequence of being in these difficult places but also, for Jim personally, more clearly defining what he was made of.

THAT NOVEMBER, HE and Crouch headed back to Patagonia, and had one of the best experiences they'd ever shared. Greg had an objective that had been burning a hole in his mind ever since he'd skied around the north end of the Torre Group the previous winter while Jim was in Antarctica. Four miles due north of Cerro Standhardt, but on the other side of the range, Cerro Pollone was a skyscraper of great-looking stone, and Greg couldn't believe its commanding west ridge had never been climbed.

When Greg described the possible route, Jim was all in—especially because of the exploring involved. To get to Pollone, they'd have to go around the north half the Torre massif, then down the west side, following the arc of the Marconi Glacier: all new terrain.

For a change, their timing was impeccable. No one had been able to climb in Patagonia for weeks, but when Jim and Greg finished their hike to a base camp on the Marconi, the skies broke open and they had a cloudless view down a stunning jawline of granite teeth. These were smaller peaks than the better-known ones to the south, but not by much; Pollone was still over 2,500 meters high, and on the Marconi side, it had huge relief.

They decided that they wanted to start with a warm-up climb and struck gold on an unclimbed and unnamed spire immediately north of Pollone with some crack systems right up the middle of its impressive west face. At first light the next day, they made fast work of a slabby approach, sorted out a detour around broken ground at the bottom of the wall, and then moved up onto the main face. The climbing was superb, and they danced through the day. Long, continuous 5.8 cracks led directly up to a rime-crusted summit—which they later named Torrecita Tito Carrasco, to honor Jim and Angela's friend—and the team was back to their tent before nightfall.

Back in camp, they turned their attention to Pollone. They knew this route was going to be a more complex adventure: the climbing looked less featured, and the summit was far back from the top of the ridge. They planned for a couple of nights high, and that's exactly what happened. The rock was fantastic. Perfect 5.10 cracks led to a solid and well-protected 5.11 face that led to new crack systems. Seven pitches up, a palace of a ledge offered an ideal launching pad for a trip to the summit and back.

"Of all the climbs that I've done in Patagonia," Jim said, "I think this one and *Old Smuggler's* were the best: the best climbing, best rock, best experience." The weather on Pollone was flawless, and so was the magnificent panorama: for the first time in all their years in the area, both men had clear views not only of all the Fitz Roy and Torre Group summits but also of the vast Southern Patagonian Ice Field.

It was, as they indicated in the name they bestowed on the route, *A Fine Piece* of climbing.

THOSE PERFECT DAYS standing in the sky on Pollone and Tito Carrasco would prove to be far more important over the coming months than Jim could possibly know. Tragedy has a terrible capacity to overpaint our lives and darken even the memories of things that came before, but those two summits kept their shine, even through the unimaginable pain that followed.

CHAPTER 26

THE SADNESS OF VALLEYS, PART THREE

ONE AUTUMN NIGHT in his trailer on the east side of Arizona's Dragoon Mountains, as a sorrowful wind whined through the thorn trees outside, I asked Jim the date of his son's death.

The answer seemed to catch in his throat. He gave an audible gasp, the color left his face, and he stared off into the far corner of the trailer, slowly shaking his head.

"I can't . . . ," he started to say, then shook his head again. A keening cry boiled up from somewhere deep inside, and for several minutes he sobbed agonized moans, tears streaming down his face. "I can't even say the date," he finally said.

I knew I'd eventually have to walk through this terrible place with him. We'd agreed from the start that we'd have to talk about Montana's death, but it was still hard to bring it up. I'd been warned by Jim's friends that even after more than twenty years, he still struggles to make any sense of the loss, still feels every poisonous ounce of the pain that he's felt since he first got the news. But the torment that came out of Jim that night in the trailer seemed to catch even him off guard.

"I really didn't know that it was going to feel like this," he said.

And then he caught his breath and started the story.

HE BEGAN WITH the good things, because that is his nature, and because he could: even though terrible things happened in 2000, there were a lot of positives, too. He and Angela had settled into a happy rhythm. Work was going well, and Jim was more than proud when Montana got admitted to Santa Barbara City College.

And then there was climbing. In the late spring, Jim managed a healing of sorts with a return to Thunder Mountain—not just healing the experience on that mountain with Malcolm the summer before, but also an old wound in another important relationship.

Out of the blue, John Bragg had reached out and asked whether Jim would be interested in doing another alpine route together. Jim said yes right away. They had been such close friends and strong partners in the past. But after Torre Egger, they really hadn't done anything together again for twenty-two years, and that bothered both men.

Jim proposed an unclimbed line on Thunder that he'd seen from base camp the year before, a pure-rock route that might offer a safer path up the wall, tackling a spur up the middle of the face immediately right of the previous year's route.

I asked both men what it was like to be out in the mountains together again. John remembered that he'd turned to Jim as they cooked supper their first night on the glacier below Thunder and asked, "Why did we stop being friends?" Through the moment of uncomfortable silence that followed, both men measured what to say: Jim didn't bring up the story of the tussle they'd had in the Egger base camp, and John didn't say that he'd heard that Jim had been criticizing him in Egger slideshows. Instead, both men just shrugged, said they didn't really remember, agreed to have a great climb, and continued their dinner. The past was past.

When I asked about climbing in the shadow of Malcolm's accident, those responses were just as telling: John said that Jim never really brought up the incident, and if Jim didn't need to talk about it, then neither did he. Jim explained: "There really wasn't anything *to* say. I didn't have anything I needed to work through anymore, and I thought that the best way of moving on was to just get to the top of the damn thing."

So up they went. The lower wall was steep, but for the Alaska Range it had stretches of solid, decently featured rock. They made progress over a couple of days, climbing up to 5.11 and resorting to only a few points of aid.

Halfway up the wall, they met a snowy ramp system that rose diagonally from the base to the right, and they set up a bivouac. By the next morning, a storm had settled into the valley, so they retreated to camp for a couple

John Bragg leading on Thunder Mountain in 2000 (**Photo by Jim Donini**)

of days. When the clouds cleared again, the men thought that it would be much faster to climb the ramp instead of reascending the wall, and they were back to their bivy site before the end of the day. By the next evening, they stepped onto the summit ridge, a stone's throw higher than the point where Malcolm had fallen.

It would have been great to summit, but that just wasn't going to happen. The ridge was covered in fresh, unconsolidated snow, which they weren't going to get up in rock shoes. They started rappelling. Because they hadn't gone to the true summit, Jim didn't name the route or suggest it was complete. But still, he said, it had been a good climb, and it was great to be out with John again.

There was also a sweet public affirmation for Jim that year, acknowledging his contributions to the mountain community. In November 1999, he was the recipient of the Robert and Miriam Underhill Award, given by the American Alpine Club (AAC) for outstanding lifetime achievement in American mountaineering. Jim was thrilled to be recognized, and it was all the richer that Jack Tackle was named as co-recipient of the award that year.

AFTER HE WALKED through the uplifting stories of the year, Jim started on the harder ones.

The puzzle with Sage had a new layer of complexity now. In the autumn of 1999, she'd given birth to twins. They were premature and were kept in hospital for several weeks, and everyone involved with Sage struggled to determine how to offer the children the best possible chance in life. Sage herself clearly couldn't look after them, and she was pregnant again within months of the twins' birth.

With Jim's support, Janet went through the process of gaining legal guardianship of the twins. She took them to Bolivia, where she was working with a cultural nonprofit as an environmental consultant, until she could arrange a permanent adoptive home back in the United States a few months later. Jim insists it was several years before he learned about the placement of the children with their new family—while Janet says he never asked—but he's since spent considerable time with them.

Surprising and sad news of another sort came in the early spring of 2000. Jim's oldest friend, Ross Johnson, died at the end of April. Ross was fine one day and then lost to liver disease in a matter of months. He was only fifty-four. It really felt like the whole year had been pushing messages about mortality and impermanence.

Then, late on the night of August 17, 2000, a phone call drove that point home in the worst possible way.

THE PHONE RATTLED Jim out of a deep sleep. At first, he couldn't make sense of what he was hearing. Janet's new husband, David Inglis, was on the phone, saying that he was in Montana's apartment in Santa Barbara, that paramedics were there, that Montana was dead. "All I could think," Jim told me, "was, 'Why is *he* calling me? I barely know him. Why is he at Montana's and what the *fuck* is he talking about?'"

But paramedics in the room confirmed the worst. Based on what they saw and had heard from another man who'd been in the apartment throughout the day, Montana had overdosed on cocaine, likely sometime that afternoon.

"What could be worse than hearing that?" Jim said with a sob. "You go from everything is fine, and you *know* you know your son, to nothing will ever be fine again, and you don't know what the hell you know."

This is what Jim understood: On the morning of August 17, Montana and a friend had started doing cocaine. Montana was still conscious by midafternoon, but when Inglis, who was briefly back in the United States from Bolivia, dropped by the apartment at 9:30 p.m., Montana was unresponsive. Inglis called 911, called Janet's brother, who lived nearby, and then phoned Jim. Janet was in South America, and no one had been able to reach her.

As Jim and Angela rushed to get to Santa Barbara from Boulder, more details emerged: Montana had toxic levels of cocaine and its metabolites in his blood. The coroner's report also noted that Montana had a mild coronary stenosis, or a narrowing of a cardiac artery, but the coroner concluded—as did the pathologist—that the stenosis was incidental and that the cause of death was "acute toxicity" and "accidental death from substance abuse."

Jim sobbed again when he talked about what he *didn't* know: that his boy was using street drugs; whether this was a one-time thing; and most difficult of all, if Montana died in pain.

As soon as Janet got the news, she flew north. Jim's friends from the mountain community mobilized immediately. A service was set for Santa Barbara, and Greg Crouch and his wife, who lived there, offered their home to Jim and Angela and anyone else who needed a bed. Jack Tackle jumped on the first plane, as did Steve Wunsch, and people from all over the country called.

Many of the climbers had experienced the tragic deaths of young friends, but this gathering seemed to have a much different tenor, so sad and raw, so ineffable. The platitudes that were familiar at mountain funerals—*at least he died doing something he loved; at least he understood the risks*—didn't work here. There wasn't a shared understanding or acceptance of the *why* of this death; instead, there was anger at the pointlessness of it, bitterness about the tragic consequences for so many people, and few ideas about how to help.

Many people described one particularly heartbreaking moment from that day: After the service, a close group of friends gathered at Crouch's house after the service. In the house, the living room where everyone gathered shared a wall with the master bathroom, and when Jim went in there to shower, the conversations in the living room were drowned out by agonized wails coming through the wall. "I've never heard anyone cry like that," Crouch said. "It was the sound of someone being ripped apart from within, and it was excruciating to listen to." It went on for many minutes, and everyone felt helpless. Jim came back out not knowing that people had heard him, but it wouldn't have mattered—he couldn't have held his grief back.

The unique tone of the gathering stood out for Jim's sister, Sandy, who had flown in from New Jersey and who was experiencing Jim's mountain people for the first time. "My brother had just gone through the worst kind of tragedy," she said, "and when I walked around and listened to all these climbers who were supposed to be his friends, all they were talking about were the mountains that they'd climbed." Still able to conjure her frustrated puzzlement twenty years later, she asked me, "What the hell is *wrong* with you people?"

Jim laughed when I shared that story. He appreciated that his sister might not quite get it, but telling stories about being up on some beautiful, faraway mountain was exactly what he wanted his friends to be doing that day.

It was exactly what he wished *he* could be doing.

CHAPTER 27

THE MENTOR

IN THE WEEKS and months after his son's death, people—both friends who knew Jim well and others who just casually bumped into him at the crags—struggled to make sense of what had happened and how to support him.

For Jim's close friends, the loss seemed like yet another hugely unfair hit on someone who had already dealt with so much. For the strangers, it was hard to know where to begin, as the information that was floating around was spotty, and at first glance, when they saw Donini racing up the cracks at Indian Creek, he just seemed his normal garrulous self. It was difficult to step forward and say anything, and Jim shared their discomfort. It was hard for *him* to know what to say. The whole thing felt almost incomprehensible.

But by the end of the year Jim felt ready to bridge the gap, and perhaps even share some lessons. He wrote a letter to *Climbing* that was printed in the December 2000 issue.

"My son, Montana, was found dead in his apartment on August 17," he began. "He would have been twenty-one on October 3. I turned fifty-seven recently, and while my level of climbing continues to surprise me, I know the day is not too far away when pushing the edges of hard alpinism will have to be replaced with some of the compensations of growing older. I so looked forward to watching my son's life unfold before me."

He continued with a few nods to how Montana walked through the world: "He had a rare combination of openness and sweetness. He liked to climb, but that was only one of a galaxy of things that he enjoyed. He was more than a son to me; he was my best friend . . . he was a great kid with the world spread out in front of him . . ."

And then he spoke of the hard-to-bear realities of the death, and all that it meant. Jim wrote that Montana, at least to his knowledge, wasn't a heavy

drug user. "He didn't use intravenous drugs, crystal
witches' brew of hard drugs that haunt parents nationw
mention that the witches' brew had already spilled int
Sage, but he did speak about the troubling parallels betv
to Montana and his own story of what he called strei
experience.

"Yes," Jim wrote about his Yosemite years, "nearly every one of us exper-
imented with drugs, [but] thirty years ago the drugs available were mostly
organic. . . . Today, the playing field is uneven; in fact, it's a minefield. . . .
Today, the price for experimentation is far greater. The price can be a life
cut short.

"Montana's death," he finished, "has left me with a void that can never be
filled, but if just one adventurous young person with his future spread out in
front of him reads these words and pauses to consider the consequences of a
momentary high, it will be a living memorial to my beloved son . . ."

Speaking out publicly was a bold step, and judging by the response the
letter generated, it helped more people than just Jim. But coming to that
depth of understanding was an agonizing journey that continues even today.
One of the hardest elements was Jim's navigation of his own role in Montana's death. "Did I do something wrong?" he asked that difficult night in the
trailer. "Did I somehow set him up for that to happen?"

Two of Montana's lifelong friends shared with me what they thought was
an—admittedly hypothesized—thread of connection between father and son.
"Montana was a really big risk-taker," they said, "and he got that from his dad."
When we spoke, they revealed that they were both terribly pained, but not at
all surprised, by Montana's overdose. They explained that since high school
they, Montana, and all their friends in Seattle had been regular drug users,
including often using cocaine. "Everybody was doing it," they said.

Then they suggested that for Montana, as for his father, pushing limits
had always been an attraction; the son just chose to push in a different way.
"Montana loved his dad's stories about taking big chances—we all did—and
he took his big chances with drugs," they told me. They said that while the
overdose that killed Montana may have been a tragic error, the potential had
been there for years—just as the potential of Jim dying on a trip had always
haunted his son.

After Jim and I talked about this revelation, Jim phoned one of these
young men, now a parent himself and established in his community. Jim

the conversation liberating, and said that the truth, no matter how difficult to hear, brought him closer to understanding his boy. That gave him some peace.

As painful as her brother's death was for Sage, it coincided with what was a long stretch of stability for her. In 2001, Jim and Angela brought Sage to Boulder and helped her get into a treatment program that seemed especially impactful. Living with them and having their help with her new baby, Sage was able to hold down a job and stay sober until the spring of 2003, when the pressures of life overtook her again. It was, Jim said, the most optimistic he'd felt about his daughter in years, and he and Angela were happy to play a role in the child's life.

Jim's close friends said that another evolution attached to Montana's death gave Jim a different sort of peace: he started mentoring a series of aspiring young alpinists. Jim himself has always said that it was never an intentional change—he jokes that he was climbing with younger partners just because it grew harder to find men his own age who still wanted to climb hard things—but his friends disagree, saying they felt Jim was seeking experiences with these young men that he'd always hoped to have with Montana.

THOM ENGELBACH LAUGHED when I asked him how he started his apprenticeship as a self-acknowledged Donini protégé. "Honestly," he said, "I think it's only because I sort of look like Crouch, and because Crouch was going through a divorce, *he* couldn't go climbing . . ."

Jim laughed at that story, but insisted there was another similarity between the men that was far more important: the Boulder-based Engelbach—thirty-eight at the time—was, like Crouch, an exceptional rock climber who seemed to have boundless energy for anything Jim proposed.

Mutual friends made the introduction, and Jim thought he'd take the eager youngster out for a test drive. He invited Thom and some of his friends to Indian Creek and was impressed with Thom's skill on the cracks. The feeling was mutual. "When you climb with Donini," Engelbach said, "you're going to realize right away how much he has to teach you—how to move, how to read the terrain, how to wait. Every single day was a master class."

Not long after, Jim suggested that the two of them do something a bit longer and proposed a route on the Diamond on Longs Peak, the alpine wall high above Estes Park, Colorado. The climb was classic Donini. *Black Dagger* includes three pitches of old-school, offwidth 5.10, each of them challenging unless you know how to finesse your way up an outsized crack. Thom remembers that he flailed a bit and that Jim seemed to find his struggles hilarious—but also inconsequential enough that, Thom remembers, Jim took him completely off belay midlead, without warning, to sort out a twisted rope.

Jim decided that if Thom was truly committed to learning the dark arts of alpinism, there was one place that would offer a real immersion course: the Kichatnas. So that's what Jim put forward in the spring of 2003: yet another attempt at a new line in the Kichatnas, this time the possible first ascent of the massive Sunshine Wall on the northwest face of Sunrise Spire above the Cul-de-Sac Glacier.

The first semester of Jim's immersion course seemed to focus only on patience: sitting around in Talkeetna, waiting out bad weather, drinking at the Fairview Inn, telling stories, changing plans. After a long week, the weather cleared enough to allow a flight into the Ruth Gorge. "We landed right near the base of *Cobra Pillar*," says Thom. "I was super-psyched to do *Cobra* and thought it would be a perfect introduction to Alaska, but there was no way Jim was going repeat something."

Jim suggested instead that they climb up to the Root Canal and try to find a new line up the striking west face of the Eye Tooth, one of the cutely named cusps on the southeast rim of the Moose's Tooth massif. It was an ambitious plan. The huge wall is almost dead vertical and nearly 3,000 feet high.

The climb offered its own Alaskan lessons. There was excellent rock low down on the face, but higher up there were frightening sections of garbage. "We were tying off spears of rock that looked like shards of broken glass, trying to convince ourselves that they'd hold," Thom said. "I couldn't believe people climbed this stuff, but it didn't seem to bother Jim at all." Finally, eight pitches up, even Jim had doubts and they bailed.

By the time they reached the glacier, the weather had improved dramatically, so they had Paul Roderick come pick them up and fly them west to the Kichatnas, where Jim, knowing the moods of that range, felt they needed to start climbing as soon as possible. The towering Sunshine Wall rose a short walk from the tent, so after just a bit of gear sorting, they crossed to the base and started up an obvious line of weakness.

They were surprised by the quality of the rock, but more surprised that they kept coming across evidence of a previous attempt that, yet again, had never been written up. By the time Jim and Thom reached a large ledge atop the fifth pitch, they had passed several bolted anchors, a few fixed pieces, and an empty bottle of Tooth Sheaf Stout (which hinted that the previous team might be Australian). Still, Jim and Thom convinced themselves that those traces didn't mean that anyone had actually finished the route. After they sussed out a few more pitches, they fixed ropes back to base to get the gear for a blast to the top.

Because the weather still looked good and they'd made fair time, they decided to pack light, with no bivy gear, and climb through the half-lit night. "That was a good idea in principle," says Thom, "but as soon as we got to the top of the fixed lines, the climbing was much harder. We started aiding and slowed to a crawl."

About 800 feet higher, the pair saw the final evidence of a previous *ascent*—a tattered remnant of rope hanging from the edge of a big overhang—but as they moved beyond the rope, they continued to come across bolted stations every fifty meters, puzzlingly suggesting that someone had rappelled the route even if it hadn't been climbed.

The attempt by Jim and Thom finally came to an end when Thom came to a huge flake that shifted dramatically when he touched it. Jim was directly below, a sitting duck if the flake released. Thom lowered down and asked Jim if he wanted to try to get around the flake, and the mountain itself answered the question with a minute-long roll of thunder and a spit of rain. It was time to get the hell off this thing. The pair spent the rest of the long night rappelling.

Thom was surprised at how easily Jim took it all in stride, but he was starting to understand what Jim meant when he said that patience might be a more important ingredient in the alpine recipe than talent or drive.

Both men's patience was tested through the next ten days. While the rest of Alaska had clear skies, the Kichatnas were draped with a cold blanket of drizzle. Between card games, mathematical puzzles they dreamed up, and a carefully measured ration of foul Highland Mist whisky every day at precisely 6 p.m., there were long stretches of silence.

I asked Thom whether Montana entered their conversations. He said he didn't think so, adding, "You could see Jim disappear inside of himself, and I guessed that's where he went—but I felt it was still a bit early in our relationship to really dive into that. I remember how Jim had once said that it was important to leave home behind when you went to do a climb like this, and I took that as a hint."

After more days of rain, it was obvious that their trip to the Kichatnas was over. Jim started discussing plans for a return to Alaska. "I'd seen that Engelbach was a really solid partner, so I suggested a bunch of things that I'd always wanted to do in Alaska," he recalled.

Thom, uninspired by the quality of the Alaskan rock and the festering through storms, fought back and proposed heading to Patagonia instead. Jim said, "Absolutely!"

"I'm sure," Engelbach laughed, "that's actually what he had planned all along . . ."

ON THE LONG flight to Buenos Aires, Engelbach was bug-eyed. Jim had decided that Greg Crouch's book *Enduring Patagonia* would be a good primer for Thom, who couldn't believe what he was reading. It seemed like every page told a story of storms and terrors, endless boredom, and countless near-misses, and in every one of those stories both Jim and Greg seemed like superheroes. "I'm thinking to myself, 'Holy shit, what have I signed up for?'" And, regarding Crouch, "I'm supposed to replace THIS guy?"

Jim didn't have any questions about Thom's abilities, but he still thought he'd offer a gentler introduction to the towers than the routes in Crouch's book. "I was feeling generous," Jim said with a laugh, "so instead of a first ascent, I agreed to a trade route"—*Supercanaleta*—"for Engelbach's first Patagonian climb."

The *Supercanaleta* (or Supercouloir) is an enormous gully that splits the west face of Cerro Fitz Roy. Ice and snow patches buried in the back can make for fast ascents, but the route is still very long, and the most difficult climbing comes at the end, on the devious technical ground of the spiky summit ridge. The *Supercanaleta*, Jim suggested, would help Thom appreciate Patagonia's "special" character.

It was "special" just reaching the far side of Fitz Roy. After a hike to a base camp on the north side of the massif, climbers are obliged to carry their gear 4,000 vertical feet up a trail called "Heartbreak Hill" to the Paso Cuadrado saddle, descend 1,000 feet to the North Fitz Roy Glacier, then reclimb all the lost elevation to reach the wall.

And then there was the weather. Locals said that they hadn't ever seen barometer readings so low, but the constant roar of the wind swore the readings were true. Jim voted that caching their gear at the base was a better use of time than just sitting around bullshitting with other climbers at base camp. So they carried loads over the pass in marginal conditions, understanding they were committed to going back up in potentially worse weather if things didn't improve.

When a small bubble of higher pressure finally promised a chance to climb, all the climbers sharing the camp raced up toward their routes, and Jim's suggestion of a high cache, which let them now approach with lighter packs, seemed to be vindicated. Thom and Jim flew past the others and got the prime tent site below *Supercanaleta*, settling in to bivy before gunning for a one-day ascent the following day.

Then the grand plan fell apart. The wind roared that afternoon, ripping the fly off the tent and carrying it off toward Chile. "And that was that," Jim said. "We couldn't get another tent, so our trip was over without having done a thing except hauling crap over that damn pass."

But as they were retreating back across the upper Fitz Roy Glacier, Jim spotted a superb-looking crack system on the south side of the Goretta Pillar, a great strut of unclimbed rock that leans against the first two-thirds of Fitz Roy's north face.

"We *have* to do that," Jim said, tracing the crack. The line was so compelling that despite the absence of any climbing at all on this trip, Thom was convinced it would be worth returning for.

As they were walking away, Jim added, "The weather is sure to be better next time."

Thom laughed again: "I must have forgotten everything I'd read in Crouch's book . . ."

AS WE DROVE one day through high desert scrub west of his Colorado home, Jim started telling the story of his next trip to Patagonia—which was in 2002, and not with Engelbach, but with John Bragg. Both described the trip as coming close to their shared notion of a perfect climb. "I think this was the trip that really helped me see what I wanted to be doing with the rest of my days," Jim said. Echoed John, "That was the best trip I ever did in my life."

Many things, over many years, fell into place to make that magic happen.

In 1977, after Bragg had made the first alpine-style ascent of Cerro Torre with Jay Wilson and Dave Carman, he'd headed north into Chile on his own, looking for a purer experience, unconstrained by the narrow objective of a single summit. He found what he was seeking in the untamed land between the eastern edge of the great Patagonian Ice Field and the western shores of Lago O'Higgins, a huge, spider-armed lake that sprawls north of El Chaltén. He vowed he'd come back one day to explore the beautiful, barely known valleys and glaciers, but he hadn't managed to live up to that promise until he sent feelers out to Jim years later.

It seemed to Jim that kismet was at play. Not long before John reached out, an old Yosemite friend of Jim's, Peter "Cado" Avenali, had shared his own experience exploring the same region. Cado had moved to Chile years before and built a guiding business in Coyhaique, and he knew the backcountry north of El Chaltén as well as any other Westerner. Jim suggested they all combine forces.

There was only spotty information about what had been done in the area, but John had seen photographs of two compelling peaks at the head of the western arm of O'Higgins. Cado believed that the higher of the peaks, Cerro Steffen (3,056 meters), had been climbed in 1965 by the only team known to have explored the area, so the plan sharpened to focus on the other summit, 2,800-meter Cerro Krüger.

Cado's wife, Ruth, organized a boat ride up a steep-walled fjord to a beautiful forest below the tongue of the Bravo Glacier, which gave them access to the icefield. "It was just fantastic," said Bragg. "We were completely on our own; we had no idea where we were and had to figure everything out ourselves. It was like the Torre Group in the 1970s."

The three men set up camp in a pristine forest just an hour from the lake and spent a week exploring the walls around the glacier. When they finally decided on a route on Krüger, Cado wasn't feeling 100 percent and elected to stay in camp while John and Jim headed up the peak. It was a stiff day, but both men loved it, errors and all. They started climbing later than they should have, the rock was bad, the route-finding complex and the weather distinctly Patagonian. Just below the summit, in driving wind and sleet, they turned around and began a serious descent. They had no food and the wrong clothing for the roaring storm, and they spent several dark hours lost on the glacier before committing to spending the night out. They were benighted well above the campsite. Still, by the time they reached their camp the next morning, both men agreed this was exactly what they'd been look-ing for. They weren't fussed that they hadn't summitted; the landscape and the feeling of being the first people to ever touch the mountain were what they'd come for.

For Jim, the best part of the adventure was the future it created. When he'd come to Patagonia with Angela in December 1999, they'd met up with Cado, who told them that he and Ruth were looking for land. The idea of actu-ally owning property in this place that he loved so much, with unexplored terrain out his front door, seemed like an impossible dream to Jim, but now, just a few years later, Cado was looking for partners to buy lots.

The land in question sat on a bench a few hundred feet above Lago Gen-eral Carrera, another large, glacier-fed lake straddling the Chile-Argentina border, about 200 miles north of El Chaltén. On a peninsula just east of the small but growing tourist town of Puerto Guadal, Chile, the property had a magnificent view across the big lake to a sky-to-sky panorama of peaks and glaciers, most untouched. Rising above all the mountains was Monte San Valentín, at 13,314 feet the highest point in Patagonia.

Jim leapt at the chance to buy in. The home that Cado eventually built for him became a launching pad not just for Jim's own explorations but also for teams of climbers coming from around the world, many lured by Jim's reports about the area's potential for first ascents.

IF THERE HAD been doubts about a return to Fitz Roy, they evaporated in the beautiful sun of a spectacular day in 2006. Far up on the Goretta Pillar, Jim and Thom were sliding their hands into clean and unbroken cracks that ran far up a wall of golden granite. There wasn't even a rumor of wind.

This time, they had the secret weapon of a new era: precise weather fore-casts. The great German climber Thomas Huber was in El Chaltén, and he had a hotline to Karl Gabel, a meteorologist from Innsbruck, Austria, whose forecast algorithms made him an oracle for climbers around the world. "Karl told us what day and time the weather was going to change," Jim explained, "and sure enough, we started the hike in and the skies cleared right up."

To take advantage of the weather window, Jim and Thom bypassed the main camp, going over the Paso Cuadrado and straight up to the Goretta. They dug a snow cave and started up in the windless morning that followed.

After eight pitches of fine new routing, they found a barely passable ledge and settled in for a calm night under an umbrella of stars. They fell asleep full of optimism and woke up to blue skies, but by midmorning, the day soured. In Patagonia, even oracles can't always get it right: Gabel's prediction didn't include the talons of cirrus that were clawing the sky.

Eight pitches higher, when they reached the shoulder of the pillar, they discovered how protected they'd been in the corner below. The winds were fiercer than anything Thom had ever experienced, and the forced bivouac was a horror show. Said Thom, "We couldn't light the stove and could barely hear each other. I'd never felt this frightened on a mountain, and that night I was sure we were going to die—and Donini was *laughing*.

"Look," Thom clarified, "when people are really down, or are close to the edge, Jim's totally reassuring, but when there's room to play—and, in retrospect, there was room that night—he thinks it's absolutely hilarious if you start to lose it. He was laughing his ass off every time the storm made me jump."

The next morning, it had stopped snowing, but the wind was still fierce. Though they were close to the top of the pillar—and though many climbers today consider an ascent of the Goretta a complete climb in its own right—Jim insisted that if they didn't reach the summit of Fitz Roy, they hadn't done the climb. Thom accepted that, and they started down.

By the time they reached the base, they had used every piece of gear they had for the single-point anchors of the descent, and worse, they only had one remaining rope—they'd had to cut the other one twelve pitches up when the malign winds snagged it on a faraway flake. The trip was done, but as Thom explained, "That was our climb, and we were definitely coming back."

Neither of them, though, expected the *way* they'd return. In late 2006, a documentary filmmaker from New York City, Dave Rosenstein, approached Jim with an idea for a project. "The theme was something like 'old guys who rock,'" Jim said, "focusing on people like me who kept active into their sixties."

It sounded like a great way to get someone else to pay for a return to the Goretta, so Jim connected Rosenstein with some climbers who could help rig and film. If the first trips to Fitz Roy were disappointments, this final one, in January 2007, was a circus. Rosenstein didn't have much wall experience, and he was completely overwhelmed. It was surprisingly hard to get footage that captured the wall's majestic scale, and every shot just took too long. A short window of really good weather was wasted low down, and even then, Jim says, they hardly got any usable footage. Three weeks after arriving in Patagonia—by far Jim's shortest trip to the towers—he headed home.

Still, Thom explained, the sorry turn of the trip offered up one last lesson from the master: "I really thought that Fitz Roy had become an obsession that was going to be really hard for Jim to let go of. But then it was just done. Enough was enough. Jim said there were other things to climb."

FROM THE BALCONY of Angela and Jim's new house on Lago General Carrera, the vast spread of ice and rock was electrifying. There were untouched peaks from horizon to horizon, and it wasn't obvious how to even get to them. This was primeval land. The terrain was topographically tortured and, thanks to the mild climate, heavily vegetated. Even the Indigenous locals who'd been there for thousands of years hadn't explored the backcountry; too much of it required navigating high-flow rivers, or the lake's many arms, or the rugged glaciers.

But Jim couldn't wait to get exploring, and he started passing the word about the area's possibilities and offered an open door at his new home. The first arrival was Morgan Boyles, a young climber from Aspen, Colorado, whose father had been a longtime friend of Cado Avenali's.

Jim excitedly told Morgan about his plan to "climb the view"—to summit every peak that he could see from his deck—and suggested they head out right away. Over the course of the next two weeks, they bagged the first ascents of three virgin summits and got a first taste of the reality of the range: not every peak that looked good from the balcony was going to be good. The rock could be excellent, but it could also get very ugly. Approaches were complex and included swarms of horseflies, endless thornbrush, and high, fast water.

But it was all new, and Jim reveled in it all enough that his nineteen-year-old partner struggled to keep up. Three first ascents in a little under two weeks seemed a brilliant start to Jim's relationship with his new world, and then Thom Engelbach arrived, psyched for harder climbs. The first objective that Jim proposed was something of a known quantity, at least by the region's standards. An enticing set of aerial photographs had inspired a chain of attempts on a hidden group of peaks. In 2004, an American team trekked in from the north and made the first ascent of the highest summit of the group, calling it Avellano Tower. The following year, John Bragg brought a small team to explore the Avellanos, but tried a much shorter approach from the southwest. They drove to the end of Bahía Murta, a deep inlet on the lake's north side, then ascended steeply up rainforest and granite slabs for ten miles. Bragg's approach was indeed shorter, but more hazardous. It rained constantly, and Bragg badly broke a leg slipping off a wet boulder. The expedition ended without actually touching a mountain.

When Jim and Thom started up the Murta approach on January 21, 2009, they agreed Bragg's hike was serious work, but the quality of the climbing over the next few days and the summit vista cemented Jim's convictions about the value of the area. He and Thom picked out a line on the group's southernmost spire, and most of the seventeen sunny and windless pitches to the summit were sublime, tapping into Jim's sweet spot: even at sixty-five, on this kind of climbing—as hard as 5.11, with plenty of route-finding and occasional head-sharpening runouts—he was as fast and comfortable as anyone. At the top, Jim proposed that they name the previously unclimbed peak Avenali Peak, and the route *Avenali Avenue*, to honor Cado Avenali's inspiration for the move to Chile, and Cado's recent death from colon cancer.

After Avenali, Jim and Thom turned their eyes to the most obvious and impressive peak visible from the balcony: San Valentín. The big mountain is encircled by the Northern Patagonian Ice Field, and its bulk and height snag the frequent storms that rise up out of the Pacific.

The plan was to attempt the mountain's impressive northeast ridge—of which Thom said, "It would be one of the classic lines in the world . . . if anyone ever actually ever saw it"—but the weather was foul, and just getting to the mountain proved terribly complex. "We vastly underestimated the challenge," Jim explained. "It's a huge mountain with nearly 13,000 feet of relief from the road-head, and going light just wasn't going to work, even with the very best weather." They slogged their way home.

The last time I spoke with Thom, I pointed out that in all his years of apprenticeship with Jim, they'd only gotten to the top of one peak—Avenali Tower. Did that bother him? Absolutely not, Thom said. There couldn't have been a better set of lessons or a better partner to learn them with. As he told me, "Every moment I had with Jim taught me something, and those were all things that have been really important in the climbing I've done since [including multiple summits in Patagonia].

"If you want to succeed on climbs like this, especially if you want to learn how to stay alive, you have to learn how to fail safely and with a good attitude. Donini's better at that than anyone I've ever climbed with."

FOR ALL THAT was new and even joyous again that winter, there was still an always-looming shadow of sadness. Although Angela was a rock in the year's following Montana's death, there was no end to the ruminating about the loss of his son, and the uncertainties surrounding Sage always simmered. She continued to be in and out of care, and she continued to have children. When Jim started spending the austral summers in Chile in 2008, Sage had already had four children, and soon after she was pregnant with her fifth. None of the fathers were involved in their lives.

It was confusing for Jim to know what role he could—or should—play as a grandparent. With the exception of the child who Janet was now raising in South America, all of Sage's children—including the grandson Jim and Angela had had in their home in 2001–2003—had been adopted, and Jim again agonized about whether he could be doing more for them. And as much as Jim loved the new winter life that he'd created for himself in Chile, he wondered, once again, whether there was more he should also be doing for his daughter.

I ASKED JIM one morning about the volunteer work he'd started doing for the climbing community in his sixties, including serving as president of the AAC from 2006 to 2009 and later organizing four years of climber cleanups in Indian Creek Canyon, Utah, for which he received a National Volunteer Award from the Bureau of Land Management. "One of the things I've always loved most about climbing is the freedom we have," he said, "but that freedom comes with a price, or at least it should. We have an opportunity—and to me an obligation—to do whatever we can to give back. If climbing has been an important part of your life, you should think about every way you can to make it as important in other people's lives as well."

The best test of those self-admittedly idealistic notions came through a series of international exchanges attached to the AAC during Jim's presidency, intriguing but complicated trips that took years to organize. In 2008, Jim started working with David Thoenen, head of the AAC's Southeast Section, to bridge an enormous political chasm and arrange a climbers' exchange with the Alpine Club of Iran. Thoenen had been working in Iran before the revolution and was married to an Iranian: he and his wife had been among the last people to leave the country.

It was an audacious time to think about connecting the two countries. Though it had been thirty years since the Islamist Revolution and the Iran Hostage Crisis, diplomatic relations remained poor, and in both the United States and Iran sentiments toward the other country were still hostile.

But everyone who had hands on this project had faith in climbing's potential to unify. The Americans felt they were exporting an important lesson about the freedoms of the hills, and the Iranians were more than happy to demonstrate that they were already quietly enjoying those freedoms.

There is a long history of connection to the high country in Iran: mountains are part of everyday life for Tehranis, who see a horizon-wide panorama of snow-covered peaks rising out of the desert north of the capital; mountains play a key spiritual role in the ancient Persian religion of Zoroastrianism; and Iran has produced many accomplished climbers.

But, as with many things, climbing had grown complicated in the new Islamic Republic. During the revolution that aimed to overthrow the Shah, climbers—most of them university students—had been activists in the rebellion, but this hadn't won them the favor of Iran's new leaders. Instead, the mullahs feared a continuation of the climbers' revolutionary zeal, and they co-opted the venerable Iran Mountaineering Federation to keep climbers controlled. Under the new regime, climbing was treated as a frivolous excess that warranted supervision.

But, as Jim well knew, control doesn't sit well with any climber, anywhere. By 1999, a loose collection of more independent-minded climbers created the breakaway Alpine Club of Iran, positioning themselves as "real climbers" who represented the future of the sport.

David Thoenen had already been involved in climber exchanges to the USSR and China, and he jumped at the chance to connect with the new group. Thoenen understood the challenges of navigating delicate political and religious protocols as well as anyone, and he had a fierce partner in Abbas Mohammadi, president of the Alpine Club of Iran.

Despite the enthusiasm, it took two long years before anyone tied into a rope. The Iranians came first, arriving in the Tetons in July 2010. Jim took an Iranian party up the Grand, and the whole experience of the visit confirmed his sense that climbers everywhere were alike. "Every difference between us disappeared once we touched rock. In the end, we're all in the same tribe," he said.

The following summer, in 2011, thirteen Americans, including Jim—and, at his request, Greg Crouch, who wrote about the exchange for *The Atlantic*—arrived in Tehran. They were planning to rock climb near the city, then head north to the striking peaks of the Alborz Range.

It was a complex plan, and the team saw that from the start. Every minute of the trip was tightly scripted, and the itinerary began with visits to mosques and museums and lectures about Iran's deep spiritual culture. That didn't bring out the best in Jim: after a couple of days of long drives out to heritage sites in the desert, he started more audibly grumbling about being there to climb, not to be hectored about the lack of civilization and history in America.

But just as Jim had imagined, out in the mountains everything changed. A weight seemed to lift off the Iranians' shoulders. Everyone was laughing. Women who were climbing stripped down to tight-fitting athletic clothing and removed their head coverings. "Up here," one of the Iranians said, "there are no men with long beards and mustaches."

Twenty-three Iranians joined the Americans, and they met many more avid climbers at the Band-e-Yakhchal crags in the hills north of Tehran. After a day of sport climbing, the team divided in two. Half headed northwest toward Iran's highest peak, Mount Damavand, an 18,405-foot volcano with a Fuji-like symmetry, while Jim and the others took on a more ambitious goal—to try new routes on Alam Kuh, the highest peak of the Takht-e-Sulaiman massif, east of Damavand.

The north wall of 15,260-foot Alam Kuh was sharp-edged, dead-vertical granite—"Like the Diamond on Longs Peak [Colorado] on steroids," Jim says—with the technical climbing starting a couple of hours' hike above the Sarchal Hut, a primitive refuge perched at 12,000 feet in a beautiful alpine cirque.

In the hut that night, Jim got to know the Iranians better and heard difficult stories of life under both recent rulers of the land. Mohammad Bahrevar, a fifty-three-year-old physicist and one of the leading climbers of the country, had been one of the students who'd organized demonstrations against the Shah. He'd been arrested by the Shah's notorious SAVAK police force, spent fifty-six days in custody, and suffered near-fatal interrogations. The hut custodian had more current experience with such oppression. He lifted his shirt and revealed long, raised scars across his back made by the whips of the Gašt-e Eršād, the morality police, who had once caught him drinking. But more of the talk was of the common ground of climbing, with the Iranians pushing the Americans to forge new lines up the main wall. "There were French, Italian, and Polish routes up there," Jim said, "and they really wanted to see an American route. So did we."

Each American climber was paired up with an Iranian, and the following day the partners hiked up to tent sites below the big face. There seemed to be an unlimited selection of new route options, and Jim was thrilled by the look of a long line of untouched cracks right above his tent. He was matched with a strong Iranian climber who "didn't speak any English but seemed like a really nice guy, even if we couldn't say a word to each other." They settled in under a star-flecked sky.

But by morning, summer had fled and the face was plastered with snow and ice. No one had the right gear for the conditions, and only one team, Mark Wilford and Mohammad Bahrevar, climbed anything of note, repeating the standard *German Flank* route up the northeast ridge, first climbed in 1936, while Jim and several others spent the day soloing the easy east ridge. Conditions were no better the following day, but Jim was still eager, so he gathered some Iranians and led them up a less technical subpeak.

The fourth day dawned beautifully, but to Jim's frustration, the strict rules of the visit meant everyone had to descend back to the road. They were scheduled to meet up with the Damavand group, who'd summitted their easier peak in a whiteout, and return to Tehran.

In Jim's grumbling mind, a half-day stop at Pol-e-Khab, a sport crag north of the city, hardly compensated for being dragged away from the mountains in great weather and, worse, being obliged to endure yet another round of mosques and museums. "We gave up that beautiful day to be back looking at the same thing we'd already seen a hundred times," he griped. "We were already in our own cathedral up in the mountains, and I couldn't understand why we had to come down and see something that didn't compare at all."

Still, the consensus, even for Jim, was that the exchange had been a great success, a model of grassroots reconciliation that other groups, particularly politicians, hadn't been able to achieve. And, for Jim and a few other climbers from the team, Iran was only the beginning of an even more exotic adventure.

THERE WAS ONE glaring absence in the team in Iran. One of the more intriguing candidates for the exchange had been Bo White, a twenty-six-year-old who had global experience beyond his years. He had a master's degree from Yale in international affairs; was fluent in several languages, including the Farsi spoken in Iran; and was a Fulbright Scholar studying in Central Asia—but for reasons that were never made clear, his visa for Iran had been turned down.

White was disappointed, but he suggested an add-on that intrigued Jim and a few other members of the Iran crew: after Iran, why not come to Tajikistan? White was completing a residency attached to his Fulbright in the former Soviet satellite, and he insisted there was some excellent climbing there. In the years that White had lived in Tajikistan, he'd spent many weeks in the high and wild Pamir Range in the eastern part of the country, and he'd become the Pamirs' most avid promoter.

Few Western climbers had visited the Pamirs at the time, but White's descriptions were compelling. Sitting at the junction of some of the biggest ranges on the planet—the Karakoram, the Hindu Kush, the Tien Shan, and the westernmost extension of the Himalaya—the Pamirs include several mountains over 7,000 meters and, most attractive to Jim, many unexplored valleys and 5,000- and 6,000-meter peaks.

Tajikistan truly met Jim's definition of an ideal place to climb. Some 97 percent of the land is mountainous, but those mountains are home to only 3 percent of the population. Thanks to a combination of both geography and politics, the mountains are almost entirely unclimbed, and they are home to a very unique group of mountain people.

White spelled out their story. Until the fall of the Soviet Union in the 1990s, Tajikistan had a paralyzed economy and an oppressive regime that controlled long-standing ethnic tensions. When Soviet rule ended, the country slid into civil war. Between 1992 and 1997, nearly 100,000 people were killed and 20 percent of the country's population was displaced. The Tajik majority took lasting control of the few cities in the country's far west, but the Ismaili Muslims who live in the deep and long valleys of the north and east won a battle of a different kind: their perilous situation in the war's aftermath got the attention of the Aga Khan, the imam of Ismailis around the world. The Aga Khan Foundation stepped in and transformed life in the Pamirs, creating jobs; building schools, hospitals, and free universities; and making great strides to eliminate poverty. In just a few years, the economy in the mountain areas stabilized, and literacy rates and health outcomes dramatically improved. The only missing ingredient was the kind of mountain tourism that had been so important throughout the Himalaya and Karakoram countries.

These kinds of historical and cultural details wouldn't normally have interested Jim—he'd often gone to other countries without researching the peaks he was going to climb, let alone the people—but as soon as he met *these* people and saw their mountains, he fell hard.

IN EARLY JUNE 2011, Jim and two other young members of the exchange, Jenn Flemming and Chris Weidner, boarded a Tajik Air flight in Tehran and flew 1,000 miles east. White was there to greet them and gently guide them through the strange madness of the Tajik capital, Dushanbe—so different from the rigid order of Tehran. Four other climbers joined the team in the city: a couple of White's university friends, Darren Benton and Jesse Burkhardt; Mikey Church, another Fulbright Scholar working on a project in the country; and Teo Kaye, a Swiss who had been working as a photographer in the area for years. The long drive to the mountains a few days later was brutal. After nearly twenty hours of bouncing and bruising, the climbers finally jarred to a stop in the town of Khorog, Tajikistan, fell out of the Land Rover, and dusted themselves off.

Everyone except for Jim was in their twenties or thirties, but from the start White was impressed by how Jim showed up. "Everyone else was griping, but Jim just took it all in stride," White said. "Tajikistan can be a bit edgy, but Jim seemed to love that, and it was really enjoyable being around him in those settings."

As they started exploring the mountains northeast of Khorog, White recalled, "None of us could keep up [with Jim]. He just pounds it out on these tough trails at 3,000-plus meters, and he always seemed more motivated than anyone else. When he puts on a pack he's got some kind of clarity of purpose that I've just never seen in anyone else."

The clarity showed up not just in getting to the peaks above the village of Gunt, just north of the Afghan border, but also in climbing them once they got there. "It was easy to be frustrated," White explained, "because rock that looked good from a distance was either choss or bulletproof quartzite with no natural lines to follow, but where the others were complaining and saying,

'I came all the way here for *this*?' Jim would just look around and say, 'Well then, what about *that*?'"

Though the area featured wave after wave of sharp ridges and steep faces, the climbing took getting used to and the weather wasn't entirely cooperative. Jim and Bo joined Weidner and Flemming for parallel attempts on the 280-meter east face of a tower they called the Tooth, perched high above Gunt and pockmarked with hundreds of body-sized, wind-carved huecos. The climbing was hard and runout, and both teams retreated when the weather soured.

Success came easier when everyone moved to the other side of the road, climbing up into a side valley called the Sizdh. On June 28, Jim and Bo made an exploratory foray up a 4,960-meter peak called Shahnameh. The approach to the southeast face was long and complicated, but the climbing above followed cracks in superb granite. Late in the day, it became obvious that there was still quite a bit of terrain to the summit, so the pair retreated, believing they'd get to the top on their next attempt. The next day, White said, was a brilliant demonstration of Jim's ingrained experience: "It was incredible how often, and easily, he just knew where to go and what to do." It was a remarkable day that gave them the first ascent of the big and complex peak.

"I THINK," JIM said one day, "that Tajikistan was one of the very best places that I ever climbed. The scene is great, the people are wonderful, and you'd never run out of things to do."

So he started talking to Bo about how to help the locals develop the systems that would encourage other climbers and trekkers to come experience the same magic. They came up with an ambitious plan to sponsor the development of a Pamiri Alpine Club, working with energetic locals White knew.

By the time Jim, Bo, and Corey LaForge (representing the gear company Black Diamond, which became a key sponsor) returned to Khorog the following year, 2012, the project had grown legs. Jim and the group were there to do some climbing—which was again excellent—but also to run climbing skills workshops.

A key player at the Tajik end was Sharaf Saidrakhmonov, a Khorog local who'd become the first president of the Pamiri Alpine Club. When we spoke, Saidrakhmonov couldn't have been clearer about Jim's role in his community: "Mr. Jim," he said, "was most important of all." A critical part of that sentiment was the honored place of elders in the Pamiri community. Jim's age meant locals saw him as the one to listen to and learn from.

In the years that followed, the Pamiri Alpine Club played a vital part in the development of a booming, self-sustaining tourism industry in the mountains of Tajikistan. Hundreds of people now come each year to trek and climb, and dozens of entrepreneurs like Sharaf Saidrakhmonov offer work in communities that had never seen a Westerner a decade ago.

White ended our call by saying, "I really don't think that Jim has any idea how big a role he played in all of this. He changed a *country*."

CHAPTER 28

THE RELUCTANT ELDER

You should serve the community with the wisdom you have of the
history, the patterns, the flow of things. Without that understanding
of history, it's too easy to think, "This is new. We've never seen this
before. We have to start from scratch." And that's just never true.
—*Jim Donini*

ONE CRISP NOVEMBER morning, Jim and I drove down through the skin of the Utah desert and followed Highway 211 along Indian Creek, into the orange-tinted bowels of Bears Ears National Monument. We passed through the shade of a cottonwood grove, and then enormous sandstone walls roared up on either side of the road. Jim grinned and said, "One of my favorite places in the world . . ."

It was easy to understand why Donini would like it here. The walls around us were lined with miles of cracks, of all sizes and shapes: Immaculate finger seams in the back of every tan corner. Perfect splitters soaring up varnished brown faces glimmering in the sun. Fierce offwidths that would scare more mortal climbers away. We slowed into a parking lot, where Jim was going to show me some of his favorite routes.

A trip to a climbing area with Jim can feel a bit like a papal visit, and that's especially true in Indian Creek, where he's been so well known for so long. As we unpacked the truck, other climbers started nodding at him and murmuring. A few came over to pay their respects, and Jim happily played along. A circle gathered, and Jim made a few route suggestions, even offering a melodramatic caution to one rope team: "Make sure you have *at least* three gold cams for the middle of that second pitch," he said. "Otherwise you're going to have to run it out like I did, and you *really* don't want to do that!"

Everyone laughed, but one of the cautioned team's members quietly counted the cams on his rack.

An hour later, we sprawled at the base of a long fist crack that looked like it had been cut with a scalpel and watched a father-son team working it. Jim turned to the father and said, "You're pretty lucky you get to do this with your boy." The father nodded back and said, "I sure am."

Jim turned to me and quietly said that he doubted the father appreciated the poignancy of that sentiment in quite the way he did.

Everyone around us, including the dad, was decades younger than Jim, and that sparked a question that I hadn't asked before: "Do you think there'll come a time when you'll be done with climbing?"

"Still love it," he answered without much of a pause, "so can't see why I would . . ."

We talked then about why some other climbers, including many of his peers, have answered the question differently. There's a fair, and even responsible, audit that climbers should put themselves through, especially in their later years: *With all the hardship and risk and time away, do I still* want *to be doing this? Is it still fulfilling me and worth it all? Can I still do this? Will my body and mind let me?* And, perhaps most nuanced of all, *Should I be doing this anymore? Am I truly still sharp enough to keep myself and my ropemates safe? Can I pay as much attention to every moment as I need to?*

It's never an easy inventory, but it has been easier for Donini than for most climbers. Thanks to an apparently blessed mix of genes, hard work, and boundless stubbornness, even in his late seventies, Jim's passion for the climbing life barely seems to have flickered. He still likes the sharp end of the rope. He swears that he still loves sleeping on the hard ground and that he's never happier than when he's battling uphill, or crashing his way through bush, or hiding from a storm. Though he'll say he doesn't endure cold so well anymore, he still itches every December for the waterfalls to freeze up around his home in Ouray, and he still dreams of even higher and colder places—and, impressively, still goes to them.

Jim insists that one thing that's kept him in the game is a happy acceptance of the many, many changes that have happened in the climbing world. With 10 million-plus climbers in the United States, the climbing scene, and the sport itself, are bound to be very different from the days when twenty-four-year-old Donini never saw a soul at High Rocks. But, he insists, all is good. "Too many people my age bitch about what climbing has become—too crowded, too safe, too regulated—and they go on about 'the good old days' and say that the new climbers don't understand what climbing's really about. I've got no time for that. I love how climbing has evolved, and how many more people get to enjoy it now. It's not the same as it was, but it sure isn't worse."

ONE AUTUMN MORNING, we sat in the kitchen of Jim and Angela's house in Ouray. Out the big windows of his living room, brilliant sun danced on the early snows that draped peaks up and down the valley. Jim was telling stories about things around the room: pictures of long-ago expeditions and some recent packrafting epics; a big panoramic shot of the view from their balcony in Chile ("This hasn't been climbed, and neither has this, or this. Never had a foot on them!"); the two cats that seem to be the masters of the house and don't much like each other; a framed speeding ticket that got canceled by a cop who was a climber and recognized Jim's name; rocks and fossils collected over the years.

"You gotta see the basement," Jim said, pulling me down a tight spiral staircase. It's a climber's basement, for sure, with the whole back wall and half the floor set into the exposed red sandstone that the house was built into. There are pull-up gadgets hanging everywhere, a collection of packrafts drying in the corner, and a pillar festooned with the biggest collection of camming devices that I'd ever seen. "You should only ever crack climb with sponsored climbers," Jim laughed. "No one else can afford this many of these things, and sponsored climbers don't worry if they have to leave gear behind on rappels!"

The phone rang. It was always ringing when I was there. Jim's more constantly connected with the climbing community around the world than anyone I've ever met—staying in weekly touch with his close people, like Crouch and Tackle; making plans to give talks across the Atlantic; offering trip advice to young climbers who've heard that Jim will always take their call; and more than anything, scheduling time to get out climbing.

Jim and Angela have been living on the outskirts of Ouray since 2003, and he's got hundreds of partners to choose from and some of the best climbing in America within easy reach. He can walk to sport climbs, there are 13,000-foot summits to slog up at the head of the valley, and two of his favorite places on the planet—Indian Creek and the Black Canyon of the Gunnison—are just a couple of hours' drive away.

Being in his seventies hasn't tamped down Donini's interest in climbs further afield either. He's got as long a bucket list as he's ever had, he says, and when the phone rings he's happy to try and twist someone's arm into coming along on a project.

I called Tad McCrea one afternoon and asked him about Jim's enticement for a series of climbs they did in northern Patagonia through the 2010s. When Tad first started climbing a few years before and was interested in becoming a guide, he'd gone looking for mentors who had lived through a time McCrea always thought was magical—the 1970s, when everything was bold and exploratory. These mentors eventually directed him to Donini, whom they said was the climber *they* most admired.

But Jim, McCrea soon discovered, wasn't interested in just talking about that past; he wanted to do new climbs. He told Tad about the unclimbed peaks visible from his house in Chile and asked whether a bit of bushwhacking or packrafting bothered him. Tad said no; Jim told him to pack his bags.

The pair did a couple of first ascents of remote 2,000-meter peaks that included ugly terrain, dangerous river runs, and, Tad said, a lot of *acceptance*. "I think that's been a huge part of Jim's success," Tad suggested. "He really likes it when struggles and disappointments happen, because he believes they always lead to great stories."

Tad was particularly impressed by Jim's accommodation of his own aging. He saw Jim slow down a bit even during the years between their trips, but he appreciated how Jim remained able to laugh at himself and never made excuses, complained, or went on about the "good old days." Said Tad, "You really get the sense that, for him, *these* are the good days."

ONE AFTERNOON, I mentioned McCrea's observation about his lack of nostalgia to Jim. He growled. "I don't have time for what happened forty years ago. I'm busy enough with the stuff I want to do today." Even if he's sometimes returned to familiar places—to Yosemite, to Chile, to the Karakoram—he wasn't going to those places to conjure a better past; he was going to *climb*.

That was true even about a return to the scene of one of his great epics: China. At sixty-nine, Jim went back into Siguniang's Changping Valley with

Angela and a friend of Crouch's, and he brought gear in case he could rustle up a climbing partner and finally get to the top of something in the range. The valley was different—easy road access and a very manicured trail now bring in thousands of trekkers every year—but Jim's enthusiasm was little changed. He found an American from Flagstaff, Arizona, Cameron Kern, who was waiting for the rest of his team, and the pair bagged the first ascent of a technical 5,182-meter peak that had a great view of Siguniang.

The next spring, Jim headed to Yosemite with sixty-nine-year-old George Lowe and climbed *The Nose* of El Cap. By far the oldest pair to climb the big route, they flew up, shaving hours off the time Jim managed when he did the first two-day ascent forty years before.

Through his midseventies, right up until the time COVID-19 ground the world to a halt, "climbing the view" from his balcony in Chile also stayed his joyful focus. He reveled in the opportunity to explore virgin ground, often on his own with his packraft, though a posse of visitors passed through and joined Jim on several first ascents across the remote range.

BUT THERE WAS one trip in the past decade that had a nostalgic poignancy that even Jim acknowledged.

In 2016, thirty-eight years after their remarkable attempt on Latok I, Jim and George Lowe returned to the Choktoi. They came at the invitation of Thomas Huber, who had become obsessed with completing a new line on the north face of Latok I and asked if Jim and George would join him in base camp. When we spoke, Huber bubbled with admiration about the 1978 climb and about George and Jim: "That was an incredible thing. One of the very greatest climbs ever, by the best climbers." Jim and George weren't interested in just coming in for the trek though. There were scores of 6,000-meter peaks all along the edges of the Choktoi, and despite their age, the pair were still looking for a suitable challenge: "And not just some snow-and-ice thing," Jim insisted. "We wanted a rock climb to sink our teeth into." They invited Thom Engelbach along as a quiet concession to the ambitiousness of the plan.

When they got to the Choktoi, good conditions helped them settle on trying Suma Brakk, a beautiful 6,166-meter rock-and-snow peak just down-valley from Latok I. The peak had impressive relief, and the recent first ascent had found water ice and long stretches of 5.10 rock.

Jim on the first ascent of Cerro Chueco in Patagonia, at seventy-four (Photo by Tad McCrea)

They did admirably well, but just short of the top, common sense won out. "We got really close," Jim explained, "but we hadn't been moving as fast as we needed to be, and we were tired and cold, and at 20,000 feet a bivouac without bags was going to be bad." Then he laughed and added, "In another time, we would have continued, but George and I are just better able to make sensible decisions these days."

During the climb, they could look across at the mammoth rise of the north ridge of Latok I, where they'd had to make so many decisions of a different magnitude so long ago. Before they left the valley, Jim and George spent a final morning with Huber, and the trio walked over to the foot of the ridge. All of them—even the typically taciturn George—described the shared moment as one of the most moving of their long mountain lives. Huber said, "All three of us started to cry, thinking of all that mountain had given all of us."

IN THE EARLY spring of 2021, another life loop closed when Jim finally got the call he'd been expecting for more than thirty years—albeit a gentler version than he'd long been dreading. Out of the blue, Sage phoned, wondering if they could spend time together, explaining that she'd been diagnosed with melanoma.

It was only days before Jim found out that that the cancer had metastasized into her brain and spine, and then he jumped into a familiar role, offering his daughter the chance to come live with him, looking for hospice care near Ouray for when her days worsened. Although the circumstances were tragic, Jim stepped up yet again.

But like so many of Jim's plans with his daughter, this last one never worked out. A stroke caused by the metastasis left Sage unresponsive, and she couldn't be moved into hospice in Colorado. Jim made one last visit to California to say goodbye and Sage passed just after he left. There wasn't pain for him losing a child this time, as there had been for so long with Montana; there was just a sense of relief that his child had finally found peace.

A few months later, Janet flew north with Sage's teenage daughter Rosie, whom she'd been raising since birth with Sage's blessing. They gathered with Jim and some old friends on the water in Santa Barbara, where they kayaked out to spread Sage's ashes. "It brought home some sweet memories from far away and long ago," Jim said, "when Sage, Montana, Janet, and I had kayaked together in the Sea of Cortez."

ON JANUARY 11, 2023, Jim sent out a group email with a somewhat cryptic photograph attached. It showed him in a La-Z-Boy with an impish grin, gaunt as always, wearing dozens of electrodes on his head and arms. The subject line was wry, if not particularly illuminating: "Damn! Try as they might, and oh did they try, but they just couldn't find any evidence of ongoing neural activity . . ."

I called to see if he was okay. One of the most remarkable things about Donini's story is how utterly free he has been of the injuries, joint conditions, and other physical damages that plague—and often even end—the climbing careers of so many of his mountain peers. He's had a few minor age-borne issues—he had a bout of prostate cancer a few years back that still sometimes keeps him up at night, and you'll often hear the squeal of his hearing aids—but the combination of his genes, a fairly ascetic diet, and an impressive regime of cardio workouts has otherwise kept him out of doctors' offices and off medication.

He called back and growled, "I've been having some trouble walking lately. They're trying to figure out what's going on."

I remembered that when we last climbed together the previous year, he had seemed uncharacteristically unsure of his feet and had stumbled a couple of times on a boulder approach—though any hesitancy disappeared as soon as he touched rock, barely placing any gear as he glided up a 5.9.

"They're pretty sure it's Parkinson's," he said.

I asked him how it felt to hear such a diagnosis. He answered by retelling the story of crossing underneath the glacier below Aguja Poincenot, when rocks suddenly started pounding the slope all around him. "Just like *that*," he said. "Not much I can do about it other than just accept whatever is going to happen."

After all, he said, hasn't accepting *whatever* he's faced been the essence of his life in the alpine? And, he added with a shrug, if the disease was only going to get worse over time, wasn't that all the more reason to get out climbing now?

So, just a few weeks later after he heard this tentative verdict about his future, he and Angela headed back to Chile, where they had some exploring to do. Within a few days, Donini's emails, with pictures of packraft approaches and him on rocky summits in his perpetually ripped trousers, started pinging in again.

Just a few weeks later, another group email came: "I'm just back from an unintended swim down a major icy cold glacial river," Jim wrote. "Thankfully with a life preserver, but most regrettably sans either a wet suit or dry suit. Never again. This episode was followed by a sleepless night in a dense rainforest fighting off hypothermia. A successful extraction [by Angela and the friends who were along on the trip] was achieved the next day and I am back home eating anything I can find.

"It seems the older I get, the easier it is for me to epic."

Many friends—so many of them from the pages of this book—weighed in, with laughs and congratulations, headshakes, and concerns—but none of them seemed the least bit surprised. It was just Donini having another adventure. Greg Thomsen ended the thread that day with a note that included a familiar line:

"As you once said, 'Survival is not assured . . .'"

ACKNOWLEDGMENTS

I'M DEEPLY INDEBTED to the many people who informed, supported, shaped, and challenged this project over the past few years—friends, mentors, wise readers, and especially the people whose stories fill these pages.

I owe the greatest thanks, of course, to the person whose name is in the title. When I first brought him the idea of the book to Jim, I was pretty much a stranger asking permission to dig into his life and share it with the world, and thanks to his openness, honesty, and trust in the process—even through some very real moments of personal pain along the way—he's come to fill all the roles in the list above.

I've been equally impressed by the willingness of several others close to Jim to help me share the rich complexities of his remarkable life. As she has been all through her years with Jim, Angela Goodacre Donini has been a beacon of pragmatism and insight through this project, clarifying and fact-checking a thousand details that have blurred in Jim's great stories and other people's minds over the years, and gently guiding him, and his story, along the way. "I never could have made it through all I have without her," Jim said.

I was deeply moved by Janet Oakley Hunter's candor and her commitment to ensuring that I got the family story right, especially when it came to the mental health issues involved. She was a fierce advocate for herself and her children, and for everyone who has suffered mental health challenges and addictions, and I hope the reader can see how much richer the book is thanks to her voice.

Jim's sister, Sandy Yanosov, was a wellspring of information about the Donini family and shared rich stories about her brother's roots, including several that Jim had never heard.

Donini family friends helped me understand the complex stories of Jim's children, and I want to especially thank Jeremy Caradona and Robby and Barbara Wood for their recollections and perceptions.

Jim has a remarkable legion of friends who stepped up with far more tales than could possibly be included here—about his family life, his work in the outdoor industry, and especially his climbs. It was a joy to hear all the stories, and particular thanks go to Yvon Chouinard, Rick Ridgeway, George Lowe, Jeff Lowe, John Long, Conrad Anker, Greg Thomsen, Thom Engelbach, Tad McCrea, Malcolm Daly, Mark Chapman, Steve Arsenault, Rick Black, Peter Lev, Thomas Huber, Phil Gleason, Rab Carrington, Bo White, John Barker, Brian Wyvill, Ben Campbell-Kelly, Stefan Hiermeier, Steve Swenson, Roger Breedlove, Sharaf Saidrakhmonov, Sibylle Hechtel, Kelly Cordes, Jim Bridwell, Tom Livingstone, Mike Hoover, Peter Pilafian, Mike Graber, and Anders Ourum. And from the opening of this book, Guy Lacelle. Miss you every day, mon frère.

A few of Jim's friends offered me a commitment of time that reflected the depth and quality of the relationship that they have had with Jim for decades—in particular, Jack Tackle, Greg Crouch, Michael Kennedy, and John/Jonna Bragg. Their love for Jim was obvious every time we spoke.

I had the privilege of having several of my own friends help this book evolve. I especially want to thank some very wise readers: James Little, Peter Tucker, and Sharon Roberts read entire drafts and helped immensely. David Roberts, David Smart, and Bernadette McDonald—superb biographers—all offered key counsel. Karen McDiarmid, Sharon Wood and Garrett Brown, Doug Leonard and Caroline Marion, Tom Dickey and Mark Abbott, Will Gadd and Sarah Hueniken, and Saul Greenberg and Judy Otton all sat through early readings of chapters, and knew exactly how to respond. Thanks for the hard truths and gentle touches, folks . . .

The team at Mountaineers Books offered incredible support for this project from the outset. In particular I want to thank Matt Samet and Sarah Currin for their editing prowess, and Tom Helleberg, Mary Metz, Janet Kimball, Emily White, and Kate Rogers for their unwavering guidance through some complex terrain.

At its heart this is a book about family, and I'm immensely grateful for all the wisdom and support that came from my own family: Jaine and George Buse, and Chris Edgelow and Alison Oakley Edgelow patiently sat through a couple of years of writerly angst and asked all the right questions. My stepchildren and their partners—Michael Irvine and Jessica Nelson, and Leith Irvine and Daniel Walker—were rockstars who truly seemed to understand why I'd be up in the middle of the night at their kitchen tables, sometimes typing and more often cursing. Thanks, all!

But the grand prize for patience, support, and understanding goes, once again, to my amazing wife, Kathi Irvine, who was there on every long stretch and always knew how to help me take chances and keep me safe. I could never have done this without her holding my rope.

SELECTED CLIMBS

1970–76 — Breakthrough free routes in Yosemite, before the advent of camming devices, including the most first ascents (FAs) in one year (1972) in Yosemite history

1971 — Ninth ascent, *Salathé Wall*, El Capitan

1972 — First two-day ascent, *The Nose*, El Capitan

1972 — New route, Death Canyon, Tetons

1973 — First American ascents, *Point Five Gully* and *Zero Gully*, Ben Nevis, Scotland

1974 — Ill-fated expedition to Cerro Fitz Roy, Patagonia; no climbing

1974 — Attempt, east face east chimney (now *Exocet*), Aguja Standhardt

1976 — FA, *Americana*, Torre Egger, Patagonia

1977 — FA, *No Survivors*, No Escape Buttress, Mount Moran, Tetons

1978 — FA, *North Face*, Cerro Autana, Venezuela

1978 — *North Ridge*, Latok I, Karakoram

1981 — *North Ridge*, Siguniang, Qionglai Mountains, China

1985 — FA, *Diamond Arête*, East Face, Mount Hunter, Alaska

1986 — Attempts, Puscanturpa Notre, Trapecio southeast face, and Jirishanca northeast face

1987 — FA, *Southeast Buttress*, Avalanche Peak, Kichatnas Spires

1987 — FA, *The Predator*, Death Canyon, Tetons

1988 — Attempt, the *Infinite Spur*, Mount Foraker, Alaska

1988 — FA, *P1190*, Grupo La Paz, Cordillera Riesco, Chile

1989 — *East Face*, Mount Wake, Alaska

1991 — FA, *Cobra Pillar*, Mount Barrille, Alaska

1993 — *Southwest Face*, Uzum Brakk, Biafo Glacier, Karakoram

1995 — *Compressor Route*, Cerro Torre, Patagonia

1996 — FA, *Bourbon Bottle Route*, Mount Bradley, Alaska

1996 — *West Ridge*, Innominata, Patagonia

1996 — FA, *Old Smuggler's Route*, North Face, Aguja Poincenot, Patagonia

1997 — FA, *Shaken, Not Stirred*, Moose's Tooth, Alaska

1998 — *West Ridge*, Mount Epperly, Antarctica

1999 — *South Face*, Thunder Mountain, Alaska

1999 — FA, Torrecita Tito Carrasco, Patagonias

1999 — FA, *A Fine Piece*, North Pillar, Cerro Pollone

2000 — FA, *Lightning Spur*, South Face, Thunder Mountain, Alaska

2001 — Kichatna Spires

2002 — *Sunshine Wall*, Kichatna Spires

2003 — *Supercanaleta*, Cerro Fitz Roy, Patagonia

2003 — Cerro Krüger, Chilean Patagonia

2005 — *Diamond Couloir*, Mount Kenya

2006–07 — Goretta Pillar, Cerro Fitz Roy, Patagonia

2008 — FA, *Avenali Avenue*, Avellano Towers, Aysén Region, Chilean Patagonia

2009 — FAs, Cerro Choss, Cerro Condor, Pisco Sour Tower, Aysén Region, Chilean Patagonia

2010 — Several FAs, up to 5.11d, Cerro Colorado, Aysén Region, Chilean Patagonia

2011 — Alam Kuh, Iran

2011 — Various FAs, Gunt and Sizdh Valleys, Pamir Range

2013 — FA, *Legends*, P5182, Qionglai Mountains, China

2013 — FA, Rakhsh, Pamir Range

2014 — FA, *The Tooth*, Crown Tower, Avellano Towers, Aysén Region, Chilean Patagonia

2016 — FA, *Half-Cocked*, Puño Este, Aysén Region, Chilean Patagonia

2016 — Choktoi Ri, Karakoram

2017 — Pico San Lorenzo, Chilean Patagonia

2018 — FA, Cerro Chueco, Aysén Region, Chilean Patagonia

2019 — FA, Avellano Towers, Aysén Region, Chilean Patagonia

NOTES

CHAPTER 1. A MAN ON ONE OF HIS MOUNTAINS

24 *Why not have a look at the south ridge:* While much of the south ridge had been climbed in 1973, the line that Jim was proposing was a new variation from the east, carried out alpine style—committing to climbing in one continuous push from the bottom of the route to the top, without the use of fixed ropes or multiple camps. Jim was familiar with the other end of the mountain, having already climbed a new route on Hunter, the *Diamond Arête*, in 1985.

25 *Across the valley, they spotted:* Jim knew the peak was informally called "Thunder Mountain," but he didn't know that it had been given that name by a party on Hunter who heard rockfall roar down the wall. Research would have helped. Given that Jim was, as always, gunning for a first ascent, it would have helped even more to know that the line they were trying on Thunder had actually already been ascended by two British climbers two years earlier.

CHAPTER 2. NON IL SOGNO AMERICANO

31 *He never met the man:* Jim is also his paternal grandfather's namesake: James is Giacomo in Italian.

35 *Beautiful, charismatic, and effervescent, Betty:* Jim has legions of stories about the Donini side of the family but far fewer about the Deatores, save that they also brought shadows into his own story: alcoholism was a problem on their side, and members of different generations had criminal histories.

CHAPTER 3. AMERICAN IDYLL

37 *She took a job at a local country club*: Jim's friends who'd met his mother told me that they see Betty in Jim's ability to connect with people and win them over, and to that Jim says, "Oh yeah, that's all her . . ."

CHAPTER 5. SPECIAL FORCES

45 *Jim has endless stories*: One member of the squad, Ross Johnson, would go on to play one of the most important and enduring roles in Jim's life. Ross was there on the first day Jim climbed and for Jim's first wedding, and they even lived together, first as young men and then again much later in life. Ross was a larger-than-life character, a big man with a surfer's mop of hair, and the source of many raucous stories pulled from the next thirty years of friendship.

47 *After Golden Hawk dissolved*: The hostages were finally freed in November 1964 by a Belgian force aided by the notorious British mercenary "Mad Mike" Hoare, who claimed to have personally killed as many as 10,000 rebels during his time in the Congo.

CHAPTER 7. THE SUMMER OF LOVE AND MOUNTAINS

57 *They had no idea where the route went*: To be entirely fair to the men's ambitions—though Jim and his friends knew nothing of this story—the first ascent of one of the harder routes on Robson, the *Wishbone Arête*, had been made twelve years earlier by a party from California that included one member who'd only ever rock climbed.

CHAPTER 8. A YOUNG MAN GOES WEST

62 *Some climbing areas were clannish*: Regional differences in grades—some of which still continue—spring from a few predictable sources: provincialism ("We've never climbed anywhere else, and so have no idea what a 5.9 is"), insecurity ("There can't be anything here as hard as in Yosemite, so it can only be a 5.9"), and pretentiousness ("Let's call this just a 5.10 and let those Yosemite climbers come see what a *real* 5.10 feels like"). All of these possibilities made entering a new area an adventure.

CHAPTER 10. DAYS IN EDEN: THE YOSEMITE YEARS, PART ONE

71 *Better than anyone else, Bridwell*: I've always been intrigued that chroniclers of Yosemite climbing haven't focused on what has to be one of the most magical short stretches of achievement in climbing history—May 1975. In just over three weeks, *The Nose* of El Capitan was climbed in a day by Bridwell, John Long, and Billy Westbay; *Pacific Ocean Wall* on El Cap—a big leap in aid climbing difficulty—was climbed by Bridwell, Westbay, Jay Fiske, and Fred East; and Long, John Bachar, and Ron Kauk freed *Astroman* on Washington Column, brilliantly redefining the possible when it came to freeing aid lines.

Even Long, one of the most articulate narrators of that time, hadn't caught that connection until I pointed it out to him. He cursed when he remembered that he had turned down Bridwell's offer to join the *Pacific Ocean Wall* team. If he'd said yes, Long would have been part of all three of those transformational climbs.

75 *It's too slow, too mechanical*: The irony of hearing this complaint about the slow pace and work of aid climbing from someone who would later spend months waiting out storms and ferrying loads up big mountain walls isn't entirely lost on Jim.

75 *"I've done grade IVs . . ."*: Grade IVs are long climbs that can be done in a single day; grade VIs require multiple days on the wall.

76 *By the end of his sixth season*: One important route that too few people know about is Jim's first ascent of a steep two-pitch corner on Lower Cathedral Rock called *Overhang Overpass*. Though Jim gave it a grade of 5.11c, many people have called it the first 5.12 in Yosemite—and Jim climbed it years before camming devices were invented. Few people would, or could, climb it today without cams.

CHAPTER 11. WORK, WHISKY, AND AN UNEXPECTED OFFER

78 *He'd really only been on a few peaks*: When I mentioned Jim's lack of mountain experience to Peter Lev—one of the lead Exum guides at the time—Lev laughed and said he had no idea this was the case. The pair of them did the difficult *North Ridge* of the Grand in near winter conditions early that season, and Lev said Jim "seemed to be an exceptional talent"—without knowing it was one of Jim's very first alpine climbs.

79 *That shift meant several guides*: Most American-born guides were uncertified at that point, while Europeans and Canadians went through a rigorous licensing process. But in another appearance in key moment in the story of American climbing, Jim was very much involved in the first steps of the creation of the American Mountain Guides Association, when he, Peter Lev, Yvon Chouinard, and nine other guides sat down over beers in Jackson, Wyoming, on August 12, 1980, and scribbled the fabled "Moose Bar Charter" on napkins. The charter grandfathered in the twelve climbers in the bar, along with six others, as the first certified members of the American Mountain Guides Association—to the fury of several people who had been guiding for years but did not make the list.

80 *Chouinard shared some of his new ideas:* Chouinard would go on to found the apparel company Patagonia, but in 1971, he was still running a garage-sized business. Great Pacific Iron Works (later Chouinard Equipment) was forging pitons and making a few ice axes every year, as well as importing the rugby shirts that would become the ubiquitous uniform of 1970s American climbers. The ascendance of the Patagonia brand was scarcely imaginable, even to the prophetic Chouinard.

CHAPTER 12. DAYS IN EDEN: THE YOSEMITE YEARS, PART TWO

87 *St. Louis native Steve Wunsch:* Wunsch would go on to put up some of the hardest routes across the country, including *Psycho Roof* in Eldorado Canyon, Colorado, and *Supercrack*, a fearsomely overhanging finger crack at the Shawangunks that was originally graded 5.13.

87 *I got along with him:* Another revelation of even greater courage came during the conversations for this book, when Bragg told Jim for the first time that he had spent the last several years transitioning to life as a woman. She now goes by the name Jonna, but she told me that she is comfortable with the book referring to her as "John" and "he," given that was how she was leading her life at the time.

89 *If we'd wanted to:* Had they continued to the top that day, it would have been a monumental achievement. When Bridwell, John Long, and Billy Westbay made the first one-day ascent two years later, it was heralded as one of the most significant milestones of the decade. Jim's first two-day ascent, and near-one-day, is barely known, if only because he never really spoke of it.

89 *"I love the climbing . . .":* Minks ended up loving it all enough that, as Jim recalls, "I literally had to shove him to the gate" when he took Minks to the airport. Minks permanently returned to the United States not long after, working as a handyman at ski resorts across the American West for years until cancer took him in 2012.

Minks's point about loving the drugs is a refrain that comes up in many accounts of Valley climbing in the 1970s. The place and role of drugs in the Yosemite scene in 1970s, especially when it came to hallucinogens, has been a sparky debate. At the very least, it's a compelling storyline, ostensibly about young revolutionaries who were set free, fueled by magical potions that let them see possibilities on the walls that were otherwise invisible and let them do things they couldn't otherwise do. Stories about some of the best-known climbers tripping on acid while doing complex, dangerous leads on El Cap have become the stuff of campfire legend, celebrated in the psychedelic names that some of their big routes were given: *Magic Mushroom*, *Mescalito*, *Tangerine Trip*.

While it seems true that, yes, there was acid dropped and peyote chewed on some climbs by some people, everyone I spoke with who was actually there in the era—Jim included—insisted that climbing high was absolutely the exception rather than the rule. John Long put it this way: "We were athletes working at a really high level, and there was simply no way that we could have done what we did if we were getting high all the time. It's a good story, but it just wasn't the way that it's been portrayed."

CHAPTER 13. AN OBSCENE JOURNEY TO AN UNSEEN MOUNTAIN

91 *There's this thing called the Darién Gap*: The Darién Gap is a roadless and lawless stretch of swamp and jungle between Panama and Colombia.

91 *It will cost hundreds of dollars*: A Carnet de Passage is a document that allows travelers to bring vehicles into participating countries without incurring importation tariffs.

91 *When the men arrived in New York*: In this, and just about every single aspect of this entire story, accounts differ. Jim insisted that the Brits had done no research and fully expected to drive without any problems, while Rab Carrington insisted that he had looked into the problems of logistics and insurance and was fully aware that they wouldn't be driving. Then again, as Rab himself proposed, "If at least two of us say something happened, and it's a good story, let's call *that* the truth . . ."

92 *But the troubling and sad irony of the celebration*: It's not lost on a lot of climbers from the era. Several climbers from both the United States and the United Kingdom have come forward in their later years to speak about the costs of their drinking and drug use, and they have been candid about the social pressures that underlaid the celebrations of the lifestyle of excess. Two courageous examples are a piece written by the great British climber Al Evans—a piece for *UKC* online entitled "A Slippery Slope (Confessions of a Climbing Alcoholic)"—and one by John Long himself—an equally brave admission at *Climbing.com* about his own struggles with addiction.

97 *As strange as their journey was*: Mike Geddes was the exception. He died of esophageal cancer only a few years later at the age of thirty-four.

CHAPTER 14. TOWERS OF PATIENCE

99 *It was a common climbers' trick*: El Chaltén, which is barely ten miles from the climbers' camp at the foot of the glaciers, offers significant advantage to today's climbers: a well-equipped, comfortable refuge from bad weather, with hotels, bars, cafés, and internet service. In the 1970s, well before a trekking boom built the town, the closest settlement with provisions, Tres Lagos, was seventy-five miles away. Travel to the towers in the 1970s involved river crossings that were often washed out and dangerous, and climbers would have to wait out storms in makeshift huts in the forests, quite far from the walls and very far from civilization.

101 *John increasingly felt that Jim*: It didn't take long, John remembered with a chilled laugh, before he realized that he was likely going to get a lot more than emotionally hurt on his proposed solo. The conditions were terrible, he fell into a crevasse, and he returned to camp chastened.

103 *The location of his body*: It has even been suggested that the location of Egger's body is more consistent with the accident happening on a completely different peak than Cerro Torre. Patagonian master and guidebook author Rolando Garibotti raised this complicated possibility in a 2015 *Alpinist* online post. All kinds of conspiracy theories followed, including a suggestion that Egger had been murdered.

103 *"Honest accounting of what we do . . ."*: With a laugh, Jim also copped to a more parochial rationale for his acceptance of Maestri's claim: "I'll always say that good Italian boys like Maestri don't lie!"

104 *But they simply didn't have enough gear*: In the moment it seemed true that their options were limited, but as Jim points out with hindsight, if they'd just traversed a little further left of their chimney, they would have found a much better ice runnel—which would later be climbed by Jim Bridwell, who called the brilliant line *Exocet*.

104 *When Janet Oakley Hunter returned*: When she met Jim, Janet called herself Juanita. She's since reverted to her birth name, and she's called Janet throughout the book for consistency.

106 *Through some Washington connections*: Janet also shaped a plan to document the wildlife of Los Glaciares National Park and shoot photos of the expedition. Pictures of hers eventually appeared in the *National Geographic* article.

110 *Jim clipped into the rope*: The revelations from Jim's team about Maestri's 1959 climb were hardly the end of that story. Angry at the challenges to his honor, Maestri returned to Cerro Torre in 1970 and made an ascent that, in his eyes, presented incontrovertible proof that he could climb the peak. But Maestri's siege of the southeast ridge in 1970 was even more scandalous than the 1959 disaster. In one of the worst examples of conceit and obsession ever seen in the mountains, Maestri dragged a gasoline-powered compressor up the wall and drilled more than 400 bolts in a continuous ladder that reached just below the summit mushrooms. There he stopped the climb, proclaimed that "the mushroom is not part of the mountain," and declared vindication.

Nothing about either ascent vindicated Maestri, and nor did subsequent climbs of Cerro Torre by other people. No one has found any physical evidence that Maestri ever climbed above the gear cache on the 1959 route, and, despite the irony that most ascents of Cerro Torre were made using the 1970 bolts (until they were almost all chopped in 2012), Maestri's decision to place those bolts is still condemned.

Despite all the evidence, Maestri stayed firm in both his claim and his anger right up until his death in January 2021. If anyone doubted him, they were "sons of bitches" who were simply jealous that he was "the strongest climber in the world."

A sad coda to the Torre Egger story came in 1987, when Jay Wilson died when a rappel anchor failed in Indian Creek, Utah. With all the superb climbing in hard places he had done over the years—particularly two successful trips to the Torre Group—Jay's death on far simpler terrain was unnerving. But, as Jim pointed out, "That's where the bad stuff happens—when you least expect it, not when you most expect it."

CHAPTER 16. LATOK I: THE MAGNIFICENT FAILURE

122 *Then there were the doctors*: Ralph Richards's connection to the mountain community and to the Karakoram continues to this day: his grandson, Cory Richards, is a renowned climber and photographer who participated in the first winter ascent of Gasherbrum II (26,230 feet) in 2011.

126 *Unlike some historic climbs*: Consider, for instance, the *West Buttress* on Denali being climbed in eleven hours and forty-five minutes in 2019 versus twenty-one days during the first ascent in 1951 or Everest's *Southeast Ridge* in ten hours and fifty-six minutes in 2003 versus forty-six days in 1953. Though speed is obviously not the only measure of a climb, those are striking differences that dramatically shift perceptions of the climbs.

126 *Since 1978, thirty-nine expeditions*: I say "likely" because there is some uncertainty about a Russian ascent in 2018. In July of that year, Sergey Glazunov and Alexander Gukov definitely reached the top of the north ridge proper, finally surpassing the 1978 highpoint, but initial claims that Glazunov had summitted alone in a whiteout were later retracted by Gukov, who said Glazunov's description of the terrain didn't fit what was known about the summit. Glazunov himself never had the chance to debate the claim, as he died in a rappelling accident at about 20,800 feet during the descent from the mountain. After Glazunov's fall, Gukov spent six days stuck on a ledge before being plucked off the ridge by helicopter—a rescue that certainly wasn't available in 1978.

CHAPTER 18. SIGUNIANG: THE UGLY AMERICANS

135 *When the doors cracked in 1980*: As part of the push to Sinicize place names in China, Minya Konka was renamed Gongga Shan in 1957, the year a Chinese team climbed the peak.

136 *Turner disappeared into the area*: When Donini and his team came to Siguniang the trailhead village was called Zelun, later Sinicized to Rilongzhen.

CHAPTER 19. CITY WAYS

148 *The crack meccas of Squamish*: He laughed, though, when people suggested it must have been good to have Mount Rainier so tantalizingly close. It was a matter of pride, he said, that in all the years he lived in Seattle he'd never set foot on it. "With all those people, I can't think of a less appealing mountain. I never even guided the damn thing," he told me.

150 *That's a perception shared by many spouses*: The best and best-known of the books on this theme is Maria Coffey's excellent *Where the Mountain Casts Its Shadow*.

CHAPTER 20. TACKLE, PART ONE

151 *Each time Jack had been up on* Isis: At 14,573 feet, Mount Hunter is the third highest in the range and is also known by its Dena'ina name Begguya, meaning "child" (of Denali).

155 *They decided to get off the snow*: That steep wall is now known as the Mini-Moonflower Buttress, home to several excellent routes, but when Jack and Jim started their descent, the huge face was completely unexplored.

CHAPTER 21. TACKLE, PART TWO

157 *Their prime target was one*: Jim had a special connection to the magnificent spire Nevado Jirishanca. In 1957, just eighteen months before Toni Egger perished in Patagonia, and nineteen years before Jim discovered his corpse, Egger made the first ascent of the mountain via its east ridge, completing what was called "one of the boldest climbing feats ever performed." The climb of Jirishanca was the reason that Cesare Maestri chose the young Austrian as his partner for Cerro Torre, and thus why Egger eventually came into Jim's life.

CHAPTER 22. DEL MAR A LAS TORMENTAS

164 *Jim liked and admired both men*: A very talented climber and filmmaker, Ridgeway would go on to work with both Chouinard and Donini at Patagonia, where he'd have a senior role as a sustainability officer. Jim had been part of a televised expedition led by Ridgeway to a Venezuelan rock tower that isn't covered in this book.

171 *They reached Puerto Natales the following day*: Given the fierce challenges of the team's paddle home from the towers, there was a particularly sad knot in the last thread of their shared story.

In early December 2015, Chouinard, Ridgeway, and Tompkins came back to Patagonia for a five-day paddle on Lago General Carrera, a huge finger lake that bridges the Argentine-Chilean border. On day four, the winds that had plagued their paddle back from Grupo Los Cerros La Paz rose up on the lake, and Tompkins and Ridgeway's boat capsized. Though a rescue helicopter came, it was already clear that Tompkins had spent too long in the glacial water. He died in the hospital early that evening.

"It was just so sad," Jim said, "that after all Tompkins had done on dangerous rivers around the world, he died on flat water in sight of shore. It made us all understand what we'd gotten away with, all those years before."

CHAPTER 23. TACKLE, PART THREE

172 *North of Dickey, he saw*: The name Mount Barrille, and that of several other peaks in the Ruth Gorge—and in much of the Alaska Range— reflect historical controversies that have been debated for years (not to mention that fact that most of the peaks in the range already had Dena'ina names).

Several of the cases involve the notorious Dr. Frederick Cook, who, it has been conclusively proven, lied about making the first ascent of Denali in 1906. Cook's companion on that infamous trip was Edward Barrill, a Montana-based horse wrangler. Cook named the peak after Barrill, but incorrectly added an "e" to the end in his submission to the US Geological Survey (USGS). The official designation for the peak keeps the "e," and so it is spelled that way here, but many climbing reports and guidebooks spell the name properly. The misspelling of Barrill's name wasn't the only slight: Cook never paid the man his wages for the trip.

Despite acknowledgment of Cook's fraud, the USGS also kept several other names that Cook had given to features: The Ruth Glacier was named for Ruth Hunt, Cook's youngest daughter. Mount Wake, Jim's warm-up climb on this trip, was named for Cook's friend Charles Wake. And Mount Bradley, a peak that Jim would climb in 1996, was named for John R. Bradley, a Florida casino owner who funded Cook's expedition.

185 *Both times, he conceded, he was carrying heavy burdens*: "Carrying" even literally—on Uzum Brakk, Jim had Bill's ashes in his pack, hoping to send his brother into the wind at the summit.

CHAPTER 25. REINVENTION: CROUCH

190 *". . . It's unbelievable"*: An important point to make here: Jim's guiding clients, and some of his less experienced partners, all told me exactly the opposite. They insisted that Donini's one of the most cautious and methodical people they'd seen in the mountains—and several of them have been guided by the very best guides. The issue seems to arise when Jim climbs with peers, whom he simply assumes won't fall, or will fix an anchor to meet their needs when they arrive at a belay. I experienced that myself on a long route in Arizona. I arrived at a belay six pitches off the ground and found that Jim's only anchor was a single piece of Dyneema sling hitched around a rotten chickenhead of rock when there were many cracks for gear right in front of him.

When I asked Jim about that, without a pause, and utterly without guile, he suggested, "Then don't fall." I stuck in more gear.

197 *It was another twenty-four hours*: Like many of Jim's routes, there haven't been many suitors for a repeat of this climb that they called the *Bourbon Bottle Route*—named in honor of the Maker's Mark bourbon they carried to the top, while also poking fun at Andreas Orgler's *Wine Bottle Route* on nearby Mount Dickey. They kept up the fun with the grade they gave *Bourbon Bottle*: 5.8+, A1+, with the "+" being the operative element. Jim explained: "It's 5.8, plus a lot harder than that, and A1, plus you're going to shit yourself."

198 *Ross was often over*: There was a touch of sadness to Ross's availability, though: A few years before, Sandy had passed away from pancreatic cancer. "I went to see her in hospice," Jim said, "and though Ross had warned me, I was still stunned. She looked like someone from concentration camp photographs. It was so terrible to see her like that, so young." Sandy died not long after Jim's visit, at only fifty-one years old.

199 *They had their eyes on the first ascent*: The peak was renamed Rafael Juárez after the death of a young Argentine climber in 1974, but climbers still most often refer to it by its original name, Fitz Roy.

201 *"Greg and I each got a 'Medal of Honor' . . ."*: A Medal of Honor lead, they explained, was a crack five inches or wider, when they had no protection bigger than four inches.

203 *It had been a great year*: Continuing the booze theme of the year, they called the route on Poincenot *Old Smuggler's*, in honor of the whisky they brought along on the climb (though the whisky is actually named Old Smuggler, without the possessive).

The route on Innominata wasn't completed until 2005, when two Canadians, Jon Walsh and Paul McSorley, carried past the ridgeline to the summit.

205 *Whatever transpired, Jim and Greg left*: These days, most climbers get flown up onto this upper glacier, known as the Root Canal. Discovering that small ski planes could land on the Root has made all the great climbs on the south face above far faster, easier, and safer.

206 *She'd already been home for a week*: Angela quickly began a course of eye movement desensitization and reprocessing therapy (EMDR), a psychotherapeutic technique that can be a great help for people who have gone through trauma.

209 *Whether intentional or not*: I once asked Jim to what he attributed his longevity. Not entirely kidding, he replied, "I never face the facts!"

210 *Four miles due north of Cerro Standhardt*: The west ridge of Cerro Pollone had not been climbed its entirety, but in 1988 two Swiss climbers completed the first thirteen pitches of the route, leaving behind many bolted belay anchors before bad weather ended their attempt.

CHAPTER 26. THE SADNESS OF VALLEYS, PART THREE

215 *Jim was thrilled to be recognized*: The prestige of the award itself was tarnished in the spring of 2022, when it was revealed that Robert Underhill had a recorded history of anti-Semitism. The AAC is in the process of renaming the award.

CHAPTER 27. THE MENTOR

221 *Jim suggested instead that they climb up*: Other cusp names include the Sugar Tooth, Wisdom Tooth, Missing Tooth, and Broken Tooth.

227 *The trip was done*: Thom eventually returned to make the second complete ascent of the line on Goretta to the Fitz Roy summit in 2011. The route, now called *Mate, Porro y Todo lo Demás*, is probably the most popular one on the peak.

228 *An enticing set of aerial photographs*: "Avellano" was also the name given to the whole valley. *Avellano* is Spanish for "hazel."

233 *"We were already in our own cathedral . . ."*: Other people on the trip were quick to point out that it wasn't quite true that they were taken to a place that they'd "already seen a hundred times." The tour was to Esfahãn, a fifteenth-century town considered to have some of the most beautiful architecture in the world, known especially for its intricate tiling. But, to Jim, "You've seen one tile, you've seen them all."

CHAPTER 28. THE RELUCTANT ELDER

240 *"It's not the same as it was . . ."*: The one exception to that rule for Jim is shared by most of his peers, and by many younger climbers as well: that the guided ascents of the Himalayan peaks, especially the commercialization of the 8,000-meter peaks, are a tragic development and have little to do with "real" climbing.

SELECTED BIBLIOGRAPHY

Boyles, Morgan. "Chilean Patagonia, First Ascents." *American Alpine Journal*, 2009.

Brady, James. "Open Letter to Yosemite Climbers." *Summit*, March 1974.

Bragg, John. "Torre Egger." *American Alpine Journal*, 1976.

———. "Thunder Mountain, South Face, New Route." *American Alpine Journal*, 2001.

Bridwell, Jim. "Brave New World." *Mountain*, 1973.

Brown, David. "Avellano Towers: The Tooth; Crown Towers." *American Alpine Journal*, 2015.

Campbell-Kelly, Ben. "Cerro Standhardt Attempt." *American Alpine Journal*, 1976.

Childers, Michael. "The Stoneman Meadow Riots and Law Enforcement in Yosemite National Park." *Forest History Today*, Spring 2017.

Chödrön, Pema. *Welcoming the Unwelcome: Wholehearted Living in a Broken-hearted World*. Boulder: Shambhala Publications, 2019.

Coffey, Maria. *Where the Mountain Casts Its Shadow: The Dark Side of Extreme Adventure*. New York: St. Martins Press, 2003.

Cordes, Kelly. *The Tower*. Ventura, CA: Patagonia, 2014.

Crouch, Gregory. "A Short Trip with the Donini-a-Saurus." *Climbing*, August 1997.

———. "Innominata, West Ridge, Attempt, and Aguja Poincenot, New Route." *American Alpine Journal*, 1997.

———. "Mount Bradley, Bourbon Bottle Route." *American Alpine Journal*, 1997.

———. *Enduring Patagonia*. New York: Random House, 2002.

———. "The Peaks of Persia." *The Atlantic*, April 2012.

Crouch, Gregory, and Stephen Alvarez. *Rope Diplomacy: On the Steeps of Iran* (self-published, 2013), Kindle.

Daly, Malcolm. "Thunder Mountain, Attempt and Air Time." *American Alpine Journal*, 2000.

Denny, Glen. *Yosemite in the Sixties*. Ventura, CA: Patagonia, 2007.

Donini, Jim. "Cerro Torre—The Lie and the Desecration." *Climbing*, April 2009.

———. "La Pirámide, Summary." *American Alpine Journal*, 2014.

———. "Cerro Chueco, First Ascent." *American Alpine Journal*, 2018.

Echevarria, Evelio A. *The Andes: A Complete History of Mountaineering in High South America* (self-published, Reidhead & Company, 2016).

Franklin, Jonathan. *A Wild Idea: The True Story of Douglas Tompkins*. San Francisco: HarperOne, 2021.

Garibotti, Rolando. *PATAclimb.com* (website).

———. "A Mountain Unveiled." *American Alpine Journal*, 2004.

———. "Completing the Puzzle: New Facts about the Claimed Ascent of Cerro Torre in 1959." *Alpinist* (online), 2015.

Hall, Brian. *High Risk: Climbing to Extinction*. Sheffield, UK: Sandstone Press, 2022.

Ives, Katie. *Imaginary Peaks: The Riesenstein Hoax and Other Mountain Dreams*. Seattle: Mountaineers Books, 2021.

———. Personal communication on underreporting of southeast Alaska climbing. 2022.

Johnson, Christopher E. "Wilderness Handrails: The Evolution of Search and Rescue in Yosemite" Master's thesis. University of Nevada, Las Vegas, 2007.

Kennedy, Michael. "No Summit, No Cry." *Rock and Ice*, March 2007.

———. Unpublished manuscript. 2021.

Kennedy, Terry G. *In Search of the Mount Cleveland Five: Montana's Worst Mountaineering Tragedy on Glacier Park's Highest Mountain* (self-pub, Lulu Press, 2017).

Kern, Cameron. "Point 5182, South Face, Legends." *American Alpine Journal*, 2015.

LaForge, Corey. "Sizdh Valley, Rakhsh." *American Alpine Journal*, 2014.

Long, John, and Fidelman, Dean. *The Stonemasters: California Rock Climbers in the Seventies*. Santa Barbara: T. Adler Books/Stonemaster Press, 2009.

McCrea, Tad. "Puño Este, Half-Cocked." *American Alpine Journal*, 2018.

Miller, Lauren DeLaunay. *Valley of Giants: Stories from Women at the Heart of Yosemite Climbing*. Seattle: Mountaineers Books, 2022.

Pastor, Jordi. "Roca, Mentiras y Una Fotografía." *CTXT*, September 2015.

Perrin, Jim. *Shipton and Tilman: The Great Decade of Himalayan Exploration*. New York: Arrow Books, 2013.

Phillips, Evan. *The Firn Line* (podcast). Episode 18.

Ridgeway, Rick. "Sea Kayaking and Climbing, Chilean Patagonia." *American Alpine Journal*, 1992.

Roosevelt, Theodore, III, and Kermit Roosevelt. *Trailing the Giant Panda*. Whitefish, MT: Kessinger Publishing, 2004.

Roper, Steve. *Camp 4: Recollections of a Yosemite Climber*. Seattle: Mountaineers Books, 1994.

Shipton, Eric. *That Untravelled World: An Autobiography*. Seattle: Mountaineers Books, 2015.

Smart, David. *Royal Robbins: The American Climber*. Seattle: Mountaineers Books, 2023.

Steele, Peter. *Eric Shipton: Everest and Beyond*. Seattle: Mountaineers Books, Seattle, 1998.

Tackle, Jack. "Siguniang North Face Attempt." *American Alpine Journal*, 1982.

———. "Hunter's Diamond Arête." *American Alpine Journal*, 1986.

———. "Snake-Bit in the Alaska Range." *American Alpine Journal*, 1992.

———. "Uzun Brakk Attempt." *American Alpine Journal*, 1994.

———. "Kim Schmitz, 1946–2016." *American Alpine Journal*, 2017.

Weidner, Chris. "Alam Kuh (4,805m) and Damavand (5,610m), AAC Exchange." *American Alpine Journal*, 2012.

White, Bo. "Gunt and Sizdh Valleys, Various Ascents." *American Alpine Journal*, 2012.

ABOUT THE AUTHOR

GEOFF POWTER is a climber, writer, and adventurer from the Canadian Rockies. He served as editor of the *Canadian Alpine Journal* for thirteen years and has won thirteen National Magazine Awards. Powter has authored several books, including *Strange and Dangerous Dreams*, which won the Jury Prize at the 2006 Banff Mountain Book Festival and was adapted into a radio series. His book *Inner Ranges* was shortlisted for the Boardman-Tasker Prize for Mountain Literature and won the Climbing Literature Prize at Banff in 2019 and the National Outdoor Book Award in the US. He has hosted the Voices of Adventure interview event at the Banff Mountain Festivals for twenty-five years—and counting. Powter lives in Canmore, Alberta, with his wife, Kathi Irvine.

YOU MAY ALSO LIKE

ROYAL ROBBINS
The American Climber
David Smart

STORIES BEHIND THE IMAGES
*Lessons from a Life in
Adventure Photography*
Corey Rich

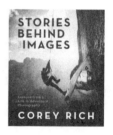

STRANGE AND DANGEROUS DREAMS
The Fine Line between Adventure and Madness
Geoff Powter

HIGH INFATUATION
A Climber's Guide to Love and Gravity
Steph Davis

VALLEY OF GIANTS
*Stories from Women at the Heart of
Yosemite Climbing*
edited by Lauren DeLaunay Miller

A FINE LINE
Searching for Balance among Mountains
Graham Zimmerman

KARAKORAM
Climbing through the Kashmir Conflict
Steve Swenson

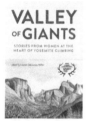